The Nonsexist Word Finder:
A Dictionary of Gender-Free Usage

by Rosalie Maggio

Phoenix • New York

ORYX PRESS

1987

The rare Arabian Oryx is believed to have inspired the myth of the unicorn. This desert antelope became virtually extinct in the early 1960s. At that time several groups of international conservationists arranged to have 9 animals sent to the Phoenix Zoo to be the nucleus of a captive breeding herd. Today the Oryx population is over 400, and herds have been returned to reserves in Israel, Jordan, and Oman.

Library of Congress Cataloging-in-Publication Data

Maggio, Rosalie.
    The nonsexist word finder.

    Bibliography: p.
    1. English language—Terms and phrases—Dictionaries.
2. English language—Sex differences—Dictionaries.
3. Sexism in language—Dictionaries. I. Title.
PE1689.M23   1987   423   87-17788
ISBN 0-89774-449-7

To DAVID
Liz, Katie, Matt

Contents

Foreword

There's an old saying that hard writing makes easy reading. As most writers know, one of their hardest tasks is to find just the right word or phrase to convey a thought clearly and compellingly, without ambiguity, without awkward repetition, and yet so smoothly readers aren't even aware a problem has been solved. Since such hard choices crop up in sentence after sentence, even word after word, anyone who writes for a living is apt to keep a few favorite reference books within easy reach: two or three dictionaries; a usage guide; some version of Roget's *Thesaurus*; an almanac. Today a new kind of reference has taken its place with those old standbys: a book like this one, designed to help writers solve the recurring problems created by sexist language.

Widespread recognition of the male bias of standard English is relatively new. In fact, the social illness this bias reflects and perpetuates was given a name only in the late 1960s when the word *sexism* was coined. Naming the disease was the necessary first step in acknowledging its extent; eradicating it involves revising our laws and customs as well as exposing and eliminating some of our most cherished cultural stereotypes. Because language screens our perception of reality, the very words we use can reinforce our sexist assumptions and attitudes.

Recognizing the sexist impact of a popular metaphor or familiar grammatical convention is one thing; finding a good alternative is another, especially when one is writing under pressure. Then the temptation is to compromise "just this once," even though the familiar term that first comes to mind may be both banal and vague, if not downright misleading.

Rosalie Maggio understands that kind of temptation, and she is exceptionally well qualified to render comfort and aid to the harassed. The author of hundreds of articles and a writer of books and stories for children, she uses language skillfully. An editor of scientific publications, she knows how difficult it is to overcome the linguistic habits that exclude and demean women. Perhaps of equal importance, she brings to the task of compiling this kind of book a passionate personal concern for the future of two daughters and a son, recognizing at first hand the disparate messages about themselves and society's expectations of them the English language conveys to boys and girls respectively.

Anyone who deliberately uses nontraditional, inclusive words in place of traditional, exclusive ones (who refers to a woman as an *actor* or addresses *the chair* instead of *the chairman*) has probably run up against some degree of resistance from defenders of the status quo. Opposition to nonsexist language usually takes the form of ridicule ("So the head of the committee is a piece of furniture, is he?") accompanied by suggestions for supposedly hilarious innovations like *personipulate* and *woperson*. But ridicule can thrive only when nonsexist writing is represented as awkward and laughable. What Rosalie Maggio demonstrates is that well-crafted inclusive language is neither.

A second, more substantive charge—that nonsexist usage is politically motivated—is, of course, true. Political realities have always shaped language, and English usage clearly reflects the exclusion from power of women as a class. The Renaissance philosopher-educators who formulated the humanist concept of the ideal citizen as a man of broad learning and artistic achievement were not interested in the education of women. The eighteenth-century political philosophers who championed the rights of man were concerned with the rights of men, not of women. When the framers of our Declaration of Independence expressed "a decent Respect to the Opinions of Mankind," they were oblivious of the fact that women, too, held valid opinions on the subject of governance.

It is sexism as a fact of history that has modified the meaning of *man*. Women's historical exclusion from such philosophical constructs as the Renaissance Man, the Common Man, and Mankind is a political reality that explains and underscores the sex-specific connotations *man*, *men*, and *mankind* have acquired in modern English. Avoiding those words today in contexts where sex is irrelevant is political, all right, but no more so than continuing to use them as though their old, inclusive meanings would still be understood.

No one can write about language and usage without expressing opinions that may strike others as overly rigid, or overly lenient, and Rosalie Maggio is no exception. If you agree, for example, that expressions like *according to Hoyle* and *wise as Solomon* so outnumber phrases like *Pandora's box* and *nervous Nelly* that it is well to avoid both varieties whenever possible (especially since the former tend to be positive and the latter negative), then you will welcome her conclusions about sex-linked metaphors. But if those terms and others like *jack-of-all-trades*, *master of arts*, and *fellowship* strike you as having moved so far from their sex-linked histories as to be gender-neutral, then you may opt to use them freely. In making such decisions logic helps very little, and a knowledge of etymology helps not at all: study after study demonstrates that the once-inclusive word *man* has so narrowed in meaning that it no longer functions generically, and yet almost all words incorporating the Old English masculine-gender suffix *-er*—as in *writer* and *teacher*—have long since moved the other way, and even the recalcitrant *waiter* appears to be following along that same road.

Fortunately, Rosalie Maggio knows that long-term changes in common usage follow no immutable laws, and the reference tool she has compiled provides the flexibility writers need to reach their own conclusions and make their own choices. Her objective is not to impose her point of view on others, but to assist people "at their own levels of understanding and commitment" to enunciate theirs. Whether you open this book to solve a particular problem or to browse through it for stimulating insights, you are in for a feast of words. Bon appétit!

Casey Miller and Kate Swift

Acknowledgments

The following wordsmiths were loving and generous with their suggestions, criticisms, and support: Sanford Berman, Joanna Cortright, Mary Kaye Cromer, Bonnie Goldsmith, Judy Johnston, Mary Maggio Pliner, Sister Judith Stoughton, and John Wall. I am particularly grateful to Irene and Paul Maggio, who knew how to raise their eight children in a gender-fair manner even before any books were written on the subject. I am also very much indebted to such pathfinding women and men as Casey Miller and Kate Swift, Cheris Kramarae, Paula Treichler, Mary Daly, Simone de Beauvoir, Dale Spender, Mary Ritchie Key, Ann Oakley, Bobbye D. Sorrels, Dennis Baron, and Alleen Pace Nilsen (among others), who have worked in powerful, insightful, and inspiring ways to tell us how our sexist language came to be, how it hurts all of us, and what we can do about it.

User's Guide

George Orwell recommended the "scrapping of every word or idiom that has outgrown its usefulness." This dictionary is designed to help you scrap outdated, stereotypical, and unrealistic sexist terminology.

Before using the dictionary to look up alternatives for sexist words and phrases, you may want to read through Appendix A, which contains guidelines on writing and speaking inclusively as well as the rationale for including words in this work. There you will also find definitions of such terms as *sexist* and *nonsexist, inclusive* and *exclusive*; information on avoiding falsely generic nouns; suggestions on replacing masculine pronouns; help with special situations (letter salutations, for example); recommendations for ensuring that your context is bias-free; and other practical, easy-to-use guidelines.

There is imperfect agreement today on which words are sexist and on what constitutes an adequate substitute for those that are. For example, some people believe the words *master, fellow*, and their compounds and derivatives are sexist; others do not. Still others accept *fellow*, but not *master*. Some people believe that no word should be gender-specific—for example, that we should use words like *member of congress* and *sales representative* instead of *congresswoman* and *salesman* even when we are speaking of a woman and a man. Other people are not at all bothered by this convention. (These issues are discussed in Appendix A.)

Some readers will choose never to use a sexist term, no matter how limited its substitutes or how difficult it is to get around it; others will believe that the use of a sexist word now and then in special circumstances is defensible. The dictionary is thus self-adjusting; readers will choose words at their own levels of understanding and commitment.

Not every entry is a sexist word. Some words are included here because they are ambiguous: Is a belly dancer always a woman? Is a Canadian Mountie always a man? Other words are included because, although they themselves are neutral, they are often used in sexist contexts. Still others are included because it is necessary to understand them before being able to use them inclusively.

When an entry word is sexist and requires a substitute, it is immediately followed by one or more alternatives. These alternatives (in italics) are listed in order of usefulness and are separated by semicolons when they are for different meanings of the entry word. Sometimes notes or comments follow the synonyms. However, if the entry word is not sexist or if alternatives are optional, you may have to read further for synonyms (if any).

Replacing sexist words and phrases with terms that treat all people respectfully can be satisfying and rewarding. It can also be difficult and frustrating, and it is good to admit that.

It is also necessary to acknowledge that there can be no solution to the problem of sexism in society on the level of language alone. Using the word *secretary* inclusively, for example, does not change the fact that only 1.6 percent of American secretaries are men. Using *director* instead of *directress* does not mean a woman will necessarily enjoy the same opportunities today that a man might. The language we use is symptomatic of our attitudes and belief systems. Changing the language does not automatically affect the way we think.

It is, however, impossible to think that we would *not* change language that "has outgrown its usefulness." Moving toward inclusive language is a small, but absolutely necessary step in encouraging the full human development of both sexes. And the payoffs are enormous: we assure justice and equal treatment to all in a country that at least nominally prizes equality; we clarify fuzzy, illogical, and unrealistic thinking; and our writing becomes more sharply expressive and dynamic. And yes, George, useful.

Why shouldn't we quarrel about a word? What is the good of words if they aren't important enough to quarrel over? Why do we choose one word more than another if there isn't any difference between them?

G. K. Chesterton

✦ ✦ ✦

abbess   the use of the feminine form of "abbott" is acceptable. This is one of the few exceptions to the rule about eliminating feminine endings; in most instances abbesses have been the equals of abbots in power, influence, and respect.

abigail   *See* lady's maid; maid.

abominable snowman   *yeti, the yeti.* "Yeti" is in any case the preferred term.

according to Hoyle   *according to/by the book, according to/playing by the rules, absolutely correct, cricket, in point of honor, on the square, proper/correct way to do things.* See Appendix A for the rationale on avoiding sex-linked metaphors, expressions, and figures.

Achilles' heel   *vulnerable point/spot, only weakness, chink in one's armor, where the shoe pinches.* See Appendix A for the rationale on avoiding sex-linked metaphors, expressions, and figures.

acid-conditioning man   *acid-conditioner.*

acid-correction man   *acid-correction hand, acid-corrector.*

acid man (explosives)   *nitrating-acid mixer.*

acolyte   usage of this word varies from one time, culture, and religion to another. In the Roman Catholic Church, for example, women can function as acolytes (one of the minor orders of the diaconate) but may not be officially installed as acolytes. Insofar as it means "attendant," an acolyte can be either a woman or a man.

act like a man   *act courageously/bravely/wisely/straightforwardly/ honorably,* etc., *show fortitude/patience/determination/strength/ vigor,* etc., *stand up for oneself, be independent/resolute/ unflinching/earnest,* etc., *sit tall in the saddle, stand tall, keep your chin up.* "Acting like a man" is a vague cultural stereotype that leaves the reader little the wiser. Identify instead the behavior you mean to describe and choose specific words for it. Note that the alternatives can also be used for a woman. *See also* manful/manfully; manlike/manly; take it like a man.

actress   *actor.* Many women today choose to call themselves actors, pointing out that they are, after all, members of the Actors' Guild. The word "actor" was used for both sexes for about seventy-five years before the general use of the word "actress," which is now commonly defined as "a woman who is an actor." The specification of gender here thus seems unnecessary and supports the male-as-norm system ("actor" being the standard and "actress" being the deviation). However, of all the words ending in "-ess" or "-ette," this is one of the least offensive today (although it will undoubtedly become more unacceptable), and if you use it out of respect for a woman who prefers to call herself an actress, you are probably not sinning grievously.

Adam's apple   leave as is; there is no easily recognized substitute for it other than a lengthy description ("the projection in the front of the neck formed by the largest cartilage of the larynx"). The term is derived from the mythical belief that the ruinous apple that Adam ate got stuck halfway down. Eve was not so afflicted, which is why generally only men have an Adam's apple.

Adam's rib   Janice Nunnally-Cox describes the two versions of the creation of woman and man in Genesis and then says, "In the Priestly account creation is simultaneous; in the Yahwist version woman comes decidedly after man, even though the term for 'man' is again *'adham,* or humankind. In the first story God blesses the people, calls them good, and then takes time to rest. The second story is filled with fear, anger, and strife: God takes no holy time of rest, and the people are not called good. The stories present us with a choice: it is for us to decide which story holds high meaning" (Nunnally-Cox 1981, p. xiv). In *Grammar and Gender* Dennis Baron discusses the concept of Adam's rib as it relates to sexism and language (Baron 1986, pp. 3–4). The phrase "Adam's rib" (as womankind's point of origin) should be set in quotes to show its dubiousness and reserved primarily for discussions of the term itself.

adjutant   woman or man.

adman   *advertising executive, creative/art director, copywriter, ad agent/ writer/creator, account executive/manager/supervisor, media buyer, ad rep; adman and adwoman* if used gender-fairly. Generic plurals: *advertising executives, ad agency staff, advertising people.* When possible, use specific job titles.

administrator   man or woman.

admiral   woman or man.

adulteress   *adulterer.*

advance man   *advance agent.*

adventuress   *adventurer.* Also: *sensation-seeker, explorer, pacesetter, globetrotter, bird of passage, gadabout, vagabond, gambler*—all equally applicable to women or men.

advertising layout man   *advertising layout planner.*

adzman   *adzer.*

aficionada/aficionado   *fan, enthusiast, devotee, nut, hound, buff.*

agent provocateur   man or woman. The French is in the masculine gender although it is used both in French and in English for women and men. If you prefer something that sounds more inclusive, use *infiltrating agent.*

agribusinessman   *farmer, agriculturist, agribusinessperson.* There are also *agribusinesswomen.* A recent news story used the last term to describe participants at the American Agri-Women national convention hosted by the Minnesota Women for Agriculture. *See also* farmer.

aide (medicine)   *nursing assistant, nurse assistant, N.A.* Traditionally, aides and orderlies did the same work, but all aides were women and all orderlies were men. Many hospitals and nursing homes now use the inclusive terms.

aide (general)   woman or man.

aide de camp   both military aides and civilian aides (for example, to an executive) can be women or men today; historically an aide de camp was a man.

aidman   *See* corpsman.

airdox man   *airdox fitter.*

airman   *aviator, pilot, flyer, airline pilot, co-pilot, test pilot, aerial navigator, flying officer, bombardier, aeronautical engineer, air marshal, aeronaut, balloonist, aviation/aircraft worker, glider, skydiver, paratrooper, parachutist, airborne trooper, member of the U.S. Air Force.* The U.S. Air Force refers to its members as airmen, although all its ranks are open to both women and men. The official Air Force publication is *The Airman.* Until the Air Force itself changes this term, it will continue to appear, although it can be circumvented by the use of "member of the U.S. Air Force."

airman basic/airman first class   man or woman.

airmanship   *aerial navigation/flying/piloting skills, flying ability, aeronautical/flying/piloting expertise.*

airplane steward/airplane stewardess   *See* steward/stewardess.

airport serviceman   *airport attendant/servicer.*

alderman   *council/city council member, city/municipal councilor; alderman and alderwoman* if used gender-fairly.

alewife (fish)   OK as is.

alimony   a woman or a man may receive alimony. In certain situations, this is referred to as back salary or reparations to avoid the old implication that one spouse is receiving unearned financial support from the other.

alleyman   *alley cleaner, bowling alley cleaner.*

all is fish that comes to his net *all is fish that comes to her/his/their net, everything they touch turns to gold, he/she/they can't lose for winning, they have/he or she has the magic touch.*

all men are created equal *all men and women/women and men are created equal, all people/we are all/all of us are created equal.* In 1848 at the first American Woman's Rights Convention, a "Declaration of Sentiments" was proposed that began: "We hold these truths to be self-evident: that all men and women are created equal; that they are endowed by their Creator with certain inalienable rights" (Anthony et al. 1889, vol. I, p. 70).

all the king's men *everybody, one and all, every last one, the whole world, everybody under the sun, all the monarch's soldiers. See also* all the world and his wife; everybody and his grandmother; every Tom, Dick, and Harry.

all the world and his wife *everyone, everybody, the whole world, every last one of them, all the world and their offspring. See also* all the king's men; everybody and his grandmother; every Tom, Dick, and Harry.

all work and no play makes Jack a dull boy *you know what they say about all work and no play; you know what they say, "all work and no play . . ."; all work and no play isn't good for anybody; all work and no play makes us pretty dull sorts; all work and no play makes Jill a dull girl/Jack a dull boy if used gender-fairly.*

alma mater this gender-specific term (it comes from the Latin meaning "fostering mother" or "bounteous mother") is not perceived as sexist. However, if you want to use strictly inclusive terminology as well as avoid a Latinate form, try *the university I (he/she/we/they/you) attended, my (your/his/her/our/their) graduating institution, my (her/his/their/our/your) college or university.* When "alma mater" refers to the school song, use such substitutes as *my school song, the school song, the University of Iowa school song.*

almsman *pauper, suppliant, mendicant, beggar, beneficiary, pensioner, recipient, welfare recipient.*

altar boy *server, acolyte.* Or, if the context requires sex-specificity, *altar girl and altar boy.*

alterations woman *alterer, tailor. See also* dressmaker; seamstress; sewing woman.

alto an alto is always a woman, although you will find both men and women singing in the alto range; the countertenor is the highest male voice and the contralto ("alto" is a contraction of contralto) is the lowest female voice.

alumna/alumnae/alumnus/alumni these Latin words, when used correctly to describe respectively a woman/women/a man/men who attended or graduated from a certain school, college, or university, are gender-fair. The most common mishandling of these terms is the use of "alumnus" to refer to either a man or a woman and the use of "alumni" to describe both women and men. To refer to men and women inclusively while also avoiding the use of the more pedantic Latin, use *graduate(s), alum(s), former student(s), ex-student(s).* If you must for some reason use the Latin, write *alumna/us* or *alumnus/a* and *alumni/ae* or *alumnae/i.*

Amazon/amazon   in Greek mythology Amazons were fabulous female warriors. As the 1970 edition of the *Encyclopaedia Britannica* explains (although later editions delete it): "The only plausible explanation of the story of the Amazons is that it is a variety of the familiar tale of a distant land where everything is done the wrong way about; thus the women fight, which is man's business." The word "amazon" is loaded with cultural and historical meanings; it has been used as a pejorative to describe certain women and certain kinds of women, but in other contexts it is a term of respect that women themselves use and appreciate. Use the term only if you have some knowledge of its history and multiple connotations. For the casual use of "amazon" meaning a tall, strong, or belligerent woman, substitute those or other descriptive adjectives. See Appendix A for the rationale on avoiding sex-linked metaphors, expressions, and figures.

ambassadress   *ambassador.*

ambassador   man or woman.

amen   the "men" in this word has nothing to do with gender; "amen" comes from the Hebrew word of the same spelling meaning "truly" or "certainly."

amiga/amigo   *friend.* If you want to use these terms, do so gender-fairly; "amiga" is feminine, "amigo" masculine.

analysis girl   *silver solution mixer.*

ancestress   *ancestor.* *See also* fathers; forefather.

anchoress   *anchorite.*

anchorman (newscasting)   *anchor, newscaster, announcer, reporter, TV reporter, commentator, broadcaster, communications artist, telecaster, narrator, news analyst.*

anchorman (black jack)   *third base.*

androgynous/androgyny   these are the ultimate nonsexist words as they contain the roots for both man ("andro") and woman ("gyn"). They are, however, often misunderstood. Those who call for an androgynous human race are thought to be promoting a unisex culture, for men and women to become indistinguishable from each other. Instead, what they hope for is the freedom for each man and each woman to be all that they are, whether that includes some so-called feminine qualities for men (sensitivity, intuition) or so-called masculine qualities for women (forcefulness, strength). "Androgyny suggests a spirit of reconciliation between the sexes; it suggests, further, a full range of experience open to individuals who may, as women, be aggressive, as men, tender; it suggests a spectrum upon which human beings choose their places without regard to propriety or custom" (Heilbrun 1973, pp. x–xi).

Gloria Steinem says the concept of androgyny "raised the hope that the female and male cultures could be perfectly blended in the ideal person; yet because the female side of the equation has yet to be affirmed, *androgyny* usually tilted toward the male. As a concept, it also raised anxiety levels by conjuring up a conformist, unisex vision, the very opposite of the individuality and uniqueness that feminism actually has in mind" (Steinem 1983, p. 158). John A. Sanford says, "Men are used to thinking of themselves only as men, and women think of themselves as women, but the psychological facts indicate that every human being is androgynous" (Sanford 1980, p. 3). And Samuel Taylor Coleridge said, "The truth is, a great mind must be androgynous." On the other hand, radical feminist Mary Daly refers to the word androgyny as a "semantic abomination": "The word is misbegotten—conveying something like 'John Travolta and Farrah Fawcett-Majors scotch-taped together' " (Daly 1978, p. xi). To use the word "androgyny" appropriately one needs to be comfortable with its various connotations. Note: androgyny is not to be confused with hermaphroditism, an anomalous condition in which a person has both female and male sex organs.

angel (referring to a woman) use with great caution. In many cultures and for many men, women are either angels (perfect and innocent) or they are witches and tempters. Our ideas of both angels themselves and women-as-angels are highly problematic, fantastic, and in some cases fairly insulting to real angels and real women.

angel of the Lord   *angel of God, angel.* **See also** Lord.

anima/animus in Jungian psychology, "anima" (the feminine form of the Latin word for "soul") refers to the female component in a man's personality, while "animus" (the masculine form) refers to the masculine component in a woman's personality. Use these as they are.

animal if you know the animal's gender and it is important for your audience to also know it, use it; otherwise refer to all animals of unknown or irrelevant gender as "it."

animal husbandman   *animal scientist.*

anthropology this word comes from the Greek words meaning "the study of human beings." Problems arise when it is mistranslated "the study of man." The Greeks (as well as Romans and Anglo-Saxons) differentiated between man-as-human-being and man-as-adult-male; the Greek word for the former ("anthropos") was used here and thus ought to be translated "human being."

antifeminist nonsexist; not all antifeminists are men.

any man's death diminishes me unless you are quoting Donne, use *anyone's death diminishes me.*

"ape-man"   *early human, prehuman, prehuman fossil, anthropoid ape.*

Apostolic Fathers leave as is; historically correct.

apprentice woman or man.

apron strings, tied to   *See* tied to [someone's] apron strings.

archfiend   man or woman. If you mean the devil, refer to it as "it."

arise as one man   *arise as one person/body, arise as one, arise of one accord, stand simultaneously, move as one/in a body, act in concert.* **See also** as one man; to a man.

armful (referring to a woman)   avoid this belittling term; it makes an object of a person.

artilleryman   *artillery personnel.* The word "artilleryman" is still used in the army, although an artilleryman can be either a man or a woman.

artiste   woman or man.

as one man   *unanimously, as one person, of the same mind, of one accord, at one with each other, willing, agreed on all hands, in every mouth, carried unanimously/by acclamation, everyone.* **See also** to a man.

asphalt-heater man   *asphalt-heater tender.*

assemblyman (manufacturing)   *assembler.*

assemblyman (politics)   *assembly member, state assembly member, member of the assembly, legislator, assemblywoman and assemblyman* (although "assembly member" is much preferred).

assembly-room foreman   *assembly-room supervisor.*

assistant cameraman   *dolly pusher.*

augerman   *rotary auger operator.*

au pair girl   *au pair, live-in family helper, family helper, live-in sitter/ child-minder.* There do not appear to be any male au pairs.

authoress   *author.*

automotive parts man   *automotive stock clerk.*

average man   *average person/citizen/human being/voter, common person/citizen/human being/voter, ordinary person/citizen/human being/voter, citizen, voter, layperson, taxpayer, resident, homeowner, landowner, passerby, nonspecialist, commoner, one of the people, one of the masses, rank and file; average woman and average man* if used gender-fairly.

aviatress/aviatrix   *aviator.* **See also** airman.

avuncular   there is no equivalent adjective for a woman; avoid "avuncular" and describe both sexes with words that convey your meaning: *indulgent, kindly, genial, expansive, friendly, conspiratorial,* etc.

axman   *axer.*

b

One must be chary of words because they turn into cages.

Viola Spolin

✦ ✦ ✦

babe/baby/baby doll (referring to a woman) avoid these terms. Women are neither babies nor dolls; using this sort of language promotes an inappropriate view of them.

bachelor *man.* Examine your need to refer to someone in terms of marital status. Something that is only one part of a person's life (being single) becomes the whole of the person when this label is used. The inclusive alternatives for "bachelor" would be *single, single person, unmarried person,* but even they should be avoided as much as possible because they tend to perpetuate the marriage-as-norm myth (the married person is the standard, the unmarried person the deviation). Note, incidentally, the nonparallel connotations of the two supposedly parallel terms, "bachelor" and "spinster."

bachelor girl/bachelorette *See* bachelor; spinster.

bachelor's degree *B.A., B.S., undergraduate degree, college degree, baccalaureate.* The last is a noun meaning a college or university bachelor's degree. It is therefore an exact synonym for "bachelor's degree" without gender-specific overtones (although its Latin roots are masculine). Dennis Baron says that the abbreviations for bachelor's degree will suggest masculinity only to the hypercritical (Baron 1986, p. 174). Eve Merriam offers "Certificate in the Arts" and "Certificate in the Sciences" as alternatives (Merriam 1974, p. 22).

backdoor man *illicit lover.*

back-shoe girl *back-shoe worker.*

back-up man *back-up, back-up worker, backer-up.*

backwoodsman *settler, wilderness settler, pioneer, woodcutter; backwoodsman and backwoodswoman* if used gender-fairly.

bad guy *See* badman; ne'er-do-well; rogue.

badman *thief, robber, outlaw, gangster, desperado, bank robber, cattle/horse thief, rustler. See also* gunman.

bad workman quarrels with his tools, a   *a bad worker quarrels with the tools, bad workers quarrel with their tools.*

bag/old bag (referring to a woman)   avoid these terms. Note that there is no parallel for a man.

baggageman   *baggage checker/handler/agent.*

bag lady/bag man (homeless)   *bag woman/bag man, street person.* The gender-fair use of "bag woman" and "bag man" (avoid the nonparallel lady/man) is sometimes appropriate, although we tend to hear a great deal more about the bag woman than we do about the bag man, even though statistically more men than women are forced into this lifestyle. In the plural, use *the homeless, street people* to place the emphasis on the central situation rather than on an incidental result of that situation.

bagman (British)   *traveling sales agent/representative.*

bagman (collector or distributor of illicit funds for someone else)   *go-between, bagger, shark, racketeer, peculator, receiver.*

bailsman   *bail/bond/bail bond/agent, provider, guarantor, bonding institution.*

balcony man   *platform worker.*

ball and chain (referring to a woman)   avoid this expression. Note that although women's being held back/enchained/weighed down by men has been a predominant feature of society for centuries, no parallel term to describe that facet of the male-female relationship ever made it into the (male-dominated) language.

ball boy   *tennis court attendant, ball/court attendant.*

ballerina   ballet companies assign narrow meanings to dancers' titles. A ballerina is a principal (but not the principal) female dancer in a company, a soloist. The term is commonly used to refer to any female ballet dancer, but this is not, strictly speaking, correct. Retain "ballerina" for its narrow meaning within ballet companies, but describe anyone who dances ballet nonprofessionally as a *ballet dancer.* **See also** danseur; premier danseur; prima ballerina.

ballet master/ballet mistress   these titles are fairly standard within professional ballet companies, but for all others, use *ballet instructor/teacher.*

ball the jack   *speed, go all out/full speed/full speed ahead, stake everything on one throw/attempt, no holds barred, all or nothing effort, anything goes.*

bandsman   *member of the band, band player, player in the band.* Or, be specific: *trumpeteer, drummer, saxophone player, pianist,* etc.

banshee   this female spirit has no male counterpart, but she plays an important part in Gaelic folklore, and the term should remain as is.

barber   man or woman.

bar boy   *bartender helper, bar helper, bar assistant/server, waiter.*

bard   *poet, poet-singer, epic/heroic poet, heroic versifier, minstrel, balladsinger.* "Bard" is not a sex-linked term, but it has acquired masculine overtones, probably from its close association with "the" bard, Shakespeare.

bargeman   *bargehand, deckhand.*

bargemaster   *barge captain.*

bark is worse than his bite, his   *See* his bark is worse than his bite.

barmaid   *bartender helper, bar assistant/server, waiter.*

barman   *bartender, bar attendant, barkeeper, barkeep.*

barren (referring to a woman)   *sterile, infertile.* These two alternatives can refer to both women and men. Avoid "barren," which carries a certain unwarranted stigma and is used only of women. Saying that someone is "childless" or "has no children" is not recommended as these phrases tend to support a children-as-norm stereotype.

barrister   woman or man.

barrow boy   *costermonger, street vendor.*

baseman (baseball)   *base player.*

bassman (music)   *bassist.*

bastard   avoid this term. Note that it is primarily an insult to a person's mother. To describe people whose parents were not married at the time of their birth, use *offspring/child/son/daughter of unmarried parents/single parent/unknown father.* Refer to the status of a person's birth only when it is relevant; too often it is gratuitous information. When it is important to your audience to know this, you may want to relay it in a neutral way, e.g., "She never knew who her father was." Or, "His birth certificate was blank after 'father's name.' " *See also* illegitimate/illegitimate child.

batboy   *batkeeper, bat attendant.* "Bat child" has also been suggested (Baron 1986, p. 189).

bathing beauty   *sunbather. See also* beauty queen.

batman   *aide.*

battered wife/battered woman   in general it is better to retain these sex-specific terms in order not to obscure the fact that it is primarily women who are battered. When an inclusive term is called for use *battered spouse/partner.*

battle-ax (referring to a woman)   *tyrant, grouch, ornery/quarrelsome/ domineering/strong-willed/high-handed/combative/hostile/ battlesome/hot-tempered person, bully, petty despot.*

bawd   *prostitute.* See Appendix A for a discussion of our language on prostitution.

bawdy   despite the connection with "bawd," this word is not exclusive to one sex.

beadsman/beadswoman (also spelled bedesman/bedeswoman)   *suppliant, licensed beggar, almshouse inmate, professional penitent.* In special instances, "beadswoman" or "beadsman" may be the correct choice. The only contravention is using "beadsmen" to indicate both men and women.

beard the lion in his den *beard the lion in its den.*

beau although "beau" and "belle" are the masculine and feminine forms of the same French word, the meanings for the two words have grown quite different from each other and are no longer parallel. *See* boyfriend for alternatives.

beau idéal although inclusive, this term looks sexist because of the masculine "beau" (the French noun "idéal" is grammatically masculine in gender and thus takes a masculine adjective). If you prefer, use *perfect model/type/example, standard model/type/example, paradigm.*

beautician/beauty school *cosmetologist/cosmetology school.* The newer terms are more inclusive and are preferred by cosmetologists.

beauty queen *beauty contest/beauty pageant winner; beautiful/attractive woman.*

bedesman/bedeswoman *See* beadsman/beadswoman.

beefeater has always been a man.

before you can say Jack Robinson *in two shakes of a lamb's tail, on the double, in a jiffy, immediately if not sooner, before you can say "knife," right off the bat, in one fell swoop, in a pig's whisper, pronto, straightaway, lickety-split, in the same breath, in the wink/ twinkling of an eye, at the drop of a hat, in double-quick time, on the spot, at once, immediately.* See Appendix A for the rationale on avoiding sex-linked metaphors, expressions, and figures.

beget in the general sense of creating something, half the time use *give birth to. See also* father (verb).

beggar man or woman.

beggarman/beggarwoman *beggar.*

be his own man *stand on one's own two feet, someone who can't be bought, be inner-directed/self-governing/independent, be one's/your/ her/his own person, be her own woman/his own man.*

bellboy *bellhop, attendant, passenger attendant.*

belle/belle of the ball *charming/popular/attractive person, flirt, center of attention, head-turner.*

bellman *bellringer, crier, herald, trumpeteer.*

belly dancer in the Middle East, belly dancing is a traditional women's folk dance and you will see no public performances by male dancers. In the United States, however, there are professional male belly dancers who perform publicly.

belt, hit a man below the *See* hit a man below the belt.

benchman *bench technician, bencher; sugar tester; bench baker.*

benefactress *benefactor.*

benjamin *youngest/favorite child.* See Appendix A for the rationale on avoiding sex-linked metaphors, expressions, and figures.

be one's own man/be your own man *stand on one's own two feet, be one's own person, be a do-it-yourselfer, be independent/ inner-directed/self-ruling/self-regulated/individualistic/outspoken/*

self-confident, be a free-thinker/free spirit, be at one's own disposal, be nobody's lackey.

best boy   *gaffer assistant, assistant to chief electrician, chief electrician's assistant.* These positions are held by both women and men.

best-laid schemes of mice and men, the   unless quoting Burns use simply *the best-laid schemes.*

best man and matron of honor/maid of honor   *best man and best woman.*

best man for the job   *best person for the job.*

better half (referring to either a man or a woman)   *spouse, partner, wife/husband, mate, best friend.* The "perfect marriage" has erroneously been held up as two half-people who are now a whole (Schaef 1981, p. 60). If you must think in halves, at least use "other half" instead of "better half."

biddy (referring to a woman)   this is ageist as well as sexist. Use instead words that can apply to persons of any age and either sex: *eccentric, character, odd duck, original,* etc.

bigot   woman or man.

billionaire   man or woman.

birdman   *aviator.* If you need to use "birdman," use also the female equivalent, "ladybird." *See also* airman.

bisexual   woman or man.

bishop   depending on the religious denomination, a bishop could be a man or a woman.

bitch (noun)   when used of a woman, this is one of the most loaded of the sexist words. It is vague and stereotypical and says more about the name-caller than it does about the name-callee since it is usually the knee-jerk response of a defensive person with a small vocabulary. To describe a trying woman, use *ruthless/aggressive/ domineering/controlling/powerful/tyrannical/overwhelming/ overpowering woman, spiteful/malicious/cruel/wicked/vicious/ cold-hearted/hard-hearted/merciless woman,* etc. When you mean the word in the sense of a complaint, use instead *gripe, complaint, problem, bone to pick, objection.* In the sense of something that is difficult, unpleasant, or problematic, use *predicament, tough one, thorny/knotty problem, uphill job, dilemma, bind.*

bitch (verb)   *complain, gripe, grouse, criticize, harp on.*

bitch goddess Success   unless quoting William James, avoid this term. Consider the psychology involved in attributing one's successes and failures to a powerful, capricious, female Other. *See also* Dame Fortune.

blackjack   in all its various meanings, this term, which comes from a man's name, has very specific associations and no substitutes. It is also rarely perceived as sexist; leave as is.

black Maria   *patrol/paddy wagon.*

black sheep   woman or man.

blindman's bluff/blindman's buff   this game has been played for many centuries under a number of different names, some of them nonsexist and more sensitive to the visually impaired: *blufty, hoodwink play, the brazen fly* (Iona and Peter Opie, *Children's Games in Street and Playground*. Oxford: Oxford University Press, 1969).

blonde   *blond.* Using "blonde" reinforces the male-as-norm pattern; that is, "blond" is the standard and "blonde" is the deviation. French-derived words of this type include brunet/brunette, divorcé/divorcée, fiancé/fiancée, all of which see.

blood brother   the term *blood sister* is also used; in the plural use *blood brothers and blood sisters/blood sisters and blood brothers.*

Bluebeard   the original Bluebeard, Gilles de Rais, abducted, raped, and murdered between forty and one hundred peasant youths. "The most amazing part of the Gilles de Rais story is that the legend of Bluebeard's Castle that we know today has metamorphosed from a terrifying account of a sex-murderer of small boys to a glorified fantasy of a devilish rake who killed seven wives for their 'curiosity' " (Brownmiller 1975, pp. 323–24). According to Brownmiller, it is more palatable to the sex in power to accept women in the role of victim than themselves. Do not perpetuate the recast Bluebeard story.

bluestocking   *intellectual, member of the literati, wit, artistic/learned person, egghead, dilettante, dabbler, amateur, culture vulture.* This derisory term for an educated or literary woman was originally used for both men and women, although no parallel term developed for men when this one became limited to women.

board boy/board girl   *board maker.*

board man   *board member.*

boatman   *boater, boat worker/dealer.*

boatswain   *ship warrant officer/petty officer, deck crew/topside supervisor, rigging boss.* The "swain" comes from "swein" meaning "boy" or "servant." However, the word seems associated with men more because virtually all boatswains have been men than because of the word's roots.

Bob's your uncle   *there you are! there you have it! voilà!* For the rationale on avoiding sex-linked metaphors, expressions, and figures, see Appendix A.

bodyguard   woman or man. Because the position of bodyguard was for so long limited to men, you may want to use a term that sounds more inclusive: *personal protection agent/operative.*

bogeyman   *bogeymonster, bogey, phantom, nightmare.*

bomb disposal man   *bomb disposal specialist, explosives expert/ specialist.*

bondman/bondwoman   *bondslave, bond servant, slave, serf.*

bondsman (law)   *bonding/bond/bail/bail bond agent, surety provider, guarantor, bonding institution.*

bondsman/bondswoman (slave)   *See* bondman/bondwoman.

bonhomie   *good-naturedness, geniality, cheerfulness, light-heartedness, optimism, happiness, joy, liveliness, friendliness, affability.* This word comes from the French for "good man" and is most often applied to men and groups of men, which is why alternatives are suggested. However, there is nothing to contraindicate using it to refer to women and to groups of both women and men.

bon vivant   *connoisseur, hedonist, epicure, aesthete, sensualist, high-liver, sophisticate, enthusiast, someone with a great deal of joie de vivre.* The French is in the masculine gender, and this term has become associated primarily with men over the years, but there's nothing to say you couldn't apply it to a woman.

bookie/bookmaker   woman or man.

bookman   *bookseller, publisher's representative, book dealer/collector/ salesperson, bookstore clerk/owner, bibliophile, bookworm, librarian.*

boom man   *log sorter.*

bootjack   OK as is; although the "jack" originally came from a man's name, it now refers to lifting, twisting, folding tools like the jackknife, the hydraulic jack, etc.

bordello   *house of prostitution.* See Appendix A for a discussion of our language on prostitution.

border patrolman   *border guard/patrol, member of the border patrol.*

born out of wedlock   avoid this dated and judgmental expression. If it is truly necessary for your audience to know the circumstances of someone's birth, use neutral terms. *See also* bastard; illegitimate/ illegitimate child.

borrow from Peter to pay Paul   *borrow from the left hand to pay the right, juggle the bills, keep one step ahead of the bailiff, indulge in creative accounting, six of one and half a dozen of the other.* For the rational on avoiding sex-linked metaphors, expressions, and figures see Appendix A.

boss man   *boss, straw/job boss. See also* foreman.

boulevardier   *See* man about town.

bowman (boats)   *bow paddler, rower, boater.*

bowman (weapons)   *archer.*

box man (gambling)   *box boss/supervisor/collector.*

boy (referring to a man)   *man, young man.* "Boy" usually refers to someone no more than sixteen and sometimes no more than twelve or thirteen, depending on the context and on the boy/ young man himself.

boy (drugs)   *heroin.*

boy and girl   half the time use "girl and boy."

boycott   nonsexist; named after Charles C. Boycott.

boyfriend   *friend, man friend* (if "woman friend" is also used), *male friend* (if "female friend" is also used), *escort, date, companion, longtime/loving/live-in companion, romantic interest, significant other, roommate, partner, partner of long standing, steady, paramour, lover, live-in lover, fiancé* (q.v.), *sweetheart.* The Census

Bureau uses POSSLQ (person of the opposite sex sharing living quarters); if this expression ever becomes popular, you may want to know how to pronounce it: POSSelcue.

boyish replace this vague word with specific inclusive adjectives for the characteristics you want to describe: *ingenuous, naive, childlike, innocent, open, friendly, eager, youthful, inexperienced, immature,* etc.

boy scout there is nothing particularly sexist about the terms "boy scout" and "girl scout" (although the goals, activities, and attitudes of the two groups have often been based on sexist concepts). You may, however, want to use another term that is gaining acceptance: *youth scout.*

boys in blue (Civil War) *Union soldiers, bluecoats, the Blue, Army blue.*

boys in blue (general) even "men in blue" (which is better than "boys in blue") is no longer correct because the armed forces consists of both women and men. Use instead *soldiers, members of the armed forces, armed forces personnel.*

boys in gray (Civil War) *Confederate soldiers, graycoats, graybacks, the Gray.*

boys will be boys *children will be children.* This expression is also sometimes used archly of men when they show their enjoyment of games, adult "toys," or practical jokes. It is a meaningless sexist stereotype and better left unsaid.

bra burner do not use this term; it is inaccurate. When feminists protested at the 1968 Miss America Pageant in Atlantic City, women threw brassieres into a trash can, thereby shedding what they considered a symbol of female oppression. Although burning was in fact outlawed by a municipal fire ordinance and never did occur, newspapers mistakenly reported "bra burning."

brakeman *brake tender/holder/coupler, braker, yard coupler.*

bravado characteristic of both men and women.

brave (Indian) always a man.

brazen usually ascribed to women, as in "brazen hussy," and therefore sexist. Use instead *fearless, dauntless, bold, daring, brash, defiant, audacious, plainspoken, outspoken, candid, frank.*

breadwinner man or woman.

brethren *brothers and sisters/sisters and brothers, people, congregation, assembly, colleagues, friends, associates, community, family, kin, believers, the faithful, neighbors.*

brewmaster *brewing director, head brewer.*

bridal consultant *wedding consultant.*

bride *See* give away the bride.

bridegroom *groom.* Note that "bridegroom" is "one of the few English masculines that seem to derive from a feminine" (Baron 1986, p. 48).

bridesmaid *bridal attendant.*

brigadier/brigadier general woman or man.

brigand   this old word referred almost exclusively to men; today's brigand is probably a terrorist, which may be either a woman or a man.

bring home the bacon   both women and men do this.

brinkmanship   *gamesplaying, gameplaying, courting catastrophe, bluff, bluffing, savvy, gambling, playing chicken.*

brothel   *house of prostitution.* See Appendix A for a discussion of our language on prostitution.

brother (drugs)   *heroin.*

brother (religion)   retain because of narrow meaning and because all orders with brothers consist of men; there are of course orders with sisters, although "brother" and "sister" do not signify entirely parallel roles.

brotherhood   *amity, society, association, organization, social organization, common-interest group, kinship, shared kinship, companionship, friendship, comradeship, unity, community, brotherhood and sisterhood.* Note that while "brotherhood" is used either as a false generic or to refer to specific all-male organizations, "sisterhood" has a sex-specific, nonorganizational significance for many women, and should be used as is in some contexts.

brotherhood of man   *human family, bond of humanity, kinship, human community/bond, solidarity, friendship, humanity, humankind.* Depending on how you feel about "fellow" there is also: *fellow-feeling, fellowship.*

brotherliness   *affection, concern, warmth. See also* brotherly love.

brotherly   this is a useful and accurate sex-specific word in most cases. Sometimes, however, it is used stereotypically when other words would be more accurate and descriptive: *affectionate, loving, kindly, protective, indulgent,* etc.

brotherly love (generic)   *kindheartedness, goodwill, philanthropy, charity, good-naturedness, generosity, benevolence, loving kindness, geniality, human feeling, benignity, beneficence, unselfishness, friendship, amiability, tolerance, consideration, affectionate/human love, love of others/of neighbor, other love, love of people.* Some people will not be bothered by the use of *fellow-feeling. See also* City of Brotherly Love.

brothers (generic)   *sisters and brothers/brothers and sisters, people, friends, the faithful, believers, neighbors, congregation, assembly, colleagues, associates, community, family, kin.*

brother's keeper   *See* I am not my brother's keeper.

brunette   *brunet.* The preferred dictionary usage is "brunet," although we tend to see "brunette" more often. However, using "brunette" reinforces the male-as-norm pattern; that is, like "blond/blonde," "brunet" is the standard and "brunette" is the deviation. *See also* divorcé/divorcée; fiancé/fiancée; habitué; protegé/protegée.

buccaneer   *See* pirate.

buckaroo   *See* cowboy.

buddy woman or man, boy or girl. Note that this word comes from the word "brother" and is a positive term denoting closeness and friendship, whereas its counterpart, "sissy" (from "sister"), is never used positively. In spite of its masculine associations, "buddy" can be used of either sex.

built (referring to a woman's figure) *See* sweater girl.

bull dyke avoid this offensive term. Note, however, that the word "dyke," q.v., is generally acceptable.

bullheaded can be said of either a woman or a man.

bullish on America *strong on America, optimistic about America.* Stock market terms using "bull" are some of the least overtly offensive sexist terms we have, and some readers will view their inclusion here as nit-picking. Others will appreciate the cumulative and largely covert effect of the many such expressions in the language, and will seek to replace them with sex-neutral expressions. *See also* bull market.

bull market *rising/improving/buy/favorable market. See also* bullish on America.

bull session nonsexist; "bull" here does not refer to the animal but to fraud or deceit, from the word "boule." However, if you want a more neutral-appearing term, try *rap/brainstorming session, free-for-all/informal discussion.*

bully man or woman, girl or boy.

bum this is nonsexist in itself, but although it can refer to either a woman or a man, it tends to be reserved for men. You may want to use more inclusive-sounding terms: *street person, homeless person, beggar, hobo, vagabond, sponger, scrounger, vagrant, parasite, loafer, idler, good-for-nothing.* Note that the word "bum" and all its traditional synonyms (the newer terms "street person" and "homeless person" are excluded) are pejorative terms, which seem insensitive; at least some of the homeless today are victims of a combination of societal values, political decisions, the economy, and bad luck. *See also* ne'er-do-well.

busboy *busser, busperson, dining room attendant, dish carrier, room service assistant/attendant.*

Bushman/Bushmen Sanford Berman, head cataloguer of the Hennepin County (Minneapolis) Library, describes these terms as not only sexist, but racist as well; the ethnic groups so described find the terms inaccurate and unacceptable. Their proper name is "San." Berman warns against replacing "Bushman/Bushmen" with "native/natives" or "tribe/tribes" as these terms are ethnocentric and racist when used in Third World contexts.

businessman *executive, business executive, member of the business community, business leader, professional, merchant, entrepreneur, industrialist, manager, investor, speculator, trader.* If used gender-fairly *businessman and businesswoman* are additional possibilities, although not high on the list, and *businessperson* comes in a poor last choice. Or, be specific: *stockbroker,* *advertising executive, chief executive officer, public relations officer,* etc.

busman/busman's holiday   *bus driver/bus driver's holiday.*

busy as a hen with one chick   *never idle, going full tilt, have many irons in the fire, have one's hands full, not a moment to call one's own, in the thick of things, doesn't let the grass grow under one's feet, on the go/move/fly, tireless, up to one's eyebrows/ears in, not have a moment to spare, in full swing, not a minute to waste.*

butch (referring to a woman)   describing one of the two roles in a dyke relationship (the other is "femme"), this word is not considered offensive to lesbians today (although it has not always been so acceptable). However, it should still be used with sensitivity and a sure knowledge of your audience.

butcher   woman or man; some seven percent of butchers are women.

butler   invariably a man.

C

The difference between the right word and the almost right word is the difference between lightning and the lightning bug.

Mark Twain

cabana boy *cabana attendant.*

cabbages and kings unless quoting Lewis Carroll use *this and that, odds and ends, threads and thrums.*

cabin boy *cabin attendant.*

cabinet member currently this term can indicate either a woman or a man. Before 1933 in the United States, however (the year Frances Perkins was appointed), all American cabinet members were men.

cabman *cabdriver.*

caddie/caddy girl or boy.

cadet in the service academies, a cadet might be a young woman or a young man. In another of its meanings, "cadet" refers specifically to a younger brother or son. If you are using it as slang, use instead *pimp.*

Caesar's wife *beyond reproach, above suspicion, someone whose conduct is impeccable, someone about whom there hovers the odor of sanctity, irreproachable, unimpeachable, innocent, blameless, sinless, clean-handed.* See Appendix A for the rationale on avoiding sex-linked metaphors, expressions, and figures.

calendar girl *calendar model.*

call boy *page, caller.*

call girl/call girl service/call house *prostitute/prostitution service/house of prostitution.* See Appendix A for a discussion of our language on prostitution.

camaraderie an inclusive term, although it has often been thought the province of men to share this feeling of unity and goodwill. The French word itself (spelled the same way) is feminine in gender. *See also* brotherhood; fellowship (companionship).

cameragirl/cameraman *photographer, camera operator.* Note the unequal "girl/man" construction.

cameramen *camera crew, photographers, camera operators.*

camp follower if you mean this term in the sense of prostitute, use *prostitute*. In the sense of a politician who switches parties for reasons of personal gain, the term can be applied to either a woman or a man.

can-can dancer this has always been a woman; there is no equivalent for a man.

candy man *drug pusher*. In addition to being inclusive, "drug pusher" is an accurate reflection of reality whereas "candy man" is a cover-up.

candy-striper *volunteer, junior/teen/hospital volunteer*. These volunteers are both girls and boys, young men and young women.

canon depending on the denomination, a canon might be a woman or a man.

canoness *canon*.

cantor man or woman.

captain woman or man.

carboy nonsexist; comes from the Persian "qaraba" meaning "large bottle."

career girl/career woman *professional, business executive, executive trainee, longtime/full-time employee*. Or, be specific: *sales representative, paralegal, scientist, career scientist, industry representative, public relations agent, social worker, professor, engineer, administrative assistant,* etc. If you are tempted to use "career woman," consider whether you would use "career man," and then handle the situation the way you would have for a man.

cart boy *cart attendant*.

Casanova *lover, great romantic, dashing lover, flirt*. See Appendix A for the rationale on avoiding sex-linked metaphors, expressions, and figures.

cash boy *cash messenger*.

Caspar Milquetoast *See* milquetoast/milksop.

castrate/castrating avoid except in its literal meaning; if you must use it metaphorically, be sure you are on sound psychological ground, but it is preferable to use a more precise alternative. For "castrate": *disarm, disable, incapacitate, undermine, unhinge, unnerve, deprive of power/strength/courage/vigor, devitalize, attenuate, shatter, exhaust, weaken, disqualify, invalidate, paralyze, muzzle, enervate, tie the hands of, draw the teeth of, clip the wings of, spike the guns of, take the wind out of one's sails, put a spoke in one's wheels*. For "castrating": *ruthless, aggressive, domineering, controlling, powerful, tyrannical, overwhelming, overpowering. See also* castrating bitch/castrating woman.

castrating bitch/castrating woman avoid these expressions. They blame women for something that takes two to accomplish. It is not possible to castrate a secure, independent person; the man is not an anesthetized patient in this type of surgery. *See also* castrate/castrating.

catechumen/catechumenate nonsexist; these words come from the Greek for "someone being instructed."

cat may look at a king, a *a person can dream, can't they?* (see Appendix A on the singular "they"), *someone who lives in a fool's paradise/has airy hopes/hopes against hope/catches at a straw/ makes sheep's eyes at/eyes wistfully/longingly.*

cattleman *cattle owner/raiser/buyer/grower/producer, rancher, farmer.*

catty *malicious, spiteful, snide, sly, underhanded, disingenuous, envious.* "Catty" is used exclusively to describe women whereas the alternatives can refer to either sex.

cavalryman *cavalry soldier/officer, horse soldier.*

caveman (man who behaves primitively toward women) *clod, slob, fumbler, boor, insensitive/ill-mannered person, masher.* It is not possible to render this concept inclusively as it refers by definition to a man, but you can use words that are less sexist-appearing than "caveman," which is also contraindicated on the grounds that it is probably ethnocentric and inaccurate.

caveman/cavewoman *cave dweller, early/Stone Age human.*

cellarman *cellar clerk/laborer, winery worker.*

centerfold girl *centerfold model.*

CEO (chief executive officer) woman or man.

chainman *surveyor's assistant, chain surveyor helper; chain offbearer; pattern assembler.*

chairman (noun) *chair, moderator, committee head, presiding officer, presider, chairer, convener, coordinator, president, department head, leader, discussion/group leader, head, speaker, facilitator, director, supervisor, manager, administrator, chairperson.* Some people do not object to *chairwoman and chairman* when they are used equally and fairly in a passage, but in general it is better to keep this term gender-free rather than gender-fair because of certain cultural overtones to the word "chairwoman." The worst offense here is to refer in the same material to a man as a "chairman" and to a woman as a "chairperson"; keep the terms parallel. Note that there is a fine precedent for the word "chair": according to the *Oxford English Dictionary*, "chair" was already being used in 1647, some seven years before the first recorded use of "chairman."

chairman (verb) *chair, head, lead, moderate, direct, supervise, officiate, preside, convene, coordinate, facilitate, control, oversee, organize, govern.*

chamberlain historically this has been a man. However, in some contexts you can use the alternatives *treasurer, chief officer,* which may denote either a man or a woman.

chambermaid *room attendant.*

champion woman or man.

chancellor man or woman.

change booth man *cashier.*

chanteuse *singer.*

chaperone *chaperon.*

chaplain woman or man.

chapman *peddler.*

chargé d'affaires man or woman.

charley horse *cramp, leg/muscle cramp, stiffness.* For the rationale on avoiding sex-linked metaphors, expressions, and figures, see Appendix A.

charwoman *char, charworker, cleaner, janitor, maintenance worker, custodian.*

chaste/chastity be sensitive to the context in which these terms are used so that there is no double standard.

chatelaine use as is in historical context.

chatter avoid this sexist term, which tends to be reserved for women, children, birds, and squirrels, and which implies a certain value judgment—that the conversation is trivial and irrelevant. Use instead terms that can be applied to both sexes: *talk idly, shoot the breeze, indulge in small talk, be talkative/loquacious/garrulous, ramble, run off at the mouth, rattle on, pour forth, talk oneself hoarse, talk at random, talk a donkey's hind leg off.*

chauffeur woman or man.

chauffeuse *chauffeur.*

chauvinist pig *See* male chauvinism/mail chauvinist/male chauvinist pig.

cheap-jack *huckster.*

checkout girl/checkout man *checkout/desk clerk, cashier.* Note the nonparallel "girl/man" construction.

checkroom girl/checkroom woman *checkroom attendant.*

cheerleader man or woman.

chef woman or man.

cherchez la femme! a mystery story favorite implying that wherever there is dirty work afoot, there must be a woman involved. On one level it is fairly harmless, but it should be used cautiously because of its covert message.

chessman *chess piece.*

Chevalier of the Legion of Honor this and other Legion of Honor orders can be awarded to both men and women.

Chicana/Chicano these acceptable gender-specific terms ("Chicana" is female, "Chicano" male) are used interchangeably with "Mexican American" to refer to members of the Mexican subculture in the United States, but use them gender-fairly.

chick (referring to a woman) avoid.

chief/chief justice/chief master sergeant/chief master sergeant of the Air Force/chief petty officer/chief warrant officer/chief of staff/chief of state man or woman.

child is father of the man, the unless quoting Wordsworth, use *the child is parent to the adult, the child begets/gives birth to the adult, the oak tree sprouts from the acorn, the seeds of the future lie in the past/present.*

chimney sweep girls and women have not historically been chimney sweeps; today in the United States both men and women own, operate, and work for chimney cleaning companies, although neither actually climb inside chimneys anymore.

china doll (referring to a woman) eschew this term; women are not dolls.

Chinaman *Chinese.* The offensive term "Chinaman" is racist as well as sexist; use "Chinese" for both men and women.

Chinaman's chance *no chance, no chance at all, not a hope in hell, fat chance, slim chance, a snowball's chance in hell, as much chance as a snowflake in hell, doomed, unlucky, ill-omened, ill-fated, unblessed.* Note that "Chinaman's chance" is racist as well as sexist.

chip off the old block the child and parent here could be either sex, but as this phrase is so often used to indicate fathers and sons, you may want to use instead *the spit and image, the spitting image, following in the footsteps of, the very image/picture of, cast in the same mold, for all the world like, a carbon copy of, as alike as two peas in a pod.*

chippie (woman) *prostitute.*

chit (girl or young woman) avoid; there is no similar word for a boy or young man.

chivalrous *courteous, considerate, protective, courtly, valiant, brave, civil, generous, honorable, gallant, kindly, heroic, mannerly, gracious, well-bred, upstanding.*

chivalry *courtesy, honor, high-mindedness, gallantry, consideration, bravery, courage, civility, valor, fidelity, mannerliness.*

choirboy *choir member/singer, member of the choir, singer.*

choirmaster *choir/music/song director, choir/music/song leader, director of the choir.*

chorine *cabaret/nightclub dancer, chorus member, member of the chorus.*

chorus boy/chorus girl *chorus member, member of the chorus, singer, dancer, musical cast member.*

chump *fool, dupe.* "Chump" ought to be inclusive, but it is invariably used for men. ***See also*** scapegoat.

church father *See* Fathers of the Church.

church/she "church" is neuter, and its proper pronoun is "it"; avoid the use of "she" and "her."

churchman *church member/worker, churchgoer, churchperson, member of a church; churchwoman and churchman* if they are used gender-fairly. Also: *clergy, ecclesiastic, priest, presbyter, pastor, minister, confessor, elder,* etc.

cigarette girl *cigarette vendor.*

city councilman *city councillor, city council member; councilwoman and councilman* if used gender-fairly.

city fathers *city leaders/founders/councillors/elders/officials/legislators/administrators/bureaucrats.*

city hostess *goodwill ambassador.*

City of Brotherly Love Philadelphia continues to use this phrase to describe itself; certain people refer to "the City of Human Love," but until Philadelphia changes its motto, it should be left as is.

claim(s) man *claim(s) agent.*

clairvoyante *clairvoyant.* Using the base word to refer to both sexes is preferred in such pairs as blond/blonde, brunet/brunette, chaperon/chaperone, divorcé/divorcée, fiancé/fiancée, protegé/protegée.

clansman *clan member, member of a clan.*

cleaning girl/cleaning lady/cleaning woman *household worker, cleaner, housecleaner, houseworker, domestic cleaner, housekeeper, office cleaner, janitor, maintenance worker, custodian, charworker.*

clergyman *clergy, cleric, member of the clergy.* Or, be specific: *pastor, minister, deacon, presbyter, elder, ecclesiastic, confessor, bishop, prelate, rector, parson, dean, vicar, chaplain, preacher, missionary,* etc.

cleric/clerical may describe either a woman or a man.

clodhopper this term tends to be used more of a man than of a woman, although it is in itself not gender-specific. However, it is a pejorative, anti-farmer stereotype and as such should be avoided.

close shave this can be used of either sex as it does not necessarily refer to shaving whiskers. "Shave" is used here in the sense of removing a thin layer of anything and proceeding with difficulty, as in "scraping by" or "close scrape."

clotheshorse as this expression invariably refers to a woman, use more neutrally perceived terms: *fashion plate, fancy/fashionable/sharp/conspicuous dresser, tailor's/sartorial dream, a person it pays to dress, one who keeps the tailor in business, clothes-conscious person.*

clothes make/don't make the man *clothes make/don't make the person/individual, clothes can break/make a person, clothes aren't everything, you must dress for success, the right clothes make a difference, don't judge a book by its cover, appearances are deceptive, all that glitters is not gold.*

clubman/clubwoman *club member, member of the club; clubber, joiner, social person.*

coachman *coach driver, driver.* In some historical contexts you may want to use "coachman."

coadjutress *coadjutor.*

coastguardsman *coastguard, coastguarder, member of the coastguard.*

co-chairman *co-chair.*

cock-a-hoop *feeling one's oats, flushed with victory, happy as a lark, merry as a cricket, lighthearted, jubilant, exultant, triumphant, jaunty; awry, out of shape, askew.*

cock-and-bull story *snow job, nonsense, a lot of nonsense, stuff and nonsense, tall tale, yarn, preposterous/improbable story, canard, moonshine, bunkum, poppycock, hot air, hogwash, banana oil, balderdash, applesauce.*

cock of the roost *arrogant, conceited, careless, overbearing, in high feather, on a high horse, sitting pretty, riding tall in the saddle.*

cock of the walk *crème de la crème, flower of the flock; tyrant, dictator, leader, ruler.*

cocksure *self-confident, overconfident, self-important, in love with oneself, pushy, overbearing, aggressive, conceited, supercilious.*

cocky *jaunty, brash, cheeky, flippant, saucy, nervy, impertinent, insolent, careless; overly confident, overbearing, arrogant, swaggering, haughty, conceited.*

coed *student.* Avoid "coed" unless it refers to both women and men. Its original meaning was simply "coeducational student," but it has since acquired pejorative overtones for women and has no male counterpart.

coeducation generally an unnecessary term. It was coined to signal the entry of women into previously all-male universities—another deviation from the "norm."

coffee girl/coffee man *coffee maker/server.* Note the nonparallel "girl/man."

co-heiress *co-heir.*

cohort woman or man.

coiffeur/coiffeuse *hairdresser, hair stylist, haircutter.*

college girl *college/university student.* Note that the masculine equivalent is usually "college man," not "college boy." Therefore, if necessary to specify sex, use "college man" and "college woman."

colonel man or woman.

colonist colonists have been both women and men; be careful of using this word generically and then implying that colonists were only men (for example, "colonists, their wives and families").

coloratura retain as is.

colporteur although this French word is masculine in gender, it is used in French and English to refer to both sexes. To avoid the masculine flavor, use *religious book peddler.*

combination girl/combination man *short-order cook.* Note the nonparallel "girl/man."

comedienne *comedian.*

come on like gangbusters this phrase comes from a 1936 radio show with startlingly loud opening music, and although the original gangbusters were male, the expression can be used of either sex today.

come to man's estate *come of age, attain majority, settle down, become adult, mature, come into one's own.*

commandant woman or man.

commander man or woman.

commander-in-chief in the United States, this is the President, and thus gender depends on the person in office.

command sergeant major woman or man.

committeeman/committeewoman   *member of the committee, committee member; ward leader, precinct leader.* "Committeewoman" and "committeeman" are not as equal as they may seem; "committeewoman" often has pejorative overtones.

commodore   man or woman.

common-law husband/common-law wife   *common-law spouse,* except when sex-specific terms are necessary. Beware of the sexist tendency to denigrate the woman in this household but not the man. In a few states, common-law spouses are in fact regarded as legally married, so disapproval based on missing marriage lines is misplaced.

common man   *common citizen/person/human/human being/voter, average citizen/person/human/human being/voter, ordinary person/ citizen/human/human being/voter, layperson, taxpayer, voter, resident, homeowner, landowner, passerby, one of the people, citizen, the nonspecialist, commoner, rank and file.*

company man   *See* organization man.

comparable worth   this term refers to pay schedules that offer equal pay for jobs that are similar in education requirements, skill levels, work conditions, and other factors. This concept differs from that of equal pay for equal work, which means that people doing the same job receive equal pay—for example, female and male nurses of equal seniority working on the same floor of the same hospital receive the same pay. Comparable worth means that a female clerk-typist might earn the same as a male warehouse employee. Comparable worth supporters seek "the expansion of U. S. civil rights laws to require that not only men and women holding the *same* jobs but those holding dissimilar jobs of comparable worth get the same pay" (Kramer 1986, p. 122). The push for comparable worth is based on the fact that women earn less than men—64 percent of men's annual earnings or 72 percent of men's hourly earnings. Some states have revised pay scales and have even paid back wages, others are studying the situation, and some businesses have halted pay disparities. *See also* equal pay/equal pay for equal work.

compatriot   man or woman. Although "compatriot" has masculine roots ("patria," the Latin word for country, actually means "land of my father," based on "pater" for father), the word seems to be used in an inclusive manner today.

comptroller   woman or man.

comrade   man or woman.

conceive   when this word is used in the generic sense of creating an idea, use alternatives that are not sex-linked: *imagine, dream up, think, invent, fashion, create, formulate, design, devise, contrive, concoct, hatch, form, originate, initiate, bring about. See also* beget; seminal.

concertmaster   *concert leader/director.* Note that some concert directors, both women and men, prefer to be called "concertmasters."

concierge woman or man.

confessor in the strictest historical sense, a confessor is and has been male; a similar function is served today by a *spiritual director,* who can be either a woman or a man. Also: *mother confessor/ father confessor, confidant, adviser, therapist, counselor, mentor, preceptor.*

confidante *confidant.* Using the base word to refer to both sexes is preferred in such pairs as blond/blonde, brunet/brunette, chaperon/chaperone, divorcé/divorcée, fiancé/fiancée, protegé/ protegée.

confidence man *con artist, confidence operator, swindler, operator, chiseler, flimflammer, fraud, cheat, charlatan, mountebank, trickster, quack, shark, crook, dodger, defrauder, sharpie, scoundrel, hoodwinker, phony, imposter, shortchange/bunko artist, snollygoster.*

confraternity *society, union, association, organization.* "Confraternity" is based on the Latin word for "brother."

confrere *colleague, associate, co-worker, teammate, collaborator, partner, companion, comrade, confederate, accomplice.* "Confrere" is based on the French (and before that the Latin) word for "brother."

congressman *member of Congress, representative, legislator, member of the United States House of Representatives, delegate.* You may also use *congressman and congresswoman* if they are used fairly, and if "congressman" is not used as a false generic. "Congressperson" is not recommended, although it is seen in print from time to time.

con man *con artist. See also* confidence man.

connoisseur man or woman.

conscript woman or man.

constable depending on locale, a constable might be either a woman or a man.

consul man or woman.

contact man *song plugger, advance agent.*

controller woman or man.

control man *control panel operator, control operator, controller.*

conveyor belt man *conveyor belt repairer/tender/worker.*

copyboy/copygirl *copy messenger/carrier.*

Cornishman use also *Cornishwoman.* Plural: *inhabitants of Cornwall, Cornishwomen and Cornishmen* (but not "Cornishmen and women"). It's generally not possible to replace words like "Cornishman," "Norseman," "Irishman," and "Dutchman" with one pithy inclusive term; you may have to either circumlocute or use the longer phrase: *Cornishwoman and Cornishman.*

corporal woman or man.

corpsman this term is still used by the Marine Corps although it may designate either a woman or a man.

cosmonaut man or woman.

costerman *costermonger, street vendor.*

councilman *councillor, council member.* You may also use *councilwoman and councilman* if they are used fairly, and if "councilman" is not used as a false generic. "Councilperson" is not recommended, although it is seen and heard from time to time.

countergirl/counterman *counter attendant.* Note the nonparallel "girl/man."

country bumpkin this term tends to be used more of a man than of a woman, although it is not in itself gender-specific. However, it supports a pejorative, anti-farmer stereotype and should be avoided on that ground.

countryman *compatriot* (q.v.), *citizen, inhabitant, native, native inhabitant, resident, indigene; countrywoman and countryman* if used gender-fairly.

courtesan *high-class prostitute.* Note that a courtesan used to be the female equivalent of a courtier; "courtier" retains most of its former meaning, but "courtesan" has been completely devalued and there is no remaining parallel.

courtier *attendant; flatterer.* See also courtesan.

couturier/couturière *high fashion designer, proprietor of a haute couture establishment.*

cover girl *cover model.*

cowboy *cowhand, cowpuncher, ranch hand, cowpoke, wrangler, range rider, cowgirl and cowboy* (in some contexts).

cowboy hat *stetson, ten-gallon hat, western-style hat, rodeo hat.*

cowboy shirt *western-style shirt, buckskin shirt, fringed shirt, rodeo shirt.*

cowgirl this term is not parallel to "cowboy." See cowboy.

cowman *rancher, cattle owner/buyer/grower/producer, farmer, cowherd.*

coxswain "swain" comes from "swein" meaning "servant" or "boy," and most coxswains are and have been men. However, "coxswain" could be used for a woman as its perceived sex link seems based more on the lack of female coxswains than on its etymology.

crackerjack (adj.) *first-rate, smashing, fantastic, marvelous, tip-top, remarkable, wonderful, super.*

cracksman *safecracker, burglar.*

craftsman *artisan, craftsworker, craftworker, skilled worker, handworker, handiworker, handicrafts worker, handicrafter, trade worker, artificer, craftsperson* (use only as a last resort); *craftsman and craftswoman* if used gender-fairly. Plurals: *craftworkers, artisans, skilled workers, handworkers, handicrafts workers, handicrafters, trade workers, handiworkers, artificers, craftspeople, craftsmen and craftswomen.*

craftsmanship *artisanry, artisanship, handiwork, skilled-craft work, crafts skills.* Or, mention the characteristics that contribute to the piece's beauty or the specific skills that went into its making.

cragsman *climber, rock/cliff climber.*

craneman *crane operator.*

crewman *crew member, member of the crew, hand, crew/deck hand.*

Croesus, rich as *See* rich as Croesus.

Cro-Magnon man *Cro-Magnon, Homo sapiens, Neanderthal, prehistoric people.*

crone avoid the pejorative use. Feminist Mary Daly speaks admiringly of Crones—strong women with powers of endurance.

crooner *pop singer, popular singer, vocalist, warbler, blues singer.* "Crooner" has become associated with male singers, which is why you might want a more inclusive term for women. Or, use "crooner" for women too.

croupier woman or man.

crown prince/crown princess OK.

cry in one's beer can be said of a man or a woman. Also: *full of self-pity, grouse, sniffle.*

cry uncle *See* say uncle.

cubmaster *cub scout/pack leader.*

cuckold avoid this term; there is no equivalent for a woman. Speak instead of one partner being unfaithful or of the other partner being betrayed.

cureman *curer.*

curmudgeon *grouch, grumbler, bad-tempered/peevish/cranky/petulant person, crosspatch, faultfinder, fire-eater, complainer, pain in the neck, nitpicker, troublemaker.* "Curmudgeon" is usually defined and used in reference to men, which is why inclusive alternatives are given.

curse this slang term for menstruation is better not perpetuated. It not only contributes to the myth that women do not operate on all cylinders throughout the month, but it also fosters incorrect and harmful attitudes in preadolescent and adolescent girls and boys.

custodian man or woman.

cut the Gordian knot *solve the riddle, solve an intricate/unsolvable problem, find the key, crack a hard nut, figure it out, find a way out, unravel something.* See Appendix A for the rationale on avoiding sex-linked metaphors, expressions, and figures.

cutthroat can refer to a man's or a woman's behavior.

d

And now we come to the magic of words. A word, also, just like an idea, a thought, has the effect of reality upon undifferentiated minds.

Emma Jung

daddy longlegs leave as is.

dairy husbandman *dairy scientist.*

dairymaid *dairy worker/employee.* However, "dairymaid" is used in fairy tales and certain older works.

dairyman *dairy scientist/farmer.*

dalesman *dale inhabitant/dweller.*

dame/damsel outdated and inappropriate; eliminate. "Dame" is belittling when used as slang.

Dame Fortune *fortune/Fortune, luck, chance, happy chance, wheels of fortune/chance, roll/throw of the dice, turn of the cards, luck of the draw, lucky stroke, the way things fall, how the cookie crumbles, the breaks, how the ball bounces, serendipity, happenstance, destiny, kismet, fate, fickle finger of fate, fortuity, whirligig of chance.*

dancing girl *dancer.*

dandy *fashion plate, fancy/sharp/conspicuous/fashionable dresser, tailor's/sartorial dream, a person it pays to dress, one who keeps the tailor in business, clothes-conscious person.*

danseur/danseuse "ballet dancer" is an inclusive term that covers anyone who dances the ballet. However, ballet companies assign strict meanings to dancers' titles. A danseur is a principal (but not the principal) male dancer in a company, a soloist, and a danseuse is a principal (but not the principal) female soloist. Retain "danseur" and "danseuse" for their narrow meaning within ballet companies, but use *ballet dancer* to describe a woman or a man who dances ballet nonprofessionally. *See also* ballerina; premier danseur; prima ballerina.

daredevil woman or man, boy or girl.

daughter cell leave as is; this is a biology term with a very specific meaning.

daughter of the horseleech *clinging vine, greedy person.*

David and Goliath *unequal contest, unequal contestants, unexpected defeat.* This phrase is impossible to replace adequately as its meaning is so specific and the picture it conjures up is so immediate and evocative. There is nothing wrong with using it in and of itself, so if you are not depending on a great many male metaphors and expressions in your speaking and writing, use this one with good cheer. See Appendix A for the rationale on avoiding sex-linked metaphors, expressions, and figures.

deaconess *deacon,* except when specific denominations designate the office for women as that of "deaconess"; in some instances "deaconess" is equal and parallel to "deacon." Note that although several translations of the Bible use "deaconess," the original Greek used the same word—*diakonos*—for both women and men. And they had the game as well as the name: in the early church both men and women functioned as deacons. Whenever possible, therefore, use the more authentic "deacon."

dead men tell no tales *the dead tell no tales.*

dean woman or man.

dear/dearie these words are patronizing when used by a man or a woman to someone (usually a woman) who has not overtly or tacitly given permission to be so addressed. In particular, these terms have no business in the workplace or in social interactions with strangers.

dear John letter, send a *give someone the air, give the gate to someone, whistle someone down the wind, send someone packing.* Also: *send a dear Jane letter.*

deathsman *executioner.*

debonair *jaunty, lighthearted, vivacious, breezy, nonchalant, free and easy, merry, cheery, sunny, sporty; well-mannered, well-bred, polite, refined, civil, charming, suave, courteous, urbane, gracious, graceful, obliging, affable.* These alternatives are suggested because the usage of "debonair" seems limited to men, although it need not be. (In *L'Allegro*, Milton used it to describe a goddess.)

debutante *debutant,* except where the "feminine" spelling is still required for a young woman making her formal debut into society. Using the base word to refer to both sexes is preferred in such pairs as blond/blonde, brunet/brunette, chaperon/chaperone, divorcé/divorcée, fiancé/fiancée, protegé/protegée.

deckman *log roller, deck worker.*

delivery boy/delivery man *delivery driver/clerk/person, merchandise deliverer, deliverer, porter, messenger, courier.*

demijohn leave as is because of its very specific meaning and lack of alternative. Note that the word is actually a mistranslation of the French "dame-jeanne" meaning Lady Jane.

demimondaine if you mean prostitute, use *prostitute.* If you mean someone on the fringes of society, use *lowlife, riffraff, outcast, down-and-outer.*

depot master *depot supervisor/chief.*

derelict man or woman.

deskman *desk clerk.*

detail man *pharmaceutical sales agent, pharmaceutical company representative, representative, sales rep.*

deus ex machina this Latin phrase, meaning "god from a machine" (because sometimes in Greek and Roman plays a god was introduced onto the stage by means of a crane to produce a "providential" ending), is appropriate for either a woman or a man. However, since "deus" is in the masculine gender and since it is used most often in masculine contexts, you may want to use an alternative: *last-minute rescuer, eleventh-hour deliverer; contrived solution.*

devil/he use "it" instead of "he" when referring to the devil.

devotee woman or man. Unlike similar words borrowed from French—divorcé/divorcée, fiancé/fiancée, habitué, protegé/protegée—this one is used in the feminine form and without its accent for both sexes. More neutral-appearing alternatives include *fan, enthusiast, nut, hound, buff.*

diamond in the rough this has always been used for men, although there is no reason it couldn't also refer to women. If you want something with less of a male association, use *rough/gauche/crude/unpolished/untutored person, raw material, someone with rough edges/a little rough around the edges, someone with hidden talents/potential.*

diamonds are a girl's best friend eliminate this phrase, which originated in the 1930s with a DeBeers ad campaign.

dike *See* dyke.

directress *director.*

dirty old man ageist as well as sexist; avoid this phrase. It is a stereotype that does not convey any real information. Describe instead what the person is doing, thinking, saying.

disc jockey woman or man.

diseur/diseuse *professional reciter.* Or, use the base term, "diseur," for both sexes.

displaced homemaker this sex-specific term has no parallel for men. However, until society eliminates the conditions that lead to such a phenomenon, the term is useful and appropriate.

display man *merchandise displayer, sign painter, displayer.*

district lineman *district line maintainer.*

divorce treat divorces as no-fault unless there is a persuasive reason to do otherwise, and be careful of such phrases as "he divorced her" or "she divorced him" absent evidence of the actual legal course of events. Use instead *they were divorced, they filed for divorce, they divorced.*

divorcé/divorcée *divorced person, divorcé.* A nonparallel situation exists here: a divorced woman is often called a divorcée, while a man is referred to as unmarried, a bachelor, or as someone who is divorced. Use parallel language in speaking of divorced women and divorced men. Also at issue is the relevancy of referring to a person's marital status at all; avoid it whenever possible. Casey Miller and Kate Swift (1980, pp. 106–07) persuasively recommend using the standard form of French words (blond, brunet, divorcé, fiancé, habitué, protegé) for both sexes.

dockman *dockhand, dockworker, docker, stevedore, shoreworker, shorehand, longshore worker, longshorehand, wharfworker, wharfhand.*

dockmaster *dock supervisor/boss.*

doctor woman or man. The two cautions here are to avoid using "the doctor/he" and to avoid specifying a female doctor's gender when it is irrelevant or when you would not do so in the case of a male doctor.

doctoress *doctor.*

doll (referring to a woman) women are not dolls; this is patronizing, belittling, and tends to make objects of women.

dollie-bird/dolly-bird women are not dolls.

dollies (drugs) *methadone.*

domestic not a sexist word in itself, but sometimes used to further a sexist context—for example, the assumption that all domestic matters belong a priori to the nearest woman. When you see the word "domestic," check the environs carefully.

domestic science this term is preferred to "home economics," which tended to become the exclusive province of women over the years. The newer term reminds us of the professional, technical, and scientific aspects of domestic management.

dominie always a man. *See also* clergyman; schoolmaster.

don in its meanings of a Spanish gentleman, grandee, or Mafia leader, "don" is correct and always refers to a man. In the sense of a university professor, however, use *professor, college/university professor, teacher, tutor, head, lecturer.*

Don Juan *lover, dashing lover, great romantic, sexually aggressive/ sexually active person, bedhopper.* See Appendix A for the rationale on avoiding sex-linked metaphors, expressions, and figures.

doorman *doorkeeper, door attendant, porter, concierge, sentry, gatekeeper, commissionaire, warder, beadle.*

doubting Thomas *skeptic, doubter, unbeliever, disbeliever, nonbeliever, cynic, questioner, pessimist, defeatist, someone from Missouri.* The tongue-in-cheek "doubting Thomasina" is sometimes seen. See Appendix A for the rationale on avoiding sex-linked metaphors, expressions, and figures.

doughboy use as is in historical context. Also: *World War I soldier.*

dowager avoid; there is no parallel for a man. One definition of "dowager" reflects on a woman's marital status (widowed) while the other reflects mainly on her age. Decide first if this information is relevant and then use descriptive terms that apply to both men and women. It should not be difficult to get along without the word; we have talked about men for centuries without using a similar term.

doyen/doyenne *dean.*

drab (referring to a woman) *prostitute.*

draftsman *drafter, artist, copyist, landscape artist, limner, drawer, sketcher, delineator, designer.*

dragoman nonsexist; the "man" is from the Italian for "hand." If the word's sexist appearance bothers you, use *interpreter, travel agent, guide.*

draughtsman *See* draftsman.

drayman *dray driver.*

dredgemaster *dredge operator.*

dressmaker *tailor, custom tailor, clothier, garment designer/worker, mender, alterer, alterations expert, stitcher.*

drillmaster *drill sergeant.*

droit de seigneur a very sexist concept that is no longer part of our vocabulary in the same way it was. However, the term may be useful as a metaphor in describing what happens in certain cases of sexual harassment of women where there is unequal power: professors and students, bosses and secretaries, etc. There is no parallel term describing the absolute power a woman has over a subordinate man, perhaps because the situation is so seldom seen.

drudge *menial, common laborer, toiler, plodder, hard worker, industrious/hard-working person.* Alternatives seem indicated since "drudge" is used for women only, although the word itself is not sex-specific.

drugstore cowboy there does not seem to be an equally pithy and colorful substitute for this phrase; sometimes *drugstore cowhand* might work, or you could, in extremis, use *drugstore cowgirl and drugstore cowboy.*

drum majorette *drum major.*

drunk/drunkard woman or man.

drunk as a lord *intoxicated, tight, loaded, well-oiled, stewed to the gills, plastered, smashed, three/four sheets to the wind, half seas over, off-color, under the table, lit to the gills, pickled, high as a kite, out of it.*

dude in the sense "vacationers at a dude ranch," both women and men can be dudes. See "dandy" for alternatives when you mean a fancy dresser. The slang term, meaning a swinging, attractive man, has no parallel for women, but is unlikely to be abandoned in casual conversation and writing in the near future.

duenna *chaperon.*

dumb blonde avoid this overworked and meaningless cliche.

dumpman *dumper.*

dustman *cleaner, sweeper, sweep.*

Dutchman *Dutch citizen, Dutchwoman and Dutchman.* Plural: *Dutch people, Dutchwomen and Dutchmen* (but not "Dutchmen and women"). It's generally not possible to replace words like "Dutchman," "Norseman," "Irishman," "Welshman," and "Cornishman" with one pithy inclusive term; you will have to either circumlocute or use the longer phrases, like "Dutchwomen and Dutchmen."

Dutch uncle, talk to like a *See* talk to like a Dutch uncle.

dyke (referring to a woman) this term with this spelling (as opposed to "dike") is considered acceptable to most lesbians. *See also* bull dyke; butch; femme.

e

Words are one of our chief means of adjusting to all the situations
of life. The better control we have over words, the more successful
our adjustment is likely to be.

Bergen Evans

✦ ✦ ✦

each man for himself *See* every man for himself.

Eagle Scout limited to boys/young men.

earth mother this is sexist insofar as there is no parallel term for a
man. Nor is there an inclusive term that conveys the same
meaning. However, "earth mother" is a positive, descriptive, and
useful concept, and can be used until nurturing men inspire the
construction of a parallel term.

ecdysiast man or woman.

effeminate this word has been and can be used in a positive sense
(and, in fact, a men's movement called Revolutionary Effeminism
has consciously struggled against masculinism), but you may want
to avoid it unless you are certain of your context. In its most
commonly understood sense, it is pejorative and sexist, loaded
with cultural stereotypes about what it means to be a man or a
woman in today's society. Choose instead some of the following
inclusive words, which seem to be what most people are trying to
convey with "effeminate": *passive, gentle, timid, weak, agreeable,
docile, fussy, particular,* etc.

elder woman or man.

elder statesman *senior/longtime/career diplomat, power behind the
throne, skilled/career/experienced politician, foreign relations
expert.*

elector man or woman.

emancipate nonsexist; from the Latin for "hand."

emasculate there may be occasions when this is the appropriate,
correct word to use, but too often it is used carelessly; it indicts
something or someone (often a woman) for a process that depends
just as importantly on a man's willingness to be emasculated, and
unflatteringly implies that he is a passive victim. Note that there

is no parallel term relating to women for such words as
"emasculate," "unman," and "castrate." For "emasculate"
substitute *disarm, disable, incapacitate, undermine, deprive of
courage/strength/vigor/power, unhinge, unnerve, devitalize,
attenuate, shatter, exhaust, weaken, disqualify, invalidate, paralyze,
muzzle, enervate, tie the hands of, draw the teeth of, clip the wings
of, spike the guns of, take the wind out of one's sails, put a spoke in
one's wheels.*

embryonic *inceptive, rudimentary, incipient, beginning, initial,
immature, undeveloped, untried, fledgling, unhatched, primary,
unfinished, imperfect, incomplete, elementary, half-finished,
developing, sketchy, preparatory, unrefined, unpolished, becoming,
unfolding, yet to come, in process.*

émigré woman or man.

empress OK as is for official titles. An empress may be not only the
wife or widow of an emperor but also an imperial title holder in
her own right.

enchantress *enchanter.*

endman this term has such a specific meaning that it is not easily
rendered gender-free, the more so since historically minstrels were
men; if for some reason a woman played this role, use *endwoman,
end comic.*

enfant terrible woman or man. Although this French expression is
masculine in gender, "enfant" refers to both male and female
babies/persons and the term is used inclusively in English-speaking
countries as well.

engineman *engine operator.*

Englishman *Britisher, Briton, Brit* (slang), *English/British
citizen/subject; Englishwoman and Englishman* if used
gender-fairly. Beware of using "Englishman" or "Englishmen" as
false generics. Plurals: *the English, English people, Englishwomen
and Englishmen* (but not "Englishmen and women").

enlisted man *enlistee, enlisted member/person/personnel; enlisted man
and enlisted woman* if used gender-fairly.

ensign man or woman.

entrepreneur woman or man. The word comes from the French and is
masculine in gender, but it is used to indicate persons of either
sex and is functionally inclusive in both English and French.

entryman *entry miner.*

equal pay/equal pay for equal work the Equal Pay Act of 1963 requires
that women and men receive equal pay for equal work. *See also*
comparable worth.

equerry equerries have always been male.

equestrienne *equestrian.*

errand boy *errand runner, messenger, gofer, page, clerk.*

escort service *prostitution service.* See Appendix A for a discussion of
our language on prostitution. If there are legitimate escort services,
they should probably consider using another term to describe

themselves, as this phrase has been preempted by prostitution services.

Esq. it is perfectly correct to address a letter to a lawyer of either sex using this courtesy title. For example: Marian Chernov, Esq.

eunuch use this word only in the literal sense of a castrated man, in which case it is a legitimate sex-specific word. Avoid its metaphorical use. Substitute *weakling, coward, wimp, pushover, doormat, lightweight, loser, craven. **See also** castrate/castrating; emasculate; namby-pamby; sissy; unman.

Eve traditionally, Eve has symbolized the tempter, the one by whom evil came into the world. Do not perpetuate this stereotype, which incidentally leaves Adam looking suggestible, inept, and easily led.

everybody and his grandmother *all the world and their offspring, all the world and their dog, everybody and their cousin, one and all, the whole world, everybody under the sun, every citizen of heaven and earth, everybody.* (See Appendix A for a discussion of singular "they.")

every dog has his day, and every man his hour *every dog has its day.* Also: *talent will out, cream will rise, to everything there is a season.*

every inch a king leave as is when referring to a king, and for a queen use *every inch a queen;* otherwise, use *a noble person, a regal bearing, an air of command.*

everyman/Everyman *the typical person, the ordinary person, the archetypical human being, Everyman and Everywoman* (always use together). **See also** average man; common man; man in the street.

every man a king *share the wealth.* This expression came from Huey Pierce Long's political campaign and referred to his share-the-wealth program.

every man for himself *everyone for themselves* (see Appendix A for a discussion of singular "they"), *the devil take the hindmost, look out for number one, no time to be lost.* Or, if you like to sprinkle your speech with foreign expressions, there is the nonsexist French equivalent: *sauve qui peut!* ("Save yourself if you can!")

every man has his price *everyone has a price.*

every man is a king in his own castle *everyone wears a crown in their own castle; we are all kings and queens in our own castles; in our own castle, each of us wears a crown; aboard our own ship each of us is captain; we are all rulers in our own castles; home is where the heart is.* (See Appendix A for a discussion of singular "they.")

every man jack *everyone, every single person, every last one of them.* **See also** everybody and his grandmother.

every man's death diminishes me **See** any man's death diminishes me.

every mother's child/son **See** all the world and his wife; everybody and his grandmother; every Tom, Dick, and Harry.

every Tom, Dick, and Harry *every stranger off the street, every so-and-so, any old body, anyone, doesn't matter who it is.* **See also** all the world and his wife; everybody and his grandmother.

evil men do, the   *the evil people do, the evil we do.* ***See also*** man's inhumanity to man.

exciseman   *excise officer/collector, tax/duty collector, excise agent, agent.*

executrix   *executor.* Note, however, that in some certain narrow legal senses "executrix" is the correct choice.

expatriate   this word comes from the Latin for "country," "patria," which in turn comes from "pater" for "father." However, the word is functionally nonsexist and its roots do not seem as obtrusive as some "pater"-based words ("paternal," for example). If you prefer, use *exile, displaced person, émigré.*

ex-serviceman   *ex-service member, ex-soldier, ex-member of the armed forces.*

f

Language makes culture, and we make a rotten culture when we abuse words.

Cynthia Ozick

factotum woman or man. *See also* handyman.

faculty wives *faculty spouses.*

fag/faggot (referring to a man) avoid these terms.

fair-haired boy/fair-haired girl *the favorite, the apple of someone's eye, privileged person, someone with pull, front runner, person after one's own heart, in one's good graces, persona grata.* The "fair-haired" phrases are problematic for three reasons: (1) making fair-haired the preferred coloring is racist and ethnocentric; (2) the phrases are used of adults, which makes the boy/girl designation inappropriate; (3) the terms are not used equally—"fair-haired boy" is common, while "fair-haired girl" is not.

fair sex, the avoid; this phrase has lost whatever meaning it ever had.

fairy (man) avoid this term.

fairy (fairy tales) fairies are both male and female, although they most often materialize in our culture as female (e.g., fairy godmother, Tinkerbell, Walt Disney's fairies, the tooth fairy).

fairy godmother retain in traditional fairy tales and add *fairy godfathers* to modern tales. Also: *good fairy/genie/genius, guardian angel, benefactor, savior, hero.*

faith of our fathers *faith of our ancestors, faith of our mothers and fathers.*

fakir *wonder-worker, ascetic, mendicant; dervish; impostor, swindler.* "Fakir" comes from the Arabic for "poor man"; a fakir is generally a man and the word is perceived as referring to a man.

fallen woman if you mean prostitute, use *prostitute*. Otherwise, eliminate the value judgment from your terms and for either sex use *someone who is unfortunate/unlucky/sexually active/promiscuous, someone who has fallen on hard/evil times/from grace.*

fall guy/fall man *scapegoat, dupe, goat, sucker, victim, fool, chump, laughingstock, loser, greenhorn, sitting duck, soft mark, mark, target, pushover, sap, nebbish. **See also** whipping* boy.

fall of Man *fall of the human race, the Fall.*

familiar to every schoolboy *familiar to every schoolchild.*

family man *homebody, stay-at-home, family head, home-lover, family-oriented/family-centered/home-centered person, someone devoted to the family.*

family of man *the human family, humanity, humankind.*

family planning the only caution here is that this neutral term not be seen as the exclusive province/responsibility of women.

fancy girl/fancy man/fancy woman *prostitute/prostitute's pimp/prostitute.* See Appendix A for a discussion of our language on prostitution.

farm boy (employee) *farm hand.*

farmer man or woman. "About two-thirds of all farmers in the world are women. . . . And yet, of all the job descriptions in the English language, few jobs have a more masculine connotation than the title 'farmer'. . . . In most cultures, agriculture becomes 'men's work' when it progresses to the point of being a successful commercial industry. When that happens, women are shoved back to perform related commercial activities, while also tending children" (Lee Egerstrom, "Third World Women Farm the Fields without Credit," *St. Paul Pioneer Press and Dispatch,* November 17, 1986, p. 3D).

farmerette *farmer.*

farmer's wife most often, this woman is a farmer in all but name; give her the name.

father ("generic" noun) *parent, progenitor, procreator; mother and father; source, ancestor, forebear. **See also** forefather.*

father (clergy) leave as is in direct address ("Father Frank Friar") but when referring to someone use the inclusive *priest, minister, pastor. **See also** priest.*

father ("generic" verb) *parent, nurture, support, protect, take care of, look after, be responsible for, rear children, caretake, supervise; procreate, create, co-create, reproduce, breed, propagate, give life to, bring to life, bring into being, bring about, call into existence, cause to exist; produce, make, found, author, originate, generate, engender, establish, invent, introduce.* Also, alternate gender-specific words such as *father/mother, beget/give birth to, conceive/beget.*

Father (God) When Jesus Christ speaks to or refers to God as his Father, the word "Father" should be retained, according to some people who believe that the name "Father" that Jesus gives to God indicates a very specific relationship and may not be changed. However, others look back to the Gnostic and Semitic traditions from which the words "Father" and "Son" emerged, and say that these words have nothing to do with roles like father and son, or indeed with any familial roles, but that they were rather the closest worshipers could come to expressing in personal terms the concepts of Uncreated Source (God) and Reflected Image (Jesus). For these people, using metaphors for God (God as nurturing mother or loving father) is acceptable, but the idea of God having a gender is not. (See "Is God Purple?" in Appendix B.) This question of God's gender or lack of it poses a dilemma for people who are equally sensitive to the Word of God, theological truth, sexist language, and the person in the pew. The latter often sees inclusive language (particularly the elimination of God as Father) as unconscionable tampering and finds the challenge to faith overwhelming. In the Old Testament, however, where the issue is not so much the Fatherness of God as the Godness of God, the word "Father" can be replaced by one of the following: *Advocate, Almighty/the Almighty, Author, Being, Creator, Creator of all things, Defender, the Deity, Divine Light, the Eternal, Eternal One, Ever-present God, First Cause, Friend, God, Godhead, God my Rock, God my Rock and my Redeemer, God of Abraham and Sarah, God of Grace, God of Heaven, God of Hosts, God of Israel, God of our ancestors/forebears, God of the Nations, Good Parent, Guide, Heavenly Creator, Heavenly Parent, Holy One/the Holy One, Holy One of Israel, the Infinite, Just One, Liberator, Living God, Maker, Merciful God, Mighty One, Most High/the Most High, Most Loving God, Nurturer, O God my God, O Gracious God, Omnipotent One, our Refuge and our Strength, Powerful One, Preserver, Providence, Redeemer, Rock, Rock of Refuge, Ruler, Savior, Shepherd, Shepherd of Israel, Source/the Source, Source of Life, Sovereign, Spirit, Supreme Being, Sustainer, Wisdom.* For a list of 196 inclusive names, titles, and phrases referring to God, send $1.50 plus $.50 handling to The Coordinating Center for Women in Church and Society, Suite D, 1400 N. 7th Street, St. Louis, MO 63106 for a copy of their thirty-page report, "Inclusive Language Guidelines for Use and Study in the United Church of Christ." Masculine pronouns referring to the Father should be avoided as much as possible in order to mitigate somewhat the strongly male orientation. *See* God/he and God/his. *See also* Father, Son, and Holy Spirit/Holy Ghost; God; Holy Spirit (Holy Ghost)/he; Lord; Son of Man.

Father Christmas *See* Santa Claus.

father figure *role model, father figure and mother figure.* "Father figure" has a very specific meaning and should be retained even though the potentially parallel term "mother figure" is not used very often (we *have* mother figures, but we are not so apt to label them). There does not seem to be any galloping sexism behind the fact that we use "father figure" but don't use "mother figure."

fatherland *homeland, native land/country/soil, home, home country, land of one's ancestors, natal place, the old country.*

fatherlike/fatherly replace these vague adjectives with ones that convey
more precisely the characteristics you want to describe: *kind,
kindly, caring, solicitous, considerate, interested, benevolent,
good-natured, fond, affectionate, devoted, loving, tender, gentle,
demonstrative, sympathetic, understanding, indulgent, obliging,
forbearing, tolerant, well-meaning, nurturing, protective, warm,
sheltering, generous.*

fathers ("generic") *ancestors, forebears, progenitors, precursors,
predecessors, forerunners, leaders, pioneers, founders, trailblazers,
innovators, fathers and mothers.*

Fathers of the Church leave as is; historically accurate.

Father, Son, and Holy Spirit/Holy Ghost *Creator, Christ, and Holy
Spirit; the grace of the Lord Jesus Christ and the love of God and
the communion of the Holy Spirit; Creator, Word, and Holy Spirit;
Creator, Redeemer, and Sustainer; the Holy Trinity; the Triune
God.*

Father Time *time/Time.*

father upon *saddle with, lay at the door of, ascribe to, bring home to,
charge with.*

favorite son candidate *state favorite, favorite candidate, favorite citizen
candidate; favorite daughter candidate and favorite son candidate* if
used gender-fairly.

fellow (noun/adj.) this is one of the most problematic words in the
area of gender-related language. On the one hand, it is often
accepted as an inclusive term; women receiving academic
fellowships are called fellows, for example. Among its dictionary
definitions are many wonderfully inclusive concepts: partner,
colleague, co-worker, companion, associate, comrade, mate,
member, etc. On the other hand, one of its definitions is "a
familiar synonym for man, male person" (*Oxford English
Dictionary*). This makes it difficult to determine whether a writer
or speaker is using "fellow" in the inclusive or exclusive sense. A
more convincing argument for its being exclusive, however, is the
common perception of the word. If you say, for example, "Today
I saw a fellow downtown throwing away hundred-dollar bills,"
there is no doubt in anyone's mind that the distributor of largesse
was a man. Substitutes for the noun include *partner, colleague,
co-worker, companion, associate, ally, comrade, friend,
acquaintance, counterpart, peer, affiliate, equal, mate, pair, match.*
For the adjective use *similar, alike, analogous, comparable,
parallel, matching, corresponding, something like, related, akin,
equal, equivalent, associate(d), united, connected.*

fellow countrymen *friends and neighbors, all of us, compatriots* (q.v.).
Rework the sentence to avoid this term if the alternatives don't
suit.

fellow feeling *sympathy, understanding, compassion, commiseration, empathy, rapport, link, bond, union, tie, closeness, affinity, friendship, agape, pity, walking in someone else's shoes, putting oneself in someone else's place.*

fellow man/men in most cases "fellow" is superfluous. We are so used to hearing this catch-all term in certain contexts that we don't stop to ask if it is necessary. Be specific: *other people, you, citizens, workers, another human being, all of us here, the average person,* etc.

fellowship (scholarship) use *scholarship* if the meaning is general; in its narrow meaning retain "fellowship."

fellowship (companionship) *association, companionship, camaraderie, friendship, comradeship, togetherness, esprit de corps, neighborliness, sharing, amity, friendliness, sodality, solidarity, human community, kinship, unity, society, assembly, community, communion, organization.*

fellow traveler *traveling companion, other traveler.*

fellow worker *co-worker, colleague, associate, teammate, partner.*

female (noun) avoid the use of "female" as a noun except in technical writing, for example, medicine, statistics, police reports, sociology. It is most often reserved for biological or nonhuman references. When using "female" as a noun, beware of nonparallel constructions, for example, "ten men and two females." Note that "female" is not at all related to "male" even though it has "male" in it; it comes from the Old French "femelle" from the Latin for "woman," "femina." *See also* female (adj.).

female (adj.) use only when you would use "male" in a similar situation or when it is necessary for clarification; this adjective is often gratuitous and belittling (for example, one sees "the female lawyer" but not "the male doctor"). Watch especially for nonparallel usage ("two technicians and a female mechanic"). *See also* female (noun).

feminine avoid this vague stereotype that conveys different meanings to different people according to their perceptions of what a woman ought or ought not do, say, think, wear, feel, look like. These subjective, cultural judgments have nothing to do with sex and everything to do with gender. Find instead words that express the characteristics you want to describe: *gracious, warm, gentle, receptive, supportive, compassionate, expressive, tender, charming, nurturing, well-mannered, cooperative, neat, soft-spoken, considerate, kind,* etc. Note that all these adjectives may be used equally appropriately of a man. See Appendix A for a discussion of the difference between sex and gender.

feminine intuition *intuition.*

feminine mystique this is a word without a true equivalent for men, although there is talk of a masculine mystique (q.v). The term comes from Betty Friedan's landmark 1963 book in which she exposed "the problem that has no name" (women's unhappiness with their role and status in society).

femininity avoid this vague, stereotypical word. Notions of femininity are based on culturally defined sex roles and how closely a woman fulfills these expectations. But because the concept is very subjective, femininity may mean different things in Alabama, New York, Iowa, and California. Identify the quality or qualities you want to describe and choose specific words for them: *warmth, graciousness, compassion, expressiveness, softness, self-confidence, strength, assurance, poise, charm, kindliness,* etc. See Appendix A for a discussion of the difference between sex and gender.

feminism generally defined as the advocacy of equal rights and opportunities for both sexes, feminism has no strictly organized agenda but does support the ERA and comparable worth and is generally pro-choice, although large numbers of women call themselves Christian feminists and are pro-life. Most people now accept feminism as a historical, enduring movement that has promoted changes beneficial to society as a whole, although other, more conservative, elements of the population see it as a destructive and inimical force. Feminism is not synonymous with the women's movement, which it predates by several centuries. The women's movement is broader and less politicized and radicalized than the feminist movement. Feminism has also been defined as "the fundamental drive of women for autonomy" (Scott and Scott 1975, p. 49).

feminist a feminist is a person who believes in "the full humanity of women" (Gloria Steinem) although most feminists advocate and work for equal rights and opportunities for both sexes. It is primarily women who identify themselves as feminists, but some men do too. The Reverend Jerry Falwell is not one of them: "I listen to the feminists and all those radical gals—most of them are failures. They've blown it. . . . These women just need a man in the house. That's all they need. Most of these feminists need a man to tell them what time of day it is and to lead them home. And they blew it and they're mad at all men. Feminists hate men. They're sexist. They hate men—that's their problem" (quoted in *Ms.,* December 1985, p. 81).

feminist theology "The critical principle of feminist theology is the promotion of the full humanity of women. Whatever denies, diminishes, or distorts the full humanity of women is, therefore, appraised as not redemptive. Theologically speaking, whatever diminishes or denies the full humanity of women must be presumed not to reflect the divine or an authentic relation to the divine, or to reflect the authentic nature of things, or to be the message or work of an authentic redeemer or a community of redemption. This negative principle also implies the positive principle: what does promote the full humanity of women is of the Holy, it does reflect true relation to the divine, it is the true nature of things, the authentic message of redemption and the mission of redemptive community" (Ruether 1984, pp. 18–19).

fem lib *feminism, women's liberation movement, women's liberation, women's movement, female liberation movement.* The use of the shortened form is insulting.

femme/fem (lesbian) this term, which describes one of the two roles (the other is butch) in a dyke relationship, is not heard so much anymore, but it is generally considered inoffensive.

femme fatale avoid; there is no parallel for a man, and this term also perpetuates the myth of woman as Eve/tempter/ siren. One of the most valuable rules in good writing or speaking is "show, don't tell." Instead of telling that someone is a "femme fatale," show how that person affects the opposite sex.

ferryman *ferry operator.*

fiancé/fiancée these sex-specific terms are acceptable to most people and are still widely used. However, the ideal is always to remove gender from situations in which it is irrelevant, and it has been suggested that fiancé can nicely include both sexes (Miller and Swift 1980, pp. 106–07). *See also* blond/blonde; brunet/brunette; devotee; divorcé/divorcée; habitué; protegé/protegée.

fickle except for that notorious finger of fate, women most often wear the "fickle" label. Avoid using it altogether unless you equally often describe men that way. The following words are not so identified with one sex: *unpredictable, changeable, unaccountable, unreliable, impulsive, impetuous, indecisive, uncertain, unsteady, irresolute, vacillating, unfaithful, disloyal, inconstant, treacherous, tricky.*

fieldman *field worker/representative/technician/contractor/buyer.*

field marshall/field officer man or woman.

fighting man *fighter, soldier, pugilist, belligerent, belligerent/aggressive individual/person.*

fill 'er up (gas tank) *fill it up.*

filmmaker woman or man.

filterman *filter press tender, filter operator/tender, ripening room attendant.*

finishing school *private school.* There are no finishing schools for boys; the cultural parallel has been the military school.

fireman *firefighter.*

fireman (locomotive) *fire tender, firer, stoker.*

fire patrolman *fire patroller/ranger/guard.*

first lieutenant/first sergeant man or woman.

fisherman *fisher, angler, fishing licensee* (for some legal purposes); *fisherman and fisherwoman* if used gender-fairly. Do not be afraid of "fisher." When you see it in a series of words like the following, you can appreciate that "fisherman" is actually the odd man out: camper, hunter, canoer, fisher, hiker, mountain climber, birdwatcher, biker, nature lover. Author, longtime library cataloger, and wordsmith Sanford Berman points out that the

Random House dictionary gives "a fisherman" as the primary definition of "fisher"; the Library of Congress has replaced the sexist subject heading "fishermen" with "fishers"; and the Hennepin County Library has been using the sex-neutral "fishers" in their catalog since 1974. He adds that a venerable example of such usage appears in Matthew 4:19 and Mark 1:17: "I will make you fishers of men" (King James Version). Incidentally, the "men" in that phrase actually comes from the Greek word "anthropos," which means "human being." There is a separate Greek word for adult male ("andros"), which is used throughout the Scriptures when "adult male" is meant; it was not used in this case, but translators still write "men" where "human beings" was meant.

fisherman's bend (knot) leave as is.

fishman *fishmonger.*

fishwife (woman) do not use. *See also* shrew.

fit for a king *fit for royalty/for the best, magnificent, noble, one in ten thousand/in a million.*

fix-it man *fixer-upper, fix-it expert, fixer, do-it-yourselfer, repairer.* Also possible but not recommended: *fix-it woman and fix-it man, fix-it person. See also* handyman.

flag girl *flag bearer.*

flagman *signaller, flagger.*

flag officer woman or man.

flapjack *pancake.* Or leave as is.

flapper use as is in historical context, but be aware that before World War I it generally referred to a sprightly, knowing female teenager. After the Great War, it developed some negative connotations, and flappers were thought to be rather "fast."

flasher *exhibitionist.* If you want to use "flasher" to describe a woman, it is acceptable. However, if you do so without any identifying pronouns, the common assumption will be that you are referring to a man.

fleet admiral man or woman.

flesh peddler *pimp.* See Appendix A for a discussion of our language on prostitution.

flight attendant woman or man.

flight engineer man or woman.

flimflam man *See* confidence man.

flirt woman or man.

floor boy/floor girl *floor worker.*

floorlady/floorman *operator, supervisor, floor worker.*

floozy *prostitute.* See Appendix A for a discussion of our language on prostitution.

flower girl (wedding) *flower carrier.*

flower girl (vendor) *flower seller/vendor, florist.*

flunky man or woman.

flyboy *high-flyer, glamorous pilot. See also* airman.

flyman *flyhand, stagehand, flyworker.*

Flying Dutchman   leave as is.

foeman   *foe, enemy, opponent, rival, competitor.*

foilsman   *fencer.*

footboy   *page, attendant.*

footman   leave as is in historical contexts; a footman was always a man.

forefather   *ancestor, forerunner, forebear, predecessor, precursor; forefather and foremother* if used gender-fairly.

forelady/foreman   *supervisor, lead supervisor, monitor, overseer, overlooker, boss, job/straw boss, superintendent, super, inspector, director, manager, line manager, chief.*

foreman (jury)   *jury supervisor/chair/representative/spokesperson/chief.* Also, "forewoman" is gaining ground so you can use *forewoman and foreman* if handled gender-fairly.

foremanship   *supervisory duties/skills, supervision.*

foremother   *ancestor, forerunner, forebear, predecessor, precursor; forefather and foremother* if used gender-fairly. *See also* foresister. While "forefather" is often used as a false generic, "foremother" may have some validity for women. Using "foremother" instead of a generic like ancestor or forebear emphasizes that there *were* women precursors even though they have so seldom appeared in the history books, classrooms, or lecture halls. For Janice Nunnally-Cox, "foremother" is a "useful word, a practical word, an everyday ordinary word" (Cox 1981, p. xi).

foresister   some people prefer this term to "foremother" when a gender-specific term is useful.

foretopman   *foretopper, sailor, foretop sailor.*

forewoman   *See* forelady/foreman; foreman (jury).

fossil man   *fossil human/remains, fossil.*

foster mother (generic)   *foster parent.*

Founding Fathers   *the Founders, writers of the Constitution, Founding Mothers and Founding Fathers; founders, pioneers, colonists, forebears, patriots* (q.v.). Be sensitive to the context in which these generic terms are used so that it is not assumed they were all men, for example, by saying "pioneers and their wives and children."

fountain girl/fountain man   *fountain server.* Note the nonparallel "girl/man."

frameman   *frame wirer, framer.*

fraternal   unless speaking of a brother, choose sex-neutral words to convey exactly what you mean: *warm, loving, teasing, protective, intimate,* etc. Use also *sibling.* The fact that there exists a feminine parallel for "fraternal" ("sororal") that is all but unknown is another example of the severe discounting of female words in our language.

fraternal order of . . .   *order of . . . .* There is no parallel for women.

fraternal organization   *organization, society, association, common-interest group.*

fraternity   *organization, society, fraternity and sorority, secret society, association, common-interest group, comradeship, unity, community, companionship, friendship, kinship.* ***See also*** fellowship.

fraternity (Greek)   there are now some coed fraternities, so a frat member is not necessary a man, and some sororities are officially titled fraternities.

fraternization   *association, socialization, mingling, banding together, keeping company, hobnobbing, mixing, consorting, clubbing together, rubbing shoulders with.* There is no parallel from the Latin word for "sister," "soror."

fraternize   *associate, socialize, mingle, band together, keep company, hobnob, mix, consort, club together, rub shoulders with.* There is no parallel from the Latin word for "sister," "soror."

frau   there is nothing in the least wrong with this word in German; the problem arises when it is used in English to convey a certain disdain for a narrowly defined role for women. ***See also*** hausfrau.

freedman   *freed slave, ex-slave, free-issue black; freedman and freedwoman* if used gender-fairly.

Freedmen's Bureau, the   this was a specific bureau whose exact title should be retained for historical accuracy.

Freedmen's schools   leave as is for historical accuracy.

freeman   *citizen, citizen of a free country; freeman and freewoman* if used gender-fairly. "Freewoman" has had other, very positive connotations in the feminist movement; *The Freewoman,* one of the earliest feminist newspapers, was published in Great Britain as a "weekly feminist review" between November 1911 and May 1912.

Freemason   the term "Freemason" (member of the Free and Accepted Masons or Ancient Free and Accepted Masons) always refers to a man; women cannot be Freemasons. The Order of the Eastern Star is an affiliate, however, to which both women and men may belong.

Frenchman   *French person; Frenchman and Frenchwoman* if used gender-fairly. Too often "Frenchman" and "Frenchmen" are used as false generics. Plurals: *the French, French citizens/people/ persons, Frenchwomen and Frenchmen.* It's generally not possible to replace words like "Frenchman," "Norseman," "Irishman," and "Dutchman" with one pithy inclusive term; either circumlocute or use the complete phrases: "Frenchwoman and Frenchman/ Frenchmen and Frenchwomen."

freshman   *first-year student, fresher, frosh; beginner, novice, newcomer.* Some people feel there is no good alternative to "freshman" when used with "sophomore," "junior," and "senior." However, "fresher" and "frosh" are becoming increasingly popular, and you will see them as the main entry in some library catalogs and in some college and high school materials. A 1987 yearbook from a large inner-city high school used *freshpeople*. Other plurals: *freshers, frosh.*

freshman congressman   *first-year member of Congress.*

frigid (referring to a woman)   avoid the word "frigid"—it is neither scientific nor accurate. Two other warnings: be leery of the orgasm-as-norm mentality (contrary to cultural myths, it is possible to live a full life without being frequently orgasmic or, indeed, orgasmic at all); men who care about their reputation as sexual athletes should be particularly careful not to label partners "frigid" as the word is out now: "frigidity" is most often directly traceable to an insensitive lover. Instead of "frigid" use inclusive, judgment-free terms: *unaroused, uninterested, unresponsive, anorgasmic, nonorgasmic,* etc.

frivolous   this term is used almost exclusively of women. Use instead *lighthearted, easygoing, trivial, insignificant, superficial, inane, vacuous, shallow, flimsy, idle, immature.*

frogman   *military diver, underwater swimmer/explorer, diver, frog; frogman and frogwoman* if used gender-fairly.

front-end man   *front-end mechanic.*

frontiersman   *frontier settler, pioneer; frontierswoman and frontiersman* if used gender-fairly.

front man (industry)   *stevedore, dockhand.* **See also** longshoreman; wharfman.

front man (music)   *lead singer, star, leader, front musician/player.*

front man   *front, figurehead.*

frump/frumpy   can describe a man or a woman.

fuddy-duddy   can describe a woman or a man.

fugleman   *file leader, lead soldier, leader.*

funnyman   *comedian.*

furnaceman   *furnace installer/repairer/cleaner.*

g

Words fascinate me. They always have. For me, browsing in a dictionary is like being turned loose in a bank.

Eddie Cantor

gabby nonsexist per se, this word is functionally sexist and ageist because it is used almost exclusively for women and elderly men. Use instead *talkative, loquacious, garrulous, voluble, fluent, glib, effusive, exuberant, wordy, verbose, long-winded, talking a blue streak.*

gaffer woman or man.

gag man *gag writer, comedian.*

gal *woman.* "Gal" has a few acceptable uses depending on the context (would "guy" be appropriate in a similar situation?).

gal-boy this prison slang has a certain limited legitimacy, although there is no parallel for women and no inclusive alternative.

gal Friday *See* girl Friday.

gambler man or woman.

gamesman *games player, gamester, gambler, someone who sails suspiciously close to the wind/skates on thin ice/cuts corners/ squeaks home.*

gamesmanship *gamestership, sailing close to the wind, suspiciously shrewd playing, sharp playing.*

gangbusters, come on like *See* come on like gangbusters.

garageman *garage worker.*

gasman *gas fitter, gas pipe repairer/installer, gas appliance repairer/ installer.*

gateman *gatekeeper, gate tender/attendant.*

gathered to one's fathers *gathered to one's ancestors/forebears/fathers and mothers.*

gaucho a gaucho is always a man; there is no parallel for a woman and no precisely similar inclusive term. *See also* cowboy.

gay/gay man   these are the terms of current preference for men with a same-sex orientation. There is no commonly preferred term that describes both men and women; neither group identifies with the omnibus term "homosexual," q.v.

gay blade/gay dog   *high-flyer, fun-lover, high-spirited person; hedonist, sensualist, flirt, bedhopper, free spirit, swinger.* The word "gay" could be ambiguous in this context, and the terms are sexist insofar as they are used only of men. *See also* ladies' man; man about town.

geisha   a geisha is always a woman; there is no parallel for a man and no inclusive term. Use only in its narrowest definition, that is, to refer to a Japanese woman with special training in the art of providing lighthearted entertainment, especially for men.

gendarme   bien sûr, when in France, use "gendarme" even though it is a masculine word (it means "men of arms"). There are, however, both female and male gendarmes with identical job descriptions. At one time the French experimented with the term "gendarmette" for its new female members because the gendarmerie had been such a completely masculine field, but the term was deemed profoundly sexist, was caricatured in a movie, and has since been given a decent burial.

gender   this is a nonsexist word, but an understanding of the difference between sex and gender is crucial to the correct use of language. See Appendix A for a discussion of this difference.

gender gap   nonsexist term used in politics, economics, sociology, etc.

general   woman or man.

gentleman   this gender-specific word is appropriate in certain instances; "gentlewoman" is its correct opposite number, although it is more commonly paired with "lady." In the plural, "ladies and gentlemen" is a popular and acceptable form of generic public address. *See* lady.

gentleman farmer   *hobby/Sunday/weekend/amateur farmer, farmer.*

gentlemanlike/gentlemanly   avoid this vague stereotype that conveys different meanings to different people according to their perceptions of what a man ought or ought not do, say, think, wear, feel, look like. These words have nothing to do with sex and everything to do with gender. Find instead terms that express the characteristics you want to describe: *civil, polite, well-mannered, mannerly, brave, thoughtful, considerate, agreeable, accommodating, decent, discreet, dependable, punctilious, civilized, cultivated, dignified,* etc. Note that all these adjectives may be used equally appropriately of a woman. See Appendix A for a discussion of the difference between gender and sex.

gentleman's agreement   *honorable/verbal/informal/oral agreement, verbal/oral promise/contract, handshake, your word.*

gentlemen of the press   *representatives of the press. See also* newsman/newspaperman.

gentle sex, the avoid this term; in its quiet way it does violence to both women and men.

gentlewoman this gender-specific word is appropriate when used together with "gentleman," but it should probably never be used alone as it has developed along very different lines than "gentleman." For example, while we might say, "He's a real gentleman," we would never say, "She's a real gentlewoman." Or, we say, "That gentleman over there is waiting to speak to you," but we would never say, "That gentlewoman over there is waiting to speak to you."

GI man or woman. This nickname for U. S. military personnel comes from "government issue" and thus is not gender-specific.

giantess *giant.*

gigolo *prostitute, lover.* This gender-specific word is difficult to replace as there is no all-purpose word describing both men and women and conveying the same meaning. *See also* kept woman.

GI Joe *GI.*

gingerbread man *gingerbread cookie/figure, gingerbread man and gingerbread woman.*

gird (up) one's loins this phrase is perceived as sexist because it is assumed to refer to men. However, it comes from Proverbs 31:17, and the loins in question actually belong to a woman. If you want something that appears more gender-free, use *prepare, prepare for battle, buckle on one's armor, get the steam up, get in gear, batten down the hatches, grit one's teeth.*

girl (referring to a woman) *woman, young woman.* "Girl" is usually reserved for pre-teens or at least for those fifteen or under. Note that some women may refer to themselves and their women friends as girls either out of long habit, local custom, or because they still think of themselves that way. However, for an outsider to refer to them this way is unacceptable. *See also* girl Friday; office boy/office girl.

girl and boy half the time use "boy and girl."

girl Friday *assistant, office assistant, clerk, right hand, secretary, aide; man Friday and woman Friday* if used gender-fairly, although it is generally only "woman Friday" that is used, and even then there is a certain reluctance to use "woman" instead of "girl." *See also* girl; office boy/office girl.

girlfriend *friend, woman friend* (if "man friend" is also used), *female friend* (if "male friend" is also used), *escort, date, companion, longtime/loving companion, romantic interest, significant other, housemate, roommate, partner, partner of long standing, paramour, lover, steady, live-in lover/companion, fiancé, betrothed, sweetheart.* The Census Bureau uses POSSLQ (pronounced POSSelcue), which means "person of the opposite sex sharing living quarters."

girlie there are no circumstances in which this word is acceptable.

girlish *ingenuous, self-conscious, young, innocent, youthful, inept, inexperienced, bright-eyed, optimistic, cheerful, adolescent, childish, sophomoric, juvenile, kiddish, infantile, callow, immature, unsophisticated, naive.* "Girlish" is an imprecise word loaded with cultural baggage; you are better served with sex-neutral terms that can express your meaning clearly.

girl scout there is nothing particularly sexist about the terms "girl scout" and "boy scout" (although the goals, activities, and attitudes of the two groups have often been sexist). You may, however, want to use another term that is gaining acceptance: *youth scout.*

girl watcher *See* ladies' man.

give away the bride *escort the bride to the altar, accompany the bride down the aisle.* Women are not "given" by their fathers to their husbands.

give someone Harry *give someone a tongue lashing/the length of one's tongue, haul someone over the coals, dress down, chew out, scold, reprimand, castigate, punish, haul on the carpet, pin someone's ears back, read someone the riot act, tell someone where to get off, skin alive.* See Appendix A for the rationale on avoiding sex-linked metaphors, expressions, and figures.

give someone Jesse *give your best effort, offer what you most hold dear, give up what you love best.* In this expression, which dates from the 1856 presidential campaign, Jesse is a woman. See Appendix A for the rationale on avoiding sex-linked metaphors, expressions, and figures.

give the devil his due *give the devil its due.*

glamour girl *glamour woman.* Use sparingly.

glassman *glassmaker, glass dealer/retailer/repairer.*

G-man *government/federal/FBI agent.*

God the words for God in both Greek and Hebrew are sex-neutral. Although some people call for balancing all the historical maleness of God with female attributes, pronouns, etc., the most appealing view for many is that in God there is no gender as we know it. It is acceptable, indeed even fruitful, to use anthropomorphic metaphors for God that embrace both sexes (God as abundant mother, as merciful father). However, God's self is neither a "he" nor a "she." *See also* Father (God); Father, Son, and Holy Spirit/ Holy Ghost; God/he; God/himself; God/his; God of our Fathers; Holy Spirit (Holy Ghost)/he; Lord; Son of Man.

God/he avoid gender-specific pronouns by: (1) replacing "he" or "him" with "God" or another name for God; (2) recasting the sentence; (3) replacing the pronouns with "you/yours" or "who/whom/that." *See also* God; God/himself; God/his.

God/himself some people are using "Godself." Since the word "God" is sex-neutral, the correct pronoun should also be sex-neutral. You can often circumlocute to avoid the reflexive pronoun (sometimes this is best done by changing the verb that takes the pronoun). *See also* God; God/he; God/his.

God/his replace such phrases as "his Goodness" or "his Mercy" with sex-neutral expressions like "Divine Goodness" or "Eternal Mercy" or with the second person: "Your Goodness," "Your Mercy." Many people believe the proper possessive pronoun for God is God's, for example, "God's goodness," "God's mercy." *See also* God; God/he; God/himself.

God of our Fathers *God of our ancestors/of all generations/of our forebears/of our mothers and fathers.*

goddess *god; god and goddess.* In some cases, it is important to retain "goddess," as, for example, in references to the goddess religions, which point to a historical truth about the importance of women in certain societies. The concept of goddess is central to feminist spirituality and the word should be retained in those cases. In some instances, however, "goddess" indicates a lesser god, and so should be replaced with "god."

gold digger avoid; there is no parallel for a man, and this term is often used carelessly. Try instead to describe the trait you have in mind with inclusive terms: *greedy, grasping, avaricious, self-seeking, rapacious, out for all one can get.*

gondolier there are only about 320 gondolas left in Venice, and all of them are plied by men.

Good Humor man *See* ice-cream man.

good Joe *good sort, agreeable/good-natured/good-humored person.* For the rationale on avoiding sex-linked metaphors, expressions, and figures, see Appendix A.

goodman/goodwife these are both obsolete. But note the nonparallel "man/wife" construction.

good old girls' network *See* old-girls' network.

good Samaritan woman or man.

good scout man or woman, girl or boy.

goody two shoes *goody-goody, do-gooder.* The original Little Goody Two Shoes from the nursery rhyme by Oliver Goldsmith was a girl who earned an undeserved reputation as a self-righteous, affected little do-gooder. See Appendix A for the rationale on avoiding sex-linked metaphors, expressions, and figures.

go see a man about a dog *See* see a man about a dog/horse.

gossip although not a sexist word per se, "gossip" is functionally sexist since the term is reserved almost exclusively for women. As Alexander Rysman (1977) points out, "gossip" used to be a positive term used for both sexes but became a negative one applied to women. It is his contention that a patriarchal society fears and resents the female solidarity created by "gossip" and thus tries to undermine it by ridiculing it. A study of a Newfoundland village showed that when women gathered, their talk was called "gossip," but when men gathered in the same way at the trading post their exchanges were called "news" (Farris

1963). Inclusive alternatives are *talk, talk idly, converse, talk over, discuss, chew the fat, shoot the breeze, spread stories, run off at the mouth.*

gossipy *talkative, curious, loquacious, garrulous, gregarious.* **See also** gossip.

gourmet woman or man.

governess when "governess" refers to a female governor, use *governor.* When it is used in the sense of a person who teaches young children, choose inclusive terms: *tutor, private teacher, teacher, child mentor, instructor.* Note what has happened to the word pair "governor/governess" over the years.

governor man or woman.

go West, young man unless quoting Greeley, use *go West.* When it needs to be sex-specific: *go West, young woman/go West, young man.*

gownsman *academic, academician, scholar, professional, licentiate.*

grand duchess use when it is an official title. Note that this can refer either to the wife of a duke or to the ruler of a duchy.

grande dame this may be appropriate in certain circumstances, but there is no equivalent for men. In some cases, you might want to use *matriarch/patriarch.*

grandfather aid leave as is. This legislative term is impossible to replace without losing its special meaning. People who have experimented with calling it "grandparent aid" find that those who need to use the term don't recognize it.

grandfather clause leave as is for its narrowest meaning. In some cases the broader term *escape clause* can be substituted. Some women who have been covered by the clause speak of being "grandmothered."

granny/grannie OK; "gramp/gramps" is for a man.

granny dress/gown *old-fashioned/Victorian/high-necked dress/gown.*

granny knot this sexist term (it describes an insecure knot made inadvertently when one is trying to tie a square knot) has no synonym.

grantsman *grantwriter; grantsman and grantswoman* if used gender-fairly.

grantsmanship *the fine art of obtaining grants, grant-getting, the knack of attracting grants, grant-getting skills.* There is no one-word substitute for this handy, but sexist, term.

grass widow/grass widower these words are almost, but not quite, parallel and thus are fairly nonsexist; however, perhaps the current gender-specific terms "widow" and "widower" will one day be replaced by one inclusive word—probably "widow" since it is the shorter term. Note that "widower" is one of the very few masculine words that is based on a feminine word.

gravamen nonsexist; comes from the Latin for "burden."

greater love than this has/hath no man *greater love than this has/hath no one.*

greenhorn woman or man.

Green Mountain Boys leave as is (historical term).

greensman *greens planter/worker, landscape artist.*

Griselda, patient *See* patient Griselda.

grisette if you mean prostitute, use *prostitute*. Otherwise use *member of the working class, working class person.* There is no male parallel for "grisette."

groceryman *grocer, grocery store owner.*

groomsman *best man, attendant.* Avoid the word "groomsman" as its opposite number ("bridesmaid") is nonparallel ("maid/man"). "Best man" is used with "best woman," and "attendant" is used when the bride's witness is also called an attendant.

groundsman *groundskeeper, grounds/yard worker, landscaper.*

groupie *admirer, fan, follower, worshiper at the throne.* "Groupie" has come to be associated almost totally with young women, and there is no parallel for young men.

guardian woman or man.

guardsman *member of the guards, guard member, guard.*

gunman *killer, armed/professional killer, assassin, slayer, gun, hired gun, gunfighter, gunner, gunslinger, gun-wielder, gun-toter, sharpshooter, sniper, attacker, outlaw, bank robber, bandit, terrorist, gangster, racketeer, mobster, hoodlum, armed person, cutthroat, liquidator; gunman and gunwoman if used gender-fairly.*

gun moll *accomplice, gun-toting accomplice, sidekick, confederate in crime, gangster's companion.* **See also** girlfriend; gunman.

gunnery sergeant man or woman.

guy *man, person.* "Guy" has a few acceptable uses depending on context (would "gal" be appropriate in a similar situation?). The ubiquitous "Hey, you guys!" could be replaced with "Hey, you people!"

Gypsy *Romani/Romany.* Although "Gypsy" is not a sexist word in itself, it is sometimes used in a sexist context, and it is always racist. "Romani" is the spelling used by the international Romani Union and by most Romani themselves, while "Romany" is the common American dictionary spelling. Either word can be used as an adjective or as a singular or plural noun. Note that the Romani peoples have suffered some of the same kinds of discrimination women have: they have been regarded as second-class citizens (and in some countries as no citizens at all) or as an invisible people. For example, there is very often little or no mention of the Romani in references to the Holocaust, although between 70 and 80 percent of the entire Romani population perished.

h

Every language reflects the prejudices of the society in which it evolved.

Casey Miller and Kate Swift

habitué woman or man. This is the masculine form in French (the feminine would be habituée) but it indicates either a man or a woman in English—a convention that has been suggested for "divorcé/divorcée," "fiancé/fiancée," and "protegé/protegee," q.v.

hackman *cabdriver.*

hag avoid because of its current pejorative meaning. Note, however, that this word's root and older meanings were not derogatory—they referred to a mature wise-woman.

hail-fellow-well-met *backslapping, hearty, jovial, breezy, extroverted, heartily informal, convivial, comradely, jocular, playful, full of life, in high spirits.*

hair-do *hair style.* "Hair-do" is used almost exclusively for women.

handmaid/handmaiden *servant, personal attendant, attendant.*

handyman *odd jobber, repairer, fixer-upper, janitor, caretaker, do-all, do-it-yourselfer, factotum; handywoman and handyman* if used gender-fairly.

hangman *executioner, public executioner, lyncher.*

happy warrior man or woman.

harbor master *harbor chief/superintendent/officer/commander.*

hard master *tyrant, iron hand/ruler, despot, martinet, disciplinarian, oppressor, stickler, dictator.*

harlot/harlotry *prostitute/prostitution.* In the beginning "harlot" (which comes from the Old French word for "rogue") referred only to men—male vagabonds, vagrants, entertainers, etc. Then it was used for a person of either sex, and finally it became restricted to women. See Appendix A for a discussion of our language on prostitution.

harpy (woman) avoid this term.

harridan (woman) avoid. *See also* shrew.

harvestman leave as is.

hatcheck girl *hatcheck attendant/clerk, hat attendant/clerk.*

hatchet man *hatchet, hired hatchet/killer/gun/attacker/assassin, killer, murderer, slayer, executioner, assassin, attacker, sniper, liquidator, bloodshedder; character assassin, scandalmonger.* **See also** gunman.

hausfrau although this term means "housewife" for both the Germans and those English-speaking peoples who have borrowed it, its use is neutral-to-positive in Germany but largely pejorative in English-speaking countries. Use it only in Germany.

hautboy nonsexist; comes from the French "bois" for "wood." **See also** highboy.

hawk (attitude toward war) woman or man.

he never use "he" when you mean "he and she," or when you are referring to someone who could be a man or a woman (for example, "the consumer/he"). Make your sentence plural, circumlocute, or use one of the suggestions given in the appendixes.

headhunter (business/personnel) man or woman. Note that the headhuntee may also be male or female.

headman *head cager/worker; traditional chief; overseer, supervisor.*

headmaster/headmistress *principal, school principal.* In some instances (e.g., an old-fashioned, conservative, or British boys'/girls' school), "headmaster" or "headmistress" might be correct.

head of family/head of household man or woman. **See also** breadwinner; bring home the bacon; family man; headship.

headship this word is used by fundamentalists in particular to denote the father's rightful and God-given status as undisputed head of the family. In the many woman-headed households today, headship properly belongs to women and in nonfundamentalist two-parent families, headship is either shared or is not an issue. The caveat is to avoid using the word lightly or without knowledge of its significance to your audience.

headsman *executioner, public executioner, beheader.*

headwaiter man or woman.

Heidelberg man *Homo erectus, early human.* The physical remains are referred to as *the Heidelberg jaw* or *the Heidelberg fossil.*

heiress *heir.*

helmsman *pilot, steerer, navigator.*

helpmate/helpmeet because these terms are so often assumed to refer to women, they are best avoided. There is nothing to contraindicate using them to refer to men, however, if you intend to use them equally of both sexes.

he-man avoid this term, first, because there is no parallel for women and, second, because it perpetuates a stereotype that appears to be false and damaging to men. Use instead adjectives that describe the individual: *aggressive, hardy, rugged, husky, hearty, robust, powerful, muscular, domineering, capable, dynamic, energetic, physical,* etc.

henchman *sidekick, hireling, underling, flunky, lackey, tool, puppet, accomplice, stooge, ward heeler; follower, supporter, helper, aide, right-hand, cohort; groom, attendant, page.*
hen party *all-women party, women-only party.*
henpecked *browbeaten, passive, dominated, subjugated, held under the thumb of, led by the nose, at one's beck and call.* These terms can apply to men or women.
herdsman *livestock manager/breeder/tender, swineherd, swineherder, cattle herder, shepherd.*
hero/heroine use "hero" to describe both men and women even though it is the masculine form of the Greek word, while "heroine" is the feminine form. However, we speak English—not Greek—and in English a heroine is defined as "a female hero"—that is, a subset of hero. There are instances when "heroine" has a specific meaning, for example, when it describes the lead role in a drama. And some sensitive writers and speakers feel there is a certain acceptability for a gender-fair use of "hero" and "heroine." But given the record of the serious devaluation and discounting of woman-associated words in our society, it seems best to support one neutral term. Note: one of mythology's best-known couples was Hero and Leander, and Hero was *not* the manly half; she was a priest(ess) of Aphrodite.
heterosexual this is the acceptable nonsexist term to describe a person of either sex with an opposite-sex sexual preference.
he that lieth down with dogs riseth with fleas *See* he who lies down with dogs rises with fleas.
hetman (Cossack leader) leave as is in historical context.
he who hesitates is lost *they who hesitate are lost, once you hesitate you are lost.*
he who laughs last laughs best *they who laugh last laugh best, when you laugh last you laugh best.*
he who lies down with dogs rises with fleas *they who lie down with dogs rise with fleas.*
he who lives by the sword dies by the sword *they who live by the sword die by the sword, if you live by the sword you will die by the sword.*
he who seeks finds *they who seek find, seek and you shall find.*
highboy nonsexist; comes from French "bois" for "wood." *See also* hautboy.
high man (game) *high, the winner, top scorer.*
high man on the totem pole *number one, second to none, front-runner, star, person on top, high-ranking individual, someone with seniority, winner, cream of the crop, influential person, big shot, hotshot, big boss, the favorite, someone at the top of the ladder/ heap/tree.* Note that this term is insensitive and ethnocentric as well as sexist. *See also* lord it over someone.
highwayman *highway robber/bandit, robber, bandit, road agent, footpad, brigand, marauder, thug, outlaw, desperado, ruffian, rogue, criminal, gangster.*

hijack/hijacker the origin of these terms is unknown, although one story has it that they come from thieves ordering victims to raise their hands by saying, "High, Jack!" They are, however, used for both women and men and have no functional sexist connotations.

hillbilly man or woman; this term is used in a nonsexist manner today even though it was originally based on a man's name. However, its use is generally derogatory and should be avoided.

him never use "him" when you mean "him and her," or when "him" might refer to either a man or a woman (for example, "the taxpayer/him"); replace with the plural, circumlocute, or see Appendix A for additional suggestions and guidelines on avoiding "generic" masculine pronouns.

himself never use "himself" when you mean "herself and himself," or when it might refer to either a man or a woman (for example, "the priest/himself"); replace with the plural, circumlocute, or see Appendix A for additional suggestions and guidelines on avoiding the "generic" masculine pronouns.

his never use "his" when you mean "his and hers," or when it might refer to either a man or a woman (for example, "the plumber/ his"); replace with the plural, circumlocute, or see Appendix A for additional suggestions and guidelines on avoiding the "generic" masculine pronouns.

his bark is worse than his bite *her/his/their/its bark is worse than her/ his/their/its bite, all clouds and no rain, all sound and no fury, empty threat, sham.*

his nibs *her nibs and his nibs, her highness and his highness, the boss, the chief.*

his own man, be *See* be his own man.

his own worst enemy *one's/your/her/his own worst enemy.*

history nonsexist; this word comes from Greek roots for such concepts as inquiring, knowing, learning. Women have pointed out the irony that history as we know it has told only one side of the story, "his story," and they have coined the tongue-in-cheek "herstory" (a word not recognized by any standard dictionaries) to "emphasize that women's lives, deeds, and participation in human affairs have been neglected or undervalued in standard histories" (Miller and Swift 1976, p. 121).

hit a man below the belt *hit below the belt.*

hit man *hired/professional/armed killer, assassin, killer, murderer, thug, gangster. See also* gunman; hatchet man.

hit the jackpot *break the bank, score a success, succeed, turn up trumps, strike it rich, hit the mark, make a killing.*

hobo woman or man.

Hobson's choice *no choice, no choice at all, not a pin to choose between/from.* See Appendix A for the rationale on sex-linked metaphors, expressions, and figures.

hoistman hoist operator.

hoity-toity invariably used of a woman. Replace with inclusive terms: *highfalutin, pretentious, pompous.*

hold the purse strings *hold all the cards, boss, lay down the law, run the place/show, call the shots/plays, be in the saddle/driver's seat, have under control, wear the crown.*

Holy Father (pope) in the past and at the present, this gender-specific term is correct.

Holy Spirit (Holy Ghost)/he eliminate masculine pronouns for the Holy Spirit altogether, replace them with descriptive adjectives, or address the Holy Spirit in prayer directly with "you" and "your." The Hebrew word "ruach," meaning "wind, breath, spirit," is usually feminine, and the Greek word for "spirit," "pneuma," is neuter, which is why some writers and speakers refer to the Holy Spirit as "she" or "it." However, the most accurate and conservative approach still seems to be eliminating any gender-specific pronouns.

homebody man or woman. *See also* family man.

home economics this term is losing favor with many people who believe that it has for too long been associated solely with women. *See* domestic science.

homemaker this unisex term is positive in itself. Use it to describe men as well as women, and examine the context in which you use it for hidden biases and prejudices that may tend to belittle homemakers.

homeroom mother *homeroom parent/aide/helper.*

hominid anthropologists use this word inclusively, and it is functionally fairly nonsexist. It is problematic only when it is defined or used as referring to "man" instead of to "human being," which is the meaning of its Latin root. For example, one dictionary defines it as "any of a family (Hominidae) of bipedal primate mammals comprising recent man, his immediate ancestors, and related forms" (*Webster's Ninth New Collegiate Dictionary.* Springfield, MA: Merriam-Webster, 1985, p. 578). The unambiguous choice here should have been: "recent human beings, their immediate ancestors, and related forms."

homo- words beginning with "homo-" come from the Greek word meaning "same" or "equal" and are not sexist—for example, "homosexual" does not refer to a man but to someone whose sexual orientation is toward persons of the same sex.

Homo erectus this "homo" (*see* homo-) comes from the Latin for "human being." The confusion and ambiguity of the English "man" also tars the Latin "homo," and gives it a sexist look. However, the term is well established—and used inclusively—in anthropology. The main problem with it is that it is so often followed by references to "man" and "mankind" when the correct references should be "human being" and "humanity." When you see "Homo erectus" check the surrounding material for sexist language.

Homo sapiens this scientific name for the human species is based on the Latin word "homo" ("human being"). It is thus inclusive, although it tends to be heard as adult-male man rather than human-being man, especially when its common definition ("mankind") underlines the males-only flavor. When using this term in nonscientific material, it is less ambiguous to use short, direct English words: *human beings, humans, humanity, humankind, member of the human race, people.*

homosexual although this term is inclusive, referring to both women and men with same-sex emotional and sexual orientations, gays and lesbians prefer those terms to "homosexual," which they reject as "alien, clinical, and much too limiting to properly denote a whole lifestyle" (Sanford Berman, letter, November 5, 1986). When an omnibus term is needed, the preferred phrase is *lesbians and gays/gays and lesbians.*

honcho/head honcho *big shot, leader, boss, hotshot, person in charge.* Although a honcho can be a woman or a man (it comes from the Japanese meaning "group leader"), we have tended to reserve it for men, which is why you may want to use alternatives. The semifacetious "honcha" is incorrect.

honey this term may be acceptable to people in intimate relationships who have implicitly or explicitly approved its use. It is always demeaning, unwelcome, and incorrect when used for a stranger or slight acquaintance.

honkie/honky avoid; it is restricted to white men, there is no female equivalent, and it is racist.

hoodlum woman or man.

hooker *prostitute.* See Appendix A for a discussion of our language on prostitution.

horseman *equestrian, trainer, cavalier, jockey, horse breeder, horseback rider, rider, hunter.*

horsemanship *riding skills, equitation.*

hostess *host.* Also: *social director, tour guide.*

hotdogger/hotdogging may refer to either a man or a woman.

hotelier man or woman.

hotelman *hotel proprietor/owner/manager/worker, hotelier.*

hotshot woman or man.

"hot stuff" man or woman. When used in a sexual context the phrase is belittling and makes an object of the partner—whether a man or a woman.

houri keep as is when referring to the women who feature in Muslim beliefs. Avoid using it to refer to a voluptuous young woman.

houseboy *servant.*

housegirl *prostitute.*

householder woman or man.

housekeeper not a sexist word in itself, this term is too often used as an all-purpose label for a woman. Professionals who manage others' homes for them call themselves *household technicians/ workers/helpers, home managers.*

housemaid *servant, domestic worker, cleaner, household helper.*

housemaid's knee *inflammation of the kneecap.*

houseman *caretaker, house cleaner, odd jobber, fixer-upper.*

housemother *houseparent, counselor, monitor, cottage parent, chaperon.*

housewife *homemaker, consumer, woman who works at home, householder, homeowner, woman, home manager, shopper, customer, parent.* This term seems to marry a woman to her house, and should be avoided altogether because of the practically endless possibilities for using it in sexist ways.

housewifery *homemaking, housekeeping, home management, domestic science.*

housework this is no longer exclusively the province of the woman who lives in the house; make no assumptions about the nature and ownership of housework. Gloria Steinem suggests we define "human maintenance and home care as a job in itself; a job that men can and should do as well as women" (Steinem 1983, p. 155).

hoyden (girl) avoid. Note that this word used to refer to members of both sexes. *See also* tomboy.

hula dancer woman or man.

human (noun) this word, which comes from the Latin "homo" meaning "human being," has been used as a noun since 1533 and is used and perceived today as an inclusive term, although most of its dictionary definitions unfortunately include the words "man/ men" instead of the correct "human being(s)."

humanity/humankind these terms come from the Latin "homo" meaning "human being" and are used and understood today as inclusive terms.

huntress *hunter.*

huntsman *hunter, hunt manager.*

husband (verb) *conserve, ration, measure, preserve, lay/put by, economize, store, reserve, hoard, save, save for a rainy day.*

husband/wife *spouse,* unless gender-specific language is necessary. One of the most glaringly unbalanced gender pairs in the language is "man and wife." Use instead *man and woman/woman and man, wife and husband/husband and wife.*

husbandlike/husbandly these vague words leave us little the wiser about the person so described; there are as many kinds of husbands as there are husbands. Choose instead specific adjectives that describe the characteristics you are thinking of: *solicitous, gentle, supportive, intimate, knowing, sensitive, protective,* etc.

husbandman *farmer, agriculturist, farm scientist, vintager, horticulturist, citriculturist, gardener, florist, cultivator, tiller of the soil, sower, reaper, forester.*

husbandry *agriculture, farming, cultivation, forestry.* Or, be specific: *arboriculture, floriculture, horticulture, landscape gardening, viniculture,* etc.

hussy avoid this term. Note that it is derived from "housewife." *See* femme fatale; Jezebel; loose woman.

hustler woman or man.

hysteria/hysterical these words are based on the Greek word for "womb" (hysteria was thought to be caused by disturbances in the womb), and they tend to be used almost entirely and often inappropriately of women. For the noun use *fear, frenzy, emotional excess, wildness, outburst, explosion, flare-up, seizure, eruption, delirium.* For the adjective use *angry, outraged, irate, incensed, enraged, furious, infuriated, livid, upset, agitated, fit to be tied, delirious, beside oneself, carried away, raving, raging, seething, distracted, frantic, frenetic, frenzied, wild, berserk, uncontrollable.*

i

I reckon there's as much human nature in some folks as there is in others, if not more.

Edward Noyes Westcott

I am not my brother's keeper *it's none of my business, I'm not responsible for anyone but myself, I'm not her/his/my sister's/my brother's keeper, it's not my responsibility.*

ice-cream man *ice-cream vendor.*

iceman *ice route driver, ice deliverer.* Use "iceman" in historical references.

idiot savant man or woman; the French is in the masculine form but has always been used for both sexes.

I'll be a monkey's uncle *See* monkey's uncle.

illegitimate/illegitimate child except for narrow legal uses, avoid these terms; no human being is "illegitimate." The word is sexist because this label is society's way of castigating the mother while the father's role is minimized or ignored. When the father assumes responsibility and remains in the picture, there is less tendency to label the child. Examine your need to mention the circumstances of a person's birth; they are very often irrelevant. If you must refer to them, use *child of unmarried parents, child of unknown father.*

I'm a monkey's uncle *See* monkey's uncle.

impotence a biologically determined (and therefore nonsexist) sex-linked term. Note that "impotence" and "frigidity," q.v., are not parallel terms.

impresario woman or man; for terms that may not hit the ear with as masculine a sound as "impresario" try *promoter, manager, director, producer.*

imprisoned in every fat man a thin one is wildly signaling to be let out *imprisoned in every fat person a thin one is wildly signaling to be let out.* (Note: Is this a "weightist" remark? Use sensitively.)

inamorata *lover.* There is no male equivalent for "inamorata." *See also* boyfriend; girlfriend.

inclusive language see discussion in Appendix A; "inclusive language" is not a precise synonym for "nonsexist language," "gender-free language," or "gender-fair language."

Indiaman *India trader, East India trading ship, merchant ship, trader;* or retain as is in historical context.

industrialist man or woman.

infantryman *footsoldier, member of the infantry, soldier, infantry; infantryman and infantrywoman* if used gender-fairly.

infertile/infertility these inclusive terms seem to be used more often for women than for men, but not in any pejorative sense. Depending on your precise shading of meaning, you might prefer "sterile/sterility," which are used equally often of both sexes. *See also* barren; sterile/sterility.

informant woman or man.

ingenue this is a well-established and fairly narrowly defined role in the theater. However, there is no male counterpart; the term "ingenu" for a man is rarely heard. When using the term in its broader sense, substitute *novice, amateur, beginner, tyro, newcomer, innocent.*

inheritress/inheritrix *inheritor.*

inkman *inker.*

inner man *inner person/self/core, soul, heart, private self.*

inspectress *inspector.*

instructress *instructor.*

insurance man *insurance agent/sales representative/rep.*

intern (advanced medical student) man or woman.

in the arms of Morpheus *fast asleep, sound asleep, sawing wood, dead to the world, out like a light, sacked out.* See Appendix A for the rationale on avoiding sex-linked metaphors, expressions, and figures.

Irishman *Irishwoman and Irishman, native of Ireland, inhabitant of Ireland.* Plurals: *Irishmen and Irishwomen/Irishwomen and Irishman, the Irish, natives of Ireland, inhabitants of Ireland.* It's generally not possible to replace words like "Irishman," "Norseman," "Welshman," and "Dutchman" with one pithy inclusive term; either circumlocute or use the longer phrases: "Irishwoman and Irishman/Irishmen and Irishwomen."

ironmaster *iron manufacturer/worker, ironmonger.*

irrational this term is too often used as a rebuttal of women's arguments or applied inaccurately to women as a catch-all condemnation; use carefully in reference to women. It is not used in the same way for men.

Isle of Man "Man" is thought to come from a Celtic word meaning "mountain"; it has nothing to do with human beings.

it is a wise father that knows his own child *it is a wise parent that knows its own child, wise parents know their own children, it is wise parents who know their own child.*

j

If thought corrupts language, language can also corrupt thought.

George Orwell

jack/jack-/-jack the word, prefix, or suffix "jack" comes from the man's name and often refers to a man or a boy. However, in some cases "jack" has come to refer to certain tools (jack, hydraulic jack, jackscrew, jackknife, and jackhammer, for example), and these terms may be used as they are. *See* specific entries: every man jack; jack of all trades, master of none; jack-tar; lumberjack/ lumberman, etc.

jackanapes *whippersnapper, smart aleck, smarty-pants, mischievous child, mischief maker, scamp, rascal, pert child, malapert, saucy person, popinjay, minx, little monkey.*

jackdaw (bird) leave as is.

Jack Frost this character has been around for too many years to throw him out abruptly, but you could begin to introduce the next generation to *the Frost Goblin, Jack and Jill Frost, the Frost Fairy* (if "fairy" isn't perceived as feminine). Also: *frost, winter.* See Appendix A for the rationale on avoiding sex-linked metaphors, expressions, and figures.

jackfruit (tree) leave as is.

jack-in-the-box the clown that pops up in the box is generally male, which makes this term acceptable; an inclusive name for the toy does not currently exist.

jack-in-the-pulpit (plant) leave as is.

jackleg *amateur, makeshift.*

jack mackerel (fish) leave as is.

jackman *printing-roller handler.*

jack of all trades, master of none *good at all trades, expert at none; generalist; someone who knows a little bit about a lot of things and not much about any of them.* *See also* handyman.

jack pine (tree) leave as is.

jackpot not a functionally sexist word although "jack" derives from a man's name. Use instead *pot, pool, kitty, stakes, bank.* **See also** hit the jackpot.

jackpot, hit the *See* hit the jackpot.

jack rabbit leave as is if referring to several genuses of large hares. However, if the term is used to indicate a male rabbit, be sure it is male and that its sex is relevant.

Jack Robinson, before you can say *See* before you can say Jack Robinson.

jacks (child's game) OK as is.

jackstay although this comes from the man's name, the term is not perceived as sexist and can be used as is.

jackstraw (game) OK as is.

jack-tar *sailor.*

jade (woman) avoid.

jailbait (referring to underage female sexual partner) avoid this term. Instead, describe the situation as it reflects reality. Using "jail bait" promotes the old Eve-tempting-poor-Adam myth, implying a certain victimization and unwilling cooperation (!) on the part of the man, and obscures the fact that the man is engaging in criminal activity (and laying the foundation for a statutory rape charge). *See also* San Quentin quail.

Jane Crow Pauli Murray said this term "refers to the entire range of assumptions, attitudes, stereotypes, customs, and arrangements which have robbed women of a positive self-concept and prevented them from participating fully in society as equals with men. Traditionally racism and sexism in the United States have shared some common origins, displayed similar manifestations, reinforced one another, and are so deeply intertwined in the country's institutions that the successful outcome of the struggle against racism will depend in large part upon the simultaneous elimination of all discrimination based upon sex. Black women, faced with these dual barriers, have often found that sex bias is more formidable than racial bias" (Murray 1973, p. 326).

Jane Doe acceptable when used for legal purposes; the male form is John Doe, q.v.

janitress *janitor.*

JAP/Jewish American Princess avoid.

Java man *Homo erectus, early human, early human found in Java, prehistoric human.* Remains are called *Java fossil, Java skull.*

jazzman *jazz musician/player, member of jazz band.*

Jekyll and Hyde *split personality, alter egos.* See Appendix A for the rationale on avoiding sex-linked metaphors, expressions, and figures.

jerrican/jerry can the word "jerry" here does not refer to a man's name but to the nickname for Germans, to reflect the can's German design. Even though it involves an ethnic reference, the term is not functionally racist. There seem to be no good alternatives to these terms for those who would like to avoid expressions that seem to be sex-linked.

jerry-built   although its origins are unclear, this term seems to be functionally nonsexist. Those who want to avoid even the appearance of sex-linked terms can use instead *shoddy/flimsy/ careless construction, cheaply/hastily/shoddily built.*

Jewess   *Jew.*

Jezebel/jezebel   avoid these terms. The biblical story of Jezebel shows a murdering, controlling, rapacious person. She is primarily an amoral manipulator and only secondarily a woman. Instead of focusing on Jezebel's viciousness, the dictionary definition of a jezebel emphasizes her sexuality (a shameless or abandoned woman) when in fact Jezebel did not in any way trade on her sex to carry out her evil deeds. Use instead *evil influence, villain, murderer, bully, plotter, scourge of the human race, devil in human form/shape.*

jiggerman   *potter.*

Jim Crow   use only in a discussion of racial discrimination, never as an epithet. *See also* Jane Crow.

jim-dandy   *terrific, super, wonderful, marvelous, fantastic, sensational, fabulous, stupendous, out of this world, far out, extraordinary.* See Appendix A for a discussion of sex-linked metaphors, expressions, and figures.

jimjams   although its origins are unclear, this term looks very sex-linked and some people may want a more neutral-appearing alternative: *jitters.*

jimmies   the origins of this term are unclear, but because it sounds sexist you might prefer an alternative: *candy sprinkles.*

jimmy (noun/verb)   *crowbar/pry (up).*

Job, patient as/poor as   *See* patient as Job; poor as Job/poor as Job's turkey.

jobmaster   *supervisor.*

jock (athlete)   woman or man.

jockey   man or woman.

john   *bathroom, restroom, toilet, washroom, privy, water closet, lavatory, W.C., comfort station, outhouse.*

john (prostitution)   *prostitute's "client."* Our language is nowhere murkier or more deceptive than in the area of words used to talk about prostitutes and prostitution (see discussion in Appendix A). There is no word equal to "prostitute" in weight, significance, and meaning that we can use to describe the prostitute's "client." Through words, as in other ways, prostitutes carry the burden of guilt and shame for a system that could not exist without "clients." While prostitutes are most often driven into the system by economic necessity or psychological coercion, their partners come to it of their own free will. If either party were able to dismantle the system, the "clients" rather than the prostitutes are the more capable of doing so, which means that certainly much of the responsibility for the continuance of prostitution falls squarely in the lap of the "clients," and our language ought to reflect this participation and responsibility instead of innocuously naming the prostitute's partner a "john," a homey, all-American name. "Prostitute's 'client'" (1) makes the connection with prostitution obvious and (2) allows the dubiousness of the word "client" show in the use of quotation marks. Avoid using language that dresses up prostitution; write and speak of it precisely and realistically.

John Bull (England) leave as is. While some countries are personified by men (for example, the United States' Uncle Sam), others are personified by women (for example, France's Marianne).

John Doe acceptable when used for legal purposes; the female form is Jane Doe. Do not use "John Doe" generically to mean "average man." *See* average man; common man; man in the street.

John Hancock *signature, name, moniker.*

johnny *hospital gown.* See Appendix A for the rationale on avoiding sex-linked metaphors, expressions, and figures.

johnnycake nonsexist; the term seems to have come either from an Indian word or from "journeycake." For more neutral-appearing words use *cornbread, journeycake, corncake.*

Johnny-come-lately *newcomer, new arrival/face, upstart, nouveau riche, arriviste, outsider, social climber.* See Appendix A for the rationale on avoiding sex-linked metaphors, expressions, and figures.

Johnny-jump-up (flower) leave as is.

Johnny-on-the-spot *friend in need, guardian angel, deus ex machina, right hand, at the ready, good Samaritan, benefactor, ministering angel, there when you need her/him.* See Appendix A for the rationale on avoiding sex-linked metaphors, expressions, and figures.

Johnny Reb *confederate soldier;* or, leave as is.

John Q. Citizen this is sexist when used "generically" to refer to the average citizen. Use instead *the average citizen, Jane Q. Citizen and John Q. Citizen. See also* average man; common man; man in the street.

jointress this is a very specific British legal term; leave as is until it is changed or replaced.

journeyman in the general sense, this word can be replaced by *trade worker, beginner, trainee, skilled craftsworker.* Or, use a specific title. However, certain uses (in labor law or trades, for example) have a very specific meaning and the term must be left as is for the present. It may be possible in such cases to use *journeyman* and *journeywoman* or *journeyperson.* ("Journeyperson" is very much a choice of last resort, but it may have some limited usefulness while the term is in transition.)

judas goat *bait, lure, decoy, trap, baited hook.* See Appendix A for the rationale on avoiding sex-linked metaphors, expressions, and figures.

judas hole/judas window   *peephole.* See Appendix A for the rationale on
   avoiding sex-linked metaphors, expressions, and figures.
judas kiss   *kiss of betrayal.* See Appendix A for the rationale on
   avoiding sex-linked metaphors, expressions, and figures.
jumping jack   the child's toy remains a "jumping jack" when the figure
   is a man; if it is a clown, call it a *jumping clown.* For the
   conditioning exercise, use *side-straddle hop.*
jumpmaster   *jump director.*
junior miss   *teenager, young woman, adolescent, high school student.*
junkman   *junk dealer/collector, rag picker.*
jury foreman   *See* foreman (jury).
juryman   *juror.*

k

A trite word is an overused word which has lost its identity like an old coat in a second-hand shop. The familiar grows dull and we no longer see, hear, or taste it.

Anaïs Nin

✦ ✦ ✦

kaffeeklatsch in Germany this expression is completely sex-neutral and refers to informal gatherings of both sexes to visit and drink coffee. In the United States, however, it has come to be used in a belittling and patronizing manner for gatherings of women. Use instead *tea, coffee, get together, gathering, social hour, visit, talk, open house, party.*

kapellmeister *choir/orchestra director.*

keelboatman *keelboater, keeler, keel/barge worker.*

keelsman *See* keelboatman.

keelson nonsexist; probably of Scandinavian origin, this word has nothing to do with male offspring.

keep a stiff upper lip this is a cultural imperative for men in our society that is sexist, unnecessary, and possibly unhealthy. *See* act like a man.

kennelman *kennel owner/operator/attendant, dog breeder.*

kept woman avoid this term as it is offensive on several counts: (1) the woman's supposed passivity (she is "kept") and (2) the lack of a word to describe her partner. Although two adults are involved here, only one of them is labeled pejoratively—or even labeled at all. The assumption is that the man is behaving "normally" and thus is still just called a man, while the woman's behavior (no different in important respects from his) is "deviant" enough to require a special term.

kewpie doll do not use for women; they are not dolls.

key man *key person/individual/executive, leading character, linchpin, leader, pivotal person, cornerstone, keystone, capstone.*

kilnman *rotary-kiln operator, annealer, kiln supervisor.*

king   use "king" only when it is the correct formal title. Otherwise, use inclusive words: *monarch, ruler, sovereign, crowned head, chief of state, potentate, commander, autocrat, tyrant, despot, protector, dictator, leader, governor, chieftain, majesty, regent.*

kingcraft   *diplomacy, statecraft, political savvy, the art of governing, holding firmly to the reins of government, wielding the scepter.*

kingdom   *country, land, reign, rule, monarchy, realm, domain, dominion, nation, state, sovereignty, principality, territory, protectorate.* Also, in some contexts: *empire, commonwealth, republic.* "Reign" is particularly good for references to the kingdom of God. Sometimes heard is "kindom," to express the meaning of "kingdom" without the triumphal male overtones. Note that during the reigns of even the most powerful and influential queens (e.g., Queen Elizabeth I), no one ever spoke of a queendom.

kingdom come   *the next world, paradise.*

kingliness   *nobility, royalty, authority, dignity, gallantry, charisma, greatness, glamour, intelligence, insightfulness.* "Kingliness" is often used vaguely and doesn't convey very much more than what we already know (i.e., that we are speaking of a crowned head). Try to identify the precise characteristic you mean to emphasize.

kingly   *regal, dignified, majestic, imperial, aristocratic, autocratic, courtly, gallant, charismatic, sovereign, royal, dynastic, royalist, monarchical, imperialistic.*

kingmaker   *power behind the throne/behind the scenes, strategist, power broker/creator, executive maker, mover, earthshaker, someone with political clout.*

king of the jungle   *monarch/ruler/majesty of the jungle.*

king of the hill/king of the mountain   when speaking of a woman, use *queen of the hill/mountain.* Other possibilities are *big shot, hotshot, big wheel, magnate, bigwig, someone on the top of the heap.*

kingpin   *key person/individual/executive, linchpin, leading character, cornerstone, leader, pivotal person.*

king post   this term has a specific architectural meaning and no substitute; leave as is.

king's blue   *cobalt blue.*

King's Counsel   when a queen is on the throne, it's "Queen's Counsel."

king's English   *Oxford English, perfect/standard/correct/pure English, standard usage, correct speech.* When a Queen is on the British throne, one technically ought to hear "the Queen's English," and one does in Great Britain, but in the United States "King's English" has become the standard, although oftentimes incorrect, usage.

kingship   *majesty, royal position, royal office, dignity, monarchy.*

king-size   *jumbo-size, gigantic, enormous, huge, extra-large, of heroic proportions, larger than normal, super-size, outsized.*

king's ransom, worth a   *See* worth a king's ransom.

kinsman/kinswoman use as is or, for gender-nonspecific terms, use *relative, blood relative, relation, kin, kinsfolk, kith and kin, connection.*

knave historically this refers to a man or boy in roughly the same pejorative sense that "boy" has been used in English for a man. When you mean a tricky, deceitful person, use inclusive terms: *mischief-maker, troublemaker, trickster, sneak, double-crosser, villain, rascal, four-flusher, cheater, crook, evildoer, traitor, betrayer.*

knavery *mischief, trickery, roguish trick, baseness, villainy, rascality, unscrupulousness, deviltry, wrongdoing, mischievousness, monkeyshines, shenanigans, hanky-panky.*

knight (noun) historically, the knight of the Round Table variety was always a man, and there was no equivalent for a woman. Women members of British orders of knighthood are called ladies and addressed as dames (for example, Dame Helen); only men are called knights and addressed as sirs.

knight (verb) generally either a woman or a man may be knighted today, although this was not always the case. *See also* knight (noun).

knight errant *rescuer, champion, hero errant; dreamer, idealist, romantic; philanthropist, altruist, humanitarian.*

knight-errantry *gallantry, nobility, bravery, quixotic conduct, generosity, altruism, philanthropy, kind-heartedness.*

knighthood historically reserved for men; today both women and men may be raised to knighthood. *See also* knight (noun); knight (verb).

knight in shining armor this is still used, although there is no good parallel for a woman; perhaps the closest is "woman of my dreams."

L

Words are all we have.

Samuel Beckett

◆ ◆ ◆

lackey historically, lackeys were footmen, male retainers, and other male servants. In today's sense of a servile follower, servant, gofer, or toady, a lackey can be a woman or a man.

lad use with "lass" in a gender-fair manner.

ladder man (gambling) *ladder supervisor, overhead spotter/checker, supervisor, spotter, checker, guard, casino employee.*

ladies' auxiliary this concept is very sexist, but as ladies' auxiliaries become less and less common, the need for this term will disappear. In the meantime, use it only when a group of women names itself an auxiliary; do not assume that a group is one.

ladies' man *popular with the women/popular with the men.* "Ladies' man" is sexist partly because there is no equivalent for women ("gentlemen's woman"?) and partly because of the use of "ladies'." *See also* lady.

lady (noun) avoid using this in place of "woman" unless you intend shadings of meanings that describe someone who is elegant, "refined," and conscious of propriety and correct behavior. In most contexts this word is perceived as (and often is) condescending. It also "often serves to trivialize" (Bebout 1984, p. 13). There appears to be a consensus that "lady" has been "banned from the approved [feminist] lexicon" (Kramer 1986, p. 121). Note that "lady" was once the female equivalent of "knight" in the social order, and it has also been paired with "gentleman," yet neither of these terms is used today in the way "lady" is.

lady (adj.) if information about gender is essential (and in most cases it is not), use instead "woman" or "female." Test yourself by asking if you would use "man" or "male" in a similar situation if the person were a man. (Under this test you would probably never use the parallel "gentleman" where one now sees "lady.") *See also* lady (noun).

lady (drugs) *cocaine.*

lady beetle/ladybird/ladybug leave as they are.

ladyfinger leave as is.

ladyfish leave as is.

lady-in-waiting *attendant, personal attendant/servant.* Use "lady-in-waiting" when it is an official title.

lady-killer this is sexist, partly because there is no equivalent for a woman and partly because of the use of "lady." Use instead for a man *popular with the women* and for a woman *popular with the men.*

ladykin this is virtually never seen today. Fortunately.

ladylike avoid this vague stereotype. The word "lady" (q.v.) is not in great favor, but additionally, "ladylike" conveys different meanings to different people according to their perceptions of what a woman ought or ought not do, say, think, wear, feel, look like. These subjective cultural judgments have nothing to do with sex and everything to do with gender. Choose instead words that express the characteristics you want to describe: *well-mannered, civil, polite, tender, cooperative, neat, soft-spoken, gentle, aristocratic, cultured, elegant, proper, correct, gracious, considerate, kind, well-spoken, courteous,* etc. Note that all these adjectives may be used equally appropriately of a man. For a discussion of the difference between gender and sex, see Appendix A.

ladylove avoid; this term has no parallel for a man. *See* girlfriend.

lady luck *luck.*

lady of pleasure *prostitute.* Note the irony of the word "pleasure"; more often, the prostitute experiences degradation, pain, or unpleasantness. See Appendix A for a discussion of our language on prostitution.

lady of the evening *prostitute.* This phrase has no parallel for a man; in addition to being sexist, it is coy and imprecise. See Appendix A for a discussion of our language on prostitution.

lady of the house *head of the house, householder, homeowner, registered voter, taxpayer, citizen, consumer.*

lady's maid *attendant, personal attendant/servant.*

ladyship used of a woman with the rank of lady; the equivalents for a man are "lord/lordship."

lady's slipper/lady's smock/lady's thumb (plants) leave as they are.

laird *landed proprietor,* except where "laird" has specific use and meaning in Scotland.

lance corporal woman or man.

landlady/landlord *proprietor, owner, manager, lessor, manager, building manager, superintendent, householder.*

landsman *landlubber; compatriot,* q.v.

lass use with "lad" in a gender-fair manner.

Latina/Latino use these gender-specific terms gender-fairly. (They are generally preferred to such terms as "Hispanic" and "Spanish.")

laundress *launderer. See also* laundryman/laundrywoman.

laundryman/laundrywoman *launderer, laundry worker/hand, washer, clothes washer.*

lawman *lawmaker, lawgiver, defender of the law, upholder of the law.* Or, be specific: *sheriff, judge, attorney, officer, police officer, officer of the law, magistrate, constable, warden, bailiff,* etc.

layman *layperson, nonprofessional, laic, member/one of the laity, average person, ordinary person, amateur, nonexpert, the uninitiated, secularist, civilian, lay Christian, congregation member.* Plurals: *laypeople, the laity, layfolk, congregation members/ membership, members of the congregation.* If no other alternative works and you use them gender-fairly try *laywoman and layman.* Although "-person" words are generally a last resort, the use of "layperson" has gained common acceptance and is one of the few "-person" words that does not seem to jar.

layman's terms *plain/nontechnical/ordinary/uncomplicated/informal language, nontechnical/easy-to-understand terms.*

layout man *layout planner/worker, patternmaker.*

lay-up man *lay-up worker, stocklayer.*

laywoman *See* layman.

lazy Susan *revolving/relish tray.* See Appendix A for the rationale on avoiding sex-linked metaphors, expressions, and figures.

leader *woman or man.*

leading lady/leading man *lead, principal.*

leading seaman man or woman. "Seaman" is still an official rank in the U.S. Navy, although it can be filled by either a woman or a man.

leadman *supervisor. See also* foreman.

leadsman *sounder, depth sounder/reader.*

leaseman *lease buyer, leaseholder.*

leatherneck since a Marine can be either a man or a woman, so can a leatherneck.

lecher by definition, a lecher is a man, so there are no synonymous inclusive terms. There are no attractive words in the language to talk about lechery, but if you want to use a less sex-specific term or if you want to describe a woman, you could try *sex maniac/ fiend.*

lector man or woman.

Legion of Honor/Legion of Merit awarded to both women and men.

legionnaire invariably a man. In the American Legion, for example, women are "full members" in the auxiliary but are not called legionnaires.

legman *gofer, assistant, reporter, courier, messenger.*

leonine can be said of a woman or a man.

lesbian (noun/adj.) this gender-specific word is the term currently preferred by most lesbians. *See also* homosexual.

let 'er rip! *let it rip!*

let George do it *let somebody else do it, pass the buck.*

letterman *letterholder, lettered athlete; letterwoman and letterman* if used gender-fairly.

leverman *lever operator.*

lib/libber *liberationist, feminist, member of the women's liberation movement.* "Lib" and "libber" are offensive terms.

liegeman *servant, subject, fiefholder, vassal.* Historically, a liegeman was always a man; his wife and children were assumed to be part of him, not separate liegemen.

lieutenant woman or man. The same is true for lieutenant colonel, lieutenant commander, lieutenant general, lieutenant governor, and lieutenant junior grade.

lifemanship *put-down artistry, superiority complex.* This is a difficult term to replace with one word; circumlocution, elaboration of the characteristic, or showing the person's orientation instead of just telling about it are all possible solutions.

liftman (British) *lift operator.*

light-o'-love for the first meaning of the word, use *prostitute. See* girlfriend for alternatives for the second meaning.

like a man replace this vague cultural stereotype with precise descriptions: *with a high/strong hand, a head for mechanics, resolutely, courageously, competitively, self-confidently, in a straightforward manner,* etc.

like father, like son *the acorn doesn't fall far from the tree, a chip off/of the old block, like parent like child, spit and image, spitting image, birds of a feather, the very image of, for all the world like, as like as two peas, take after, follow in the parent's footsteps, take a leaf out of the parent's book.*

line foreman *line supervisor.*

lineman/linewoman *lineworker, line installer/repairer/maintainer/ erector/installer-repairer, line-service attendant; line umpire.*

linesman *line tender.*

linkboy/linkman OK in historical context, as they were boys and men. Or, *torch carrier, light attendant. See* anchorman for substitutes for "linkman" as used chiefly in Great Britain.

linksman *golfer, golf player.*

little lady avoid. It is never correct to refer to an adult woman this way, and there is no acceptable substitute because the very intent is demeaning. It is also incorrect to refer to a child this way because (1) a child is not an adult and should be allowed to be a child while she is a child and (2) telling a child she is a little lady almost without exception is an attempt to perpetuate some cultural stereotype, e.g., sitting quietly and neatly in the background. There is nothing wrong per se in this behavior, but "little lady" tells the child this is the desired, best behavior for all occasions.

little man avoid. Unlike "little woman," which can also be used to refer to an adult woman, "little man" is reserved for boys. Avoid it because (1) a child is not an adult and should be allowed to be a child while he is a child and (2) telling a child he is a little man almost without exception is an attempt to perpetuate some cultural stereotype, e.g., not showing emotions. There is nothing wrong with refraining from crying in certain instances, but a boy should not be taught that this is the desired, best behavior in all circumstances.

little shaver *youngster, tyke, child.* Although the origins of this expression may not be as masculine as they sound ("shaver" deriving perhaps from the chip-off-the-old-block kind of shaving rather than from whisker shaving), it is defined either as a youngster or as a boy and it is heard as a masculine term.

little woman, the *spouse, partner, wife.* Never use this, even (especially) as intended humor.

liveryman *livery worker, liveried retainer, vehicle-rental service operator.*

living doll unlike other uses of "doll," this one refers to both men and women. Although it seems that there ought to be a general rule not to refer to people as dolls (because of all the implications of making objects of them), this particular expression has always been fairly innocuous, and there seems to be no difference in tone, intent, or significance between references to men and women.

lobsterman *lobster catcher/fisher/farmer/grower/cultivator/dealer.*

Lolita *sexually precocious; underage and seductive.* For the rationale on avoiding sex-linked metaphors, expressions, and figures, see Appendix A.

lone wolf woman or man.

longbowman in historical contexts leave as is; otherwise, *archer, longbow archer.*

longshoreman *longshore worker, stevedore, dockhand, dockworker, shorehand, shoreworker, wharfworker, wharfhand.*

loose woman avoid. If you mean *prostitute,* use it. If you mean a woman of questionable morals (which is a questionable judgment) say exactly what you mean using inclusive words: *promiscuous, sexually active, indiscriminating,* etc. Note that the language has no such expression as "loose man," yet a "loose woman" must, by definition, have a partner.

Lord one way of handling this masculine word is to retain the word "Lord" when referring to the Lord Jesus Christ, as that is part of who he is (the use of masculine pronouns when referring to Christ is of course correct); however, both Old Testament and New Testament references to the Lord God (not Christ) can be handled by substituting one of the following: *Advocate, Almighty/the Almighty, Author, Being, Creator, Creator of all things, Defender, the Deity, Divine Light, the Eternal, Eternal One, Ever-present God, First Cause, Friend, God, Godhead, God my Rock, God my Rock and my Redeemer, God of Abraham and Sarah, God of Grace, God of Heaven, God of Hosts, God of Israel, God of our ancestors/ forebears, God of the Nations, Good Parent, Guide, Heavenly Creator, Heavenly Parent, Holy One/the Holy One, Holy One of*

Israel, the Infinite, Just One, Liberator, Living God, Maker, Merciful God, Mighty One, Most High/the Most High, Most Loving God, Nurturer, O God my God, O Gracious God, Omnipotent One, our Refuge and our Strength, Powerful One, Preserver, Providence, Redeemer, Rock, Rock of Refuge, Ruler, Savior, Shepherd, Shepherd of Israel, Source/the Source, Source of Life, Sovereign, Spirit, Supreme Being, Sustainer, Wisdom. For a list of 196 inclusive names, titles, and phrases referring to God, send $1.50 plus $.50 handling to The Coordinating Center for Women in Church and Society, Suite D, 1400 N. 7th Street, St. Louis, MO 63106 for a copy of their thirty-page report, "Inclusive Language Guidelines for Use and Study in the United Church of Christ." Masculine pronouns referring to God should be avoided. *See* God/ he; God/himself; God/his. *See also* God; Father (God); Father, Son, and Holy Spirit/Holy Ghost; Lord's Prayer, the; Son of Man; Holy Spirit (Holy Ghost)/he.

lord and master do not use, even (especially) to be funny.

lord it over someone *dominate, domineer, boss around, browbeat, bully, intimidate, tyrannize, overshadow, overpower, oppress, wear the crown, ride herd on, ride roughshod over, trample underfoot, be hard upon, lay a heavy hand on, rule with a high hand, have the upper hand, deal hardly with, call the shots, run the show, crush under an iron heel, keep a tight rein on, lay down the law, bend to one's will.*

lordliness replace this vague term with words that convey precisely what you mean: *haughtiness, regal bearing, dignity, imperiousness, formality, stateliness, majesty, pomposity, elegance, arrogance,* etc.

lord mayor leave as is where used officially (as in Great Britain).

lord of the manor, playing *See* playing lord of the manor.

lordship used of a man with the rank of lord; the equivalent for a woman is "ladyship."

Lord's Prayer, the some people feel that the two sex-linked words in this prayer ("Father" and "kingdom") are not sexist, but are instead theologically and scripturally sound and necessary; they are not to be tampered with. Others feel that the spirit of the prayer is in no way violated by replacing "Father" with "God," "Mother/Father," or another title, and "kingdom" with "dominion" or some other synonym. An inclusive Lord's Prayer could look something like this: *Our God in heaven, holy be your name. Your dominion come, your will be done, on earth as it is in heaven. Give us this day our daily bread. Forgive us our trespasses, as we forgive those who trespass against us. Lead us not into temptation, but deliver us from evil. For the dominion, the power, and the glory are yours, now and forever. Amen.*

Lothario *seducer, gay deceiver, libertine, lover, great/dashing lover.* See Appendix A for the rationale on avoiding sex-linked metaphors, expressions, and figures.

lounge lizard this phrase is functionally sexist because it's used only of men. Use instead: *social parasite. See also* ne'er-do-well.

love, honor, and obey (wedding ceremony) *love, honor, and cherish; love, respect, and cherish; develop mutual love and respect; love, honor, and reverence; love, encourage, and accept; love and honor; love and cherish.*

low man *low, the low scorer, the loser, defeatee. See also* low man on the totem pole.

low man on the totem pole *lowest ranking individual, new kid on the block/street, someone with no seniority/clout, the last one in, washout, three-time loser, hard-luck case, defeatee, also-ran, plebian, neophyte, proletarian, rookie, beginner, tyro.* Note that this phrase is insensitive and ethnocentric as well as sexist.

lowboy nonsexist; "boy" comes from the French for "wood," "bois."

lumberjack/lumberman *lumber worker/cutter, logger, tree cutter, woodcutter, log roller, timber worker, woodchopper.*

lust properly (or improperly) attributed to either sex.

m

A word is not a crystal, transparent and unchanged; it is the skin of
a living thought and may vary greatly in color and content
according to the circumstances and time in which it is used.

Oliver Wendell Holmes, Jr.

✦ ✦ ✦

ma'am this contraction for "madam" is used in the same way "sir" is
used for a man. It is a useful term and in no way derogatory to
women. *See also* madam.

machismo/macho by definition, these terms apply only to men; there
are no parallels for women. As these words tend to be overused,
examine your use of them closely. Choose instead specific,
inclusive terms to describe the behavior or attitude: *aggressive,
assertive, defensive, proud, overbearing, overconfident, arrogant,* etc.

madam "madam" is a valuable term, used for a woman in the same
way "sir" is used for a man. Use it freely to address women you
don't know or know only very slightly. It is in the process of
losing its respectability altogether, however, because of its other
usage: female head of a house of prostitution. Like so many of the
female words in male-female word pairs, it has been deeply
discounted. (Notice how nice "sir" is.) Do not use "madam" to
refer to someone connected with prostitution. Use instead:
prostitute, owner/head of house of prostitution. See Appendix A for
a discussion on the way we use language to speak of prostitution.

mad as a wet hen *mad as a hornet.*

mademoiselle use only for a Frenchwoman who calls herself
"mademoiselle." In France, "mademoiselle" is generally reserved
for women in their teens or early to mid-twenties while "madame"
is used for older women—in both cases irrespective of their
marital status. This used to be the case in the United States with
"Miss" and "Mrs." *See also* Miss; Mrs.; Ms.

madman/madwoman although these terms are fairly equally weighted
for women and men, they are so inaccurate and insubstantial that
they should probably be avoided altogether. If a person's mental
condition must be mentioned, use something like "a person with

mental illness" to avoid identifying the whole person with one aspect of her or his existence. Some ex-patients or institutionalized, militant persons with a mental illness call themselves "psychiatric inmates."

maestro *conductor, orchestra leader; expert.*

magdalen *reformed prostitute.*

magistrate woman or man.

magnate man or woman.

magsman *safecracker.*

maharaja/maharani use these sex-specific words as they are.

maid *houseworker, household worker/servant, housekeeper, room attendant, cleaner, attendant, servant, house servant, custodian, janitor.*

maiden (noun) use only where necessary in historical contexts.

maiden (adj.) *first, premier.* **See also** maiden voyage.

maidenhead *hymen, virginity.*

maidenhood use only as necessary in historical contexts.

maiden lady *See* spinster.

maiden name *birth name, birth family name.*

maiden voyage *first/premier voyage, first trip.*

maid of all work *general servant.* **See also** charwoman; cleaning girl/cleaning lady/cleaning woman; handyman; maid; maidservant.

maid of honor *best woman, attendant of honor, honor/bridal/bride's attendant, attendant.* Whichever term you choose, be sure that the groom's attendant is referred to with a parallel term, for example, "best woman and best man" or "bride's attendant and groom's attendant."

maidservant *servant, house servant, houseworker, room attendant, cleaner, attendant, household helper.* **See also** charwoman; handyman; maid.

mailboy *mail messenger.*

mailman *mail/letter carrier, postal worker/clerk, mail deliverer/clerk.*

main man (slang) *best friend, mentor, hero, partner.* This has such a particular meaning that in most cases it is probably irreplaceable if you are writing or reporting street talk.

maintenance man *maintenance mechanic/repairer/specialist, maintainer.*

maitre d' *dining room/restaurant host, host, head waiter, majordomo, hotel manager.*

major woman or man.

majordomo man or woman; this term comes from the Latin for "elder of the house."

majorette *drum major, baton twirler, marching band leader.*

major general woman or man.

make a man of *be the making of, do a world of good, improve, mature, toughen someone up.*

makeup girl/makeup man *makeup artist.* Note the nonparallel "girl/man" word pair.

malapropism from Mrs. Malaprop in Richard B. Sheridan's comedy *The Rivals* (1775), the word "malaprop" has passed into the language with no rival (although "spoonerism," q.v., is a near relative) and with no pithy substitute or alternative. Retain. Few people perceive the term as sex-linked.

male (noun) avoid the use of "male" as a noun except in technical writing, for example, medicine, statistics, police reports, sociology. It is most often reserved for biological or nonhuman references. When using "male" as a noun, beware of nonparallel constructions, for example, "three women and two males." *See also* male (adj.).

male (adj.) use only when you would use "female" or when it is necessary for clarification; this adjective is often inserted gratuitously, for example, "male nurse," "male secretary," "male model," "male prostitute." Watch particularly for nonparallel usage, for example, "three male dancers and one woman dancer." *See also* male (noun).

male chauvinism/male chauvinist/male chauvinist pig *chauvinism/ chauvinist.* "Chauvinism" used to refer to the view that one's own country was vastly superior, right or wrong, to all other countries. Dictionaries now also define "chauvinism" as the view that one's own sex is vastly superior. Either a man or a woman can be a sex-chauvinist.

male climacteric *climacteric.* This concept is still somewhat debatable; however, if you need to be sex-specific use *female climacteric and male climacteric.*

male ego *ego.*

male menopause *climacteric.* *See also* male climacteric.

male nurse *nurse.*

mama's boy *spoiled/immature/irresponsible person.* The concept of a mama's boy is an unfortunate cultural stereotype that encourages many parents to deny their sons the warm nurturing they need (and that they continue to seek, often in inappropriate ways, throughout life). Daughters, on the other hand, are actually encouraged (also with sometimes unfortunate results) to be clinging and dependent and demonstrative.

"mammy" avoid. This term is sexist (there is no parallel term for a man), racist, and a stereotype that was probably always highly mythical.

Man/man ("generic") *person(s), people, human(s), human being(s), individual(s), one, creature(s), creation, mortal(s), body, somebody, someone, anyone, soul(s), living soul(s), society, human society/ nature/species, early peoples, we, us, ourselves, humankind, humanity, mortality, flesh, all generations, folk(s), the public, the general public, the world, community, the larger community, nation, state, realm, commonweal, commonwealth, republic, body politic, population, inhabitant(s), adult(s), citizen(s), taxpayer(s),* *worker(s), member(s), head(s), hand(s), party/parties, earthling, personage, participant(s).* **See also** man (adult male human being).

man (adult male human being) this narrow definition is the only acceptable nonsexist usage for the noun. Dictionaries list two major definitions for "man": (1) adult male, (2) human being. However, studies have shown that people "hear" only the first meaning of the word. See Appendix A for a complete discussion of "generic" man.

man (chess, checkers, games) *piece.*

man (verb) *operate, staff, run, supply a crew/personnel for, supply with/ furnish with personnel/crew, work, serve at/on, cover, employ staff, occupy, equip, arm.*

man about town *worldly person, sophisticate, socially active person, swinger, high-liver, high-flyer.* Any of the foregoing can be used for either women or men, whereas there is no phrase for women parallel to "man about town." A woman who has "been around" is not being complimented—au contraire. *See also* ladies' man; playboy; rake; womanize/womanizer/womanizing.

manacle nonsexist; comes from the Latin for "hand."

man, act like a *See* act like a man.

man after one's own heart, a *someone after one's own heart, someone for whom you have a soft spot, persona grata, favorite, general favorite, apple of one's eye.*

management/manager/managerial nonsexist terms; they come from the Latin for "hand."

manageress *manager.*

man alive! *good grief, gee, golly, gee whiz, wow,* etc.

man and wife never use this phrase; it is a nonparallel construction. Use instead *man and woman/woman and man, wife and husband/ husband and wife, spouses.*

man ape *See* ape-man.

man, arise as one *See* arise as one man.

man-at-arms *warrior, soldier, combatant.*

man bites dog story there is currently no good gender-free substitute for this colorful phrase; it conveys something very particular that would be lost in translation. That doesn't mean, of course, that someone won't come up with an equally pithy and evocative—but inclusive—phrase.

man-child use with "woman-child," not "girl-child," as is generally done. If "girl-child" is used, then "boy-child" is the equivalent, not "man-child."

manciple nonsexist; comes from the Latin for "purchaser."

mandarin when this term refers to a public official in the Chinese Empire, it is always male. Its other uses are nonsexist.

mandate/mandator nonsexist; these terms come from the Latin for "hand."

man-day *worker-day, workday, average worker day.*

man does not live by bread alone *we/you/people do not live by bread alone, one does not live by bread alone, not by bread alone do we/ does one live.*

mandrake leave as is.

man-eater *people-eater, human-eater, carnivore, cannibal.*

manege nonsexist; from the Italian for "horse training."

manes (deified spirits) nonsexist.

maneuver nonsexist; from the Latin for "hand."

man for all seasons *a person of many parts, woman for all seasons and man for all seasons, a Renaissance individual, all-around expert.*

man-for-man *player-for-player, one-on-one.*

man Friday *assistant, office assistant, clerk, right hand, secretary; man Friday and woman Friday* if used gender-fairly, although the convention generally remains limited to "woman Friday" and even then it seems to be difficult for people to use "woman Friday" instead of the familiar "girl Friday." (Note the nonparallel "man Friday/girl Friday.") *See also* office boy/office girl.

manful/manfully avoid these vague cultural stereotypes and instead look for precise words to convey your meaning: *strong/strongly, resolute/resolutely, brave/bravely, courageous/courageously, mighty/ mightily, vigorous/vigorously, stout/stoutly, robust/robustly, sturdy/ sturdily, hardy/hardily, powerful/powerfully, potent/potently, indomitable/indomitably, husky/huskily, energetic/energetically, bold/boldly, defiant/defiantly, earnest/earnestly, serious/seriously, unflinching/unflinchingly, inexorable/inexorably, dogged/doggedly,* etc. Note that all these adjectives/adverbs can be used equally for women and for men.

mangrove leave as is.

manhandle *mistreat, maltreat, mishandle, maul, batter, push/kick/ knock around, paw, subdue, force, handle roughly, rough up, beat up, pummel, thrash, strike, injure, abuse.*

man-hater *man-hater/woman-hater, misanthrope/misogynist.* These sex-specific terms are acceptable as long as they are used equally frequently and in gender-fair ways.

Manhattan nonsexist; it comes from an Indian word meaning "island."

manhole *sewer/utility/access hole, utility access hole.*

manhole cover *utility-hole/access/sewer-hole/access-hole cover.*

manhood this word has four general dictionary definitions: (1) It is said to mean "the condition of being human." Do not use "manhood" in this way; it is a false generic. (2) Also avoid using it as a false generic meaning "human beings." (3) When you mean manly qualities, and are referring to a man, its use is correct. But sometimes in this sense it is clearer to use more specific words: *pride, strength, self-confidence, courage, maturity,* etc. (4) Use "manhood" anytime to mean the condition of being an adult male human being. In that case, "womanhood" is the parallel term. *See also* Man/man ("generic"); man (adult male human being); mankind.

man-hours *worker/work/working/staff/labor/operator/typist hours, hours of work, labor, time.*

manhunt *dragnet, chase, person hunt, search for a fugitive, womanhunt or manhunt.* "Manhunt" is one of the more difficult sexist words in that there currently exists no equally brief and descriptive inclusive term. When possible, avoid it by circumlocution.

mania nonsexist; comes from the Greek "menos" meaning "spirit."

Manichaeism nonsexist; comes from the name of the Iranian founder, Mani.

manicure nonsexist; from the Latin for "hand," "manus."

manifest nonsexist; from the Latin for "hand," "manus."

manifold nonsexist; the "mani" here comes from an Old English word for "many."

manikin/mannikin *miniature person.* "Manikin" not only looks masculine, it means "little man." There is no parallel term for a little woman. *See also* mannequin.

man-induced *artificially/humanly induced, human-caused, manufactured, of human genesis/origin(s).*

man in office *person in authority/office, official.*

man in the moon *face in the moon.*

man in the street *average person/citizen/human/human being/voter, common person/citizen/human/human being/voter, ordinary person/citizen/human/human being/voter, citizen, voter, layperson, taxpayer, resident, homeowner, landowner, passerby, nonspecialist, commoner, one of the people, one of the masses, rank and file, average worker; average woman and average man* if used gender-fairly.

maniple/manipulate nonsexist; from the Latin for "hand," "manus."

man is known by the company he keeps, a *people/we/you are known by the company they/we/you keep, one is known by the company one keeps, birds of a feather flock together, we are judged by the company we keep, show me your company and I'll tell you who you are.*

man jack *See* every man jack.

man-killer *killer, murderer, slayer, assassin, cutthroat, sniper, silencer, dispatcher, liquidator, hired gun, bloodshedder. See also* gunman.

mankind *humanity, humankind, people, persons, humans, human beings, human creatures, human society, human species, human nature, individuals, creatures, creation, all creation, mortals, souls, living souls, all living souls, society, early peoples, we, us, ourselves, mortality, flesh, all generations, folks, the public, the general public, the world, community, the larger community, population, inhabitants, adults, citizens, taxpayers, workers, parties, earthlings, our ancestors, women and men; nation, state, realm, commonweal, commonwealth, republic, body politic.* "Mankind" is always a false generic; avoid it. *See also* Man/man ("generic"); man (adult male human being); manhood.

man, like a *See* like a man.

manlike/manly avoid these vague cultural stereotypes. By definition, whatever a man does is manly or manlike because a man is doing it. Choose instead the precise characteristics you want to describe: *courageous, strong, brave, upright, honorable, resolute, straightforward, vigorous, adventurous, spirited, direct, competitive, physical, mechanical, logical, rude, active, self-confident,* etc. Note that these words apply equally well to either sex.

manmade *artificial, handmade, hand-built, synthetic, made, manufactured, fabricated, machine-made, produced, machine-produced, constructed, custom-made, simulated, plastic, imitation, bogus, mock, spurious, counterfeit, fictitious, contrived, human-constructed, human-made, result of human activity.* This word can often be eliminated entirely without affecting the meaning of the sentence. "Manmade" is one of those words that many people believe is irreplaceable, yet much of our resistance to replacing it is habit; if, for example, you say "human-made" about fifty times, it begins to sound quite as "natural" and "right" as "manmade." Note the very special use Dale Spender has for "manmade" in her book *Man Made Language* (Spender, 1980).

manned *staffed, crewed, operated, run. See also* man (verb).

manned space flight this is one of the most difficult sexist phrases as there is currently no equally convenient and pithy description of space flight crewed by both women and men. Some circumlocution is possible; for example, "The Columbia space flight with six astronauts aboard . . . ." In print, "crewed space flight" is possible, but in broadcast journalism, "crewed" will be heard "crude." Other possibilities include: *piloted space flight, staffed space flight, live space flight, astronaut-controlled space flight.* And, finally, it is possible to speak simply of *space flight.* Sanford Berman, Head Cataloguer of the Hennepin County (Minneapolis) Library says, "Even though we lose some specificity, HCL makes 'manned space flight' simply a 'see reference' to SPACE FLIGHT. In other words, we don't use the palpably sexist term."

mannequin *model, dressmaker's/tailor's dummy, display figure, window display figure.* "Mannequin" and "manikin" come from the same Dutch word, which means "little man."

mannish avoid. Choose instead words that convey the characteristics you want to describe: *brusque, blunt, abrupt, direct, square-jawed, aggressive,* etc.

man of action *human dynamo, active/energetic/determined/ambitious/ action-oriented person/individual, ball of fire, someone on their toes, someone who works up a storm/to beat the band; woman of action and man of action* if used gender-fairly.

man of affairs avoid this term; the ersatz parallel for a woman doesn't sit well in polite society. Use instead *entrepreneur, mover, wheeler-dealer, someone with fingers in many pies/many irons in the fire. See also* businessman.

man of all work *caretaker, odd-jobber.* **See also** handyman.

man of business, one's *agent, factotum, caretaker, bailiff, factor, tax preparer, steward, clerk, attorney, broker, representative.*

man of distinction *important personage, person of distinction/note/mark/consequence/importance, prominent/high-ranking individual; man of distinction and woman of distinction* if used gender-fairly.

man of few words *strong, silent type; person of few words; close-mouthed individual.*

man of God *See* churchman; clergyman.

man of his word/man of honor *honorable person, trustworthy individual, someone as good as their word, someone on the up and up/as honest as the day is long/tried and true, truth-speaker, truth-dealer, truth-lover, square-shooter, straight-dealer; woman of her word and man of his word* if used gender-fairly.

man of letters *writer, author, scholar, literary giant, one of the literati; woman of letters and man of letters* if used gender-fairly.

man of means *wealthy individual, rich person, plutocrat, capitalist, moneyed person, moneybags, nabob, millionaire, billionaire; woman of means and man of means* if used gender-fairly.

man of my kidney, a *my kind/sort/type of person, an individual of my kidney, a person after my own heart.*

man of straw *See* straw man.

man of the church/man of the cloth *See* churchman; clergyman.

man of the hour *honored guest, star of the show, center of attention; woman of the hour and man of the hour* if used gender-fairly.

man of the house *homeowner, head of the household; man of the house and woman of the house,* although these terms have been so abused that even if they are used gender-fairly they still have a subtle sting. *See also* family man; homebody.

man of the world *sophisticate, person with wide experience, practical/sophisticated/worldly/worldly wise/well-rounded/experienced person, someone who gets around/who knows the ropes.*

man of the year *citizen/member of the year; man of the year and woman of the year* if used gender-fairly. In the fifty-plus years that *Time* magazine has been covering people of the year, three women have occupied the cover alone: Wallis Simpson in 1936, Queen Elizabeth II in 1952, and Cory Aquino in 1986.

man-of-war leave as is in historical context. Otherwise use *warship, battleship, ship of war/the line, war vessel.* Or, be specific: *cruiser, destroyer, gunboat.*

man on the street *See* man in the street.

manor nonsexist; comes from the Latin for "dwell, remain."

man or beast, not a fit night for *See* not a fit night for man or beast.

man overboard *overboard!, person/someone overboard!; woman overboard/man overboard!*

manpack *backpack, one-person pack.*

manpower *workforce, personnel, human resources, staff, available workers, workers, employees, labor, people, labor supply/force, staffing, human power/energy, staff time.*

manpowered *muscle-/human-/peoplepowered.*

man proposes, but God disposes *creation proposes, but the Creator disposes, we/people/you/the world/the individual propose(s), but God disposes, the Missourians propose but the Kansans dispose.*

manrope *handrail.*

man's best friend there is no good substitute for this phrase because it is associated like no other phrase with the dog, whereas we all know that a woman's best friend is diamonds (!), and the friend of the people could be anything from Smokey the Bear to General Electric to Karl Marx. Try instead: *the devoted dog, our canine friend, our faithful canine friends, a human's best friend.*

manservant *servant, attendant, assistant.*

-manship avoid words with this suffix. *See* airmanship; brinkmanship; craftsmanship; gamesmanship; grantsmanship; horsemanship; marksmanship; salesmanship; sportsmanship; statesmanship; workmanship; yachtsmanship, etc.

man's home is his castle, a *my home is my castle, a person's home is a castle, a woman's home is her castle and a man's home is his castle, our home is our castle.* This is a difficult phrase; look for fresher ways of saying it, for example, "Home is the place where, when you have to go there,/They have to take you in" (Robert Frost). "My heart is turning home again,/and there I long to be" (Henry Van Dyke). Also: *home is where the heart is, there's no place like home.*

man's inhumanity to man *inhumanity, the inhumanity of the human species when it turns on itself; a house divided against itself. See also* evil men do, the.

mansion nonsexist; comes from a word meaning "dwell, remain."

man-sized *hefty, husky, big, ample, large, comfortably large, sizable, massive, weighty, impressive, considerable, capacious, towering, voracious, enormous, immense.*

man's job, a *an adult's job, adult-sized job, a big job.*

manslaughter this term has a specific legal meaning—use it in that sense until a nonsexist legal term is developed; in its larger sense, use *murder, butchery, wholesale killing/slaughter, assassination, bloodletting, slaughter, carnage, massacre, slaying, killing.*

manslayer *See* man-killer.

man's man, a this has a special meaning—a man who does not threaten other men's egos, who is accepted by them, but who perhaps is not very comfortable in the presence of women—so although there is no functional parallel for women it has a place in the language.

man's work *work.* The only "work" strictly and biologically limited to men is the work they do in helping propagate the species and so far it is rarely referred to as work. All other so-called men's work is based on cultural stereotypes.

man the barricades! *mount the barricades!*

mantle nonsexist; from the Latin for "cloak."

man-to-man defense *player-to-player/one-to-one/person-to-person/ one-on-one defense.*

man-to-man talk *frank/honest/serious/straightforward/face-to-face/ one-to-one/heart-to-heart/private/on-the-level talk/discussion.*

mantrap (referring to a woman) avoid. This perpetuates the tempter-Eve/helpless-Adam stereotype.

mantrap *booby/death trap, snare.*

manual/manufacture/manumission/manumit/manuscript nonsexist; all these terms come from the Latin for "hand," "manus."

manward *peopleward, toward/in relation to people/human beings, with respect to humans.* Many words that end in "-ward" with the meaning of "toward" are awkward and should probably be replaced anyway.

manwise *humanwise, peoplewise* (if you must). Using the "-wise" suffix is Madison Avenue-ese (another example) that is better replaced or circumvented.

man who is his own doctor/lawyer has a fool for a patient/client, a *those who are their own doctors/lawyers have fools for patients/clients, if you insist on being your own doctor/lawyer, you have a fool for a patient/client.*

man without a country, a *a person without a country/with no roots. See also* expatriate.

marchioness/marquise use these sex-specific titles when necessary.

mare's nest *hoax, delusion, much ado about nothing, chaos.*

margrave/margravine use these sex-specific titles when necessary.

marine woman or man.

marksman *sharpshooter, crack/good/dead shot; markswoman and marksman* if used gender-fairly. *See also* gunman.

marksmanship *riflery skills, shooting ability/expertise, sharpshooting.*

marquess/marquis use these sex-specific titles when necessary.

marshall woman or man.

martinet man or woman.

Mary Jane *marijuana.*

masculine avoid this vague stereotype that conveys different meanings to different people according to their perceptions of what a man ought or ought not do, say, think, wear, feel, look like. These subjective cultural judgments have nothing to do with sex and everything to do with gender. Find instead words that express the characteristics you want to describe: *strong, upright, charming, robust, hearty, direct, straightforward, deep-voiced, protective, nurturing, attentive,* etc. See Appendix A for a discussion of the difference between gender and sex.

masculine mystique this term refers to society's narrow definition of a man as one who is solely concerned with protection and occupation. Lucile Duberman says men are pressured to be strivers—in their jobs, in physical exploits, or in areas of leadership (Duberman 1975, p. 228).

masher by definition a masher is a man who makes passes at women, so there is no synonymous inclusive term. Today's masher is often found in sex harassment cases. If you want to use a less sex-specific term or if you want to describe a woman, use *flirt, someone who comes on strong.*

Mason (member of fraternal organization) *See* Freemason.

mason (worker) woman or man.

masseur/masseuse *massage therapist.*

master (noun) *owner, manager, chief, head, leader, governor, superior, director, supervisor, boss; sovereign, ruler, monarch, autocrat, dictator, potentate; expert, artist, adept, teacher, trainer, instructor, tutor, specialist, proficient, connoisseur, professional; proprietor, landholder.* "Master" has many inclusive meanings—"owner," "employer," "teacher," "scholar," "artisan," "victor," etc.—but because it is perceived as (and generally is) a masculine word and because other meanings of the word are incontrovertibly masculine (for example, "male head of household"), it is an ambiguous term. More important, there is no parallel term for a woman. (Note what happened to the once-parallel male/female word pair "master/mistress": the prolific male word has become broader and more important while the female word has narrowed so much that it now speaks of the woman only in a sexual sense.) Another problem is that "master" is used as noun, verb, and adjective as well as a compound in many other words. Its overwhelmingly masculine flavor thus seasons a good bit of our language. "Master" should probably be avoided in all its uses except for its applications in trades where master has a very specific meaning and no currently acceptable substitutes. Fortunately, for all other forms of the word there are many appropriate and easy-to-use alternatives.

master (adj.) *expert, accomplished, proficient, skilled, excellent, competent, gifted, dextrous, adroit, deft, resourceful. See also* master (noun).

master (verb) *be successful at, learn, acquire proficiency at, learn inside and out/backwards and forwards, be on top of; conquer, subdue, defeat, subject, subordinate, suppress, get the upper hand, overcome, overpower, overwhelm, overthrow, surmount, triumph; rule, dominate, govern, control, command, dictate to, boss/order around. See also* master (noun).

Master (referring to Christ) *Teacher. See also* master (noun).

master bedroom this is the term used exclusively today. To get around it use *main bedroom, owner's bedroom, owner's suite, principal bedroom, largest bedroom.* Or, refer to bedrooms by their location, as do some designers and architects: *the northeast bedroom, the southwest bedroom,* etc.

master builder   *expert/award-winning builder.* This may refer to a woman or a man.

master class   this term, which describes an advanced art, music, or dance seminar led by a recognized expert in the field, is difficult to replace with a term that is equally concise, descriptive, and meaningful to those involved. Although "master" is a masculine word, master classes are led by both women and men. One alternative sometimes used is *artist class* (and it is not limited to the visual arts).

masterful   *skilled, articulate, powerful, authoritative, competent, commanding, domineering, sweeping, imperative, imperious, arbitrary, overbearing, arrogant, haughty.*

master gunnery sergeant   woman or man.

master hand   *expert, genius, major talent, professional, authority, adept, proficient, whiz, dab hand.*

master key   *universal/all-purpose/skeleton key, passe partout.*

master list   *overview, key, main/complete/primary/reference list.*

masterly   *accomplished, skilled, knowledgeable, consummate, matchless, excellent, distinguished, experienced, crack, ingenious, able, felicitous, shrewd.*

mastermind (noun)   *genius, brilliant thinker, intellectual prodigy/giant, mental giant, brains; plotter, organizer, creative organizer, instigator, originator, creator, the one who pulls the strings.*

mastermind (verb)   *oversee, direct, guide, lead, coordinate, invent, contrive, engineer, launch, originate, devise, have the bright idea.*

master of ceremonies/mistress of ceremonies   *host, emcee, leader/ coordinator of ceremonies, speaker, main/guest speaker, moderator.* Note that although "emcee" comes from these sex-specific terms, it is used for either sex and is perceived as neutral, probably because "emcee (M.C.)" could stand for either "master of ceremonies" or "mistress of ceremonies."

master of the situation   *in charge, in control, on top of things, reins firmly in hand, finger on the pulse.*

masterpiece   *great work, work of art/genius, stroke of genius, best work, consummate art, chef d'oeuvre, magnum opus, cream of the crop, crème de la crème, pièce de résistance, flower of the flock, prime, nonpareil, acme of perfection, ne plus ultra, tour de force, coup de maître.*

master plan   *overall/comprehensive plan, overview.*

"master race"   use this term only in its historical context and enclose it in quotation marks to indicate its questionable validity.

master's degree   *M.A., graduate degree, first advanced degree, first graduate degree.* Dennis Baron says that using "M.A." suggests masculinity only to the hypercritical (Baron 1986, p. 174). Eve Merriam proposes calling the master's degree "a Higher or University degree" (Merriam 1974, p. 22). However, in many

instances the spelled-out "master's degree" must be used because
there is as yet no substitute for it in its narrowest and most
official sense.

master sergeant man or woman.

masterstroke *trump card, clever idea, good move, bold/lucky stroke,
checkmate, stroke of genius, coup, complete success, stunt, exploit,
victory.*

master switch *control/lead/main switch, circuit breaker.*

master tape *pattern/final tape, template.*

master teacher leave as is where custom and usage require it. A
substitute sometimes seen is *artist teacher* (not restricted to the
visual arts). A master teacher can be either a man or a woman.

masterwork *See* masterpiece.

mastery *proficiency, understanding, knowledge, accomplishment,
acquaintance with, competency, excellence, facility, advantage,
adeptness, skill, dexterity, deftness, expertise; rule, victory,
ascendency, supremacy, authority, subjugation, conquest, control,
domination, upper hand, reins in one's hands, command, order,
sway.*

mater/materfamilias these words are gender-fair as there are parallel
terms for men, but usage today tends to replace the Latin with the
more common "mother" and "matriarch."

materialman *material supplier, supplier.*

maternal/maternity these terms have look-alike counterparts for men,
but "paternal" and "paternity" convey very different meanings,
and all four words tend to be used in gender-unfair ways and to
be found in sexist contexts. Give them a second look, and avoid
when possible.

maternal instinct *instinct.*

maternity leave *parental/child care leave.*

matriarch/matriarchy these words are nonsexist in themselves and have
counterparts for men, but they are sometimes used judgmentally.
Because patriarchy is seen as the norm, a matriarchy tends to be
viewed with suspicion, alarm, and disapproval; it doesn't seem
"natural." Until society reaches a point where neither sex needs to
dominate the other, use these terms cautiously.

matrilineal use this word when referring to descent through the
mother's line; use "patrilineal" when referring to descent through
the father's line. These are useful and necessary sex-specific words.

matrimony *marriage.* "Matrimony" comes from the Latin for "mother"
and is thus sex-specific. And although "marriage" also has
sex-linked roots (it comes from the Latin for "a woman's dowry"),
to our modern ears it is less obviously sex-linked than
"matrimony," which has the further disadvantage of being part of
a nonparallel female/male word pair, "matrimony/patrimony."

matron *warden, attendant, police officer, deputy sheriff, bailiff, guard,
jail/custodial guard, superintendent, supervisor, overseer.* In its
narrow legal sense, "matron" must be used until a nonsexist legal

term is developed. In the sense of a middle-aged woman, replace
"matron" with words that more precisely describe the woman.
Note the widely different meanings of the supposedly parallel
word pair "matron/patron."

matronly replace this vague word with precise, inclusive terms:
*dignified, gracious, ponderous, heavy-set, established,
comfortable-looking, serene, slow-moving, well-dressed,* etc. Note
that we have no such word as "patronly."

matron of honor *best woman, attendant of honor, honor/bridal/bride's
attendant, attendant.* Whichever term you choose, be sure that the
groom's attendant is referred to with a parallel term, for example,
"best woman and best man" or "bride's attendant and groom's
attendant."

maven woman or man

maverick man or woman. Although this term comes from a man's
name—a nineteenth-century Texas rancher named Samuel
Maverick with a certain reputation for straying from the herd (he
refused to brand his cattle)—its origins have been largely forgotten
and it is perceived as sex-neutral.

mayoress *mayor.*

may the best man win *may the best person win.*

meatman *butcher, meat vendor.*

"meat market" avoid this unattractive phrase, which refers to bars
where people go to meet people.

mediatress/mediatrix *mediator.*

mechanic woman or man.

medicine man *shaman, healer, magician, faith healer; medicine woman
and medicine man* if used gender-fairly.

meistersinger "mastersingers," members of German middle-class
guilds, flourished during the fourteenth to sixteenth centuries and
were all men.

memsahib always a woman; the man is a "sahib."

men ("generic") *See* Man/man; man (adult male human being);
mankind.

menagerie nonsexist; from the French for "household."

mendacious/mendacity nonsexist; from the Latin for "lie."

mendicant nonsexist; from the Latin meaning "to beg."

men of goodwill *people/those of goodwill.*

menopause nonsexist; the "men" in it comes from the Latin for
"month." "Menopause" is a neutral term describing a physical
reality that is very different for different women; avoid
stereotyping it.

menopausal avoid describing a woman as menopausal unless it is
germane to the discussion and unless you are sure she is.

menses/menstrual nonsexist; "menses" is Latin for "months."

mensh/mench/mensch this Yiddish/German word is neutral (in
Yiddish it means "human being," in German it means "person")
although it is often used only for men. Use it for women, too, to

mean a purposeful, upright, honorable person who stands up for the rights of others as well as for her own.

mentor woman or man. The original Mentor was a male friend of Odysseus charged with the education of Odysseus' son, but the term is functionally inclusive today.

men working *work zone, workers, working.*

mercenary this is still largely a male province, although you will occasionally find a female mercenary.

merchantman *merchant, merchant ship/marine.*

mermaid/merman folklore and fantastic tradition have given us these creatures, along with nonparallel designations ("maid/man"). When possible, use instead *merwoman/merman, sea creature, sea nymph, Nereid, sea god/sea goddess.*

meter maid (parking) *meter attendant/monitor.*

meter man (water/gas/electricity meter) *meter reader.*

mezzosoprano leave as is.

mice and men, the best-laid schemes of *See* best-laid schemes of mice and men, the.

Mickey Finn *knockout drops.* See Appendix A for the rationale on avoiding sex-linked metaphors, expressions, and figures.

Mickey Mouse (adj.) *cheap, inferior, small, insignificant, worthless, petty, trivial, simple, easy, childish, flimsy, piddling, paltry, trite, trifling.* See Appendix A for the rationale on avoiding sex-linked metaphors, expressions, and figures.

Midas touch *magic/golden touch, everything she/he touches turns to gold.* See Appendix A for the rationale on avoiding sex-linked metaphors, expressions, and figures.

middleman *go-between, agent, third party, negotiator, broker, mediator, arbiter, arbitrator, representative, messenger, factor, intermediary, intercessor, intervener, umpire, referee, peacemaker, contact, advocate; jobber, wholesaler, distributor, dealer.*

mid-life crisis not limited to either sex.

midshipman man or woman. This term is officially used to designate both.

midwife (noun) *birth attendant.* "Midwife" does not refer to the sex of the midwife but to that of the person being assisted: "mid" means "with" and "wife" means "woman," therefore, a midwife is someone who is with a woman. Because of the term's feminine appearance, some people prefer the more neutral-looking "birth attendant." But "midwife" enjoys strong feminist endorsement and since it is not sexist, it can and should be retained in many contexts.

midwife (verb) *give birth to/beget, assist, support, conceive of (ideas)/beget (ideas), bring forth.*

milady avoid except in historical contexts.

militant man or woman.

military man *soldier, member of the armed forces/the military, military officer. **See also** soldier.*

military police women or men.

military wife *military/soldier's/service member's spouse.*

militiaman *militia member, the militia, soldier; militiawoman and militiaman* if applicable.

milkmaid *dairy worker,* except for fairy tales or in historical contexts.

milkman *milk route driver, milk deliverer.*

millionaire man or woman.

milquetoast/milksop (referring to a man) *timid/meek/poor-spirited/ fearful/unassertive person, someone who is scared of her/his own shadow/with cold feet.*

minister depending on the denomination, this might be a woman or a man. With the introduction of women into the clergy, many members of a congregation are unsure how to address a female minister. The simplest course is to ask her, as it will vary from denomination to denomination and from person to person within a denomination. *See also* priest.

minstrel most minstrels were men. However, women belonged to some of the medieval troupes, juggling or acting out small parts. Troubadours, which flourished during the two centuries preceding the rise of the minstrels, also numbered some women among them; see Meg Bodin, *The Women Troubadours* (New York: Norton, 1976). At the height of the popularity of nineteenth-century Negro minstrelsy, women were impersonated by men (for example, in the "wench performances"), so although there appeared to be women on stage, there rarely were.

minuteman leave as is when referring to the militia of the Revolutionary War or to minuteman rockets. *See also* militiaman.

misanthrope *misanthrope/misogynist, man-hater/woman-hater.* These sex-specific words are acceptable as long as they are used equally frequently and in gender-fair ways.

miser woman or man.

miss (noun) avoid.

Miss (title) use "Ms.," except for people who indicate a preference for "Miss." Dale Spender says, "Contrary to the belief of many people, the current usage of *Miss* and *Mrs.* is relatively recent, for until the beginning of the nineteenth century the title *Miss* was usually reserved for young females while *Mrs.* designated mature women. Marital status played no role in the use of these terms" (Spender 1980, p. 27). Calling women "Miss" or "Mrs." is part of our tradition of labeling them in relation to men, although men have never been labeled in relation to women. *See also* Mrs.; Ms.

missus avoid.

missionary man or woman.

missy avoid.

mistress *lover. See also* girlfriend; kept woman.

mistress of ceremonies *See* master of ceremonies/mistress of ceremonies.

mixerman *mixer tender.*

mobster woman or man.

model man or woman.

modern man *modern people/peoples, today's people, modern civilization, the modern age. See also* Man/man ("generic"); mankind.

modiste this refers only to women and is not much used anymore. *See* couturier/couturière; dressmaker.

mogul woman or man.

moldman *machine molder, mold mover/maker/worker, fiberglass laminator.*

moll *See* gun moll.

mollycoddle (noun/verb) because of the "molly" in the word (from the woman's name) but even more because the noun is defined as "a pampered, spoiled, effeminate boy or man," this word is thoroughly sexist. *See* mama's boy; sissy, for alternatives to the noun. For the verb, use *indulge, spoil, pamper, dote on, overprotect.*

monarch nonsexist; can be either a woman or a man.

monastery most monasteries house or housed monks, but some abbeys and convents that housed nuns are also considered monasteries. Therefore, do not assume that all the residents of a monastery are male.

moneybags woman or man.

monk this is a gender-specific term because all monks are men; the approximate equivalent for women is "nun," q.v.

monkey's uncle found in such expressions as "Well, I'll be a monkey's uncle!" this term could be simply reduced to "Well, I'll be!" although it probably doesn't need to be taken too seriously. Anyone who wants to be a monkey's uncle is probably not a threat to the language.

monogamy nonsexist; either a woman or a man can enjoy monogamy.

monsignor always a man.

monster if not human, a monster can be sexless (use the pronoun "it" to refer to it). When using it figuratively to refer to humans, either a woman or a man can be one.

Montezuma's revenge *dysentery, intestinal flu, gippy tummy, travelers' scourge.* See Appendix A for the rationale on avoiding sex-linked metaphors, expressions, and figures.

Morpheus, in the arms of *See* in the arms of Morpheus.

mother (noun) with respect to parenting, too often the mother alone is mentioned, whereas mentioning the father as well might be appropriate and accurate. The best choice is *parent.*

mother (verb) *parent, nurture, support, protect, take care of, look after, be responsible for, rear children, caretake, supervise.* Note that these synonyms are the same ones used for "father ('generic' verb)."

mother cell leave as is; this is a biology term with a specific meaning. When mother cells split, they form daughter cells.

mother country *See* motherland.

mother hen *overprotective/indulgent/hovering person/parent.*

motherhood use this term gender-fairly, that is, refer to "fatherhood" as often as to "motherhood."

motherhouse useful sex-specific term, although there is no parallel "fatherhouse."

mother-in-law avoid mother-in-law jokes, and be sure that treatment afforded mothers-in-law is similar to that given fathers-in-law. It helps to ask if "mother" could be substituted for "mother-in-law" without outraging anyone's sensibilities.

motherland *homeland, native land/country/soil, home, home country, land of one's ancestors, natal place, the old country.*

mother lode *main/principal lode.*

motherly replace this vague adjective with ones that convey more precisely the characteristics you want to describe: *warm, nurturing, loving, kind, kindly, protective, supportive, caring, solicitous, considerate, interested, benevolent, good-natured, fond, affectionate, devoted, tender, gentle, demonstrative, sympathetic, understanding, indulgent, obliging, forbearing, tolerant, well-meaning, sheltering, generous,* etc.

mother-naked *stark naked, naked, without a stitch on, in the altogether/ raw/buff, in one's birthday suit, au naturel.*

Mother Nature *Nature.*

mother of pearl (mollusks) leave as is.

mother of pearl (British) rhyming slang for "girl," although it usually means wives or women friends; leave as is.

mother of vinegar leave as is.

mother superior leave as is when it is someone's title.

mother tongue *native language/tongue, birth/first/original language.*

mother wit *native wit, natural wit/intelligence.*

motorman *driver, streetcar driver, dinkey/streetcar/motor operator, motor-power connector, motoreer* (a clever older word that was put together from motor + engineer).

mountain man use as is, but do not use as a generic. If you mean more than an adult male, use *mountain people, mountain folk, mountain woman/mountain man.*

mountebank man or woman.

Mountie there are both men and women in the Royal Canadian Mounted Police Force.

Mrs. some women prefer to retain this title; respect their wishes. When their wishes or marital status are unknown, use "Ms." Dale Spender says, "Contrary to the belief of many people, the current usage of *Miss* and *Mrs.* is relatively recent, for until the beginning of the nineteenth century the title *Miss* was usually reserved for young females while *Mrs.* designated mature women. Marital status played no role in the use of these terms" (Spender 1980, p. 27). "Mrs." and "Miss" reflect a tradition of labeling women in relation to men although the converse has never been true. *See also* mademoiselle; Miss; Ms.

Mrs. Malaprop *See* malapropism.

Ms. pronounced MIZ, this title is the opposite of "Mr." Use these titles gender-fairly, that is, if you talk about Ms. Ayallah, use also Mr. Seifert, but if you call Seifert by his last name only, do likewise with Ayallah. "Ms." has gained wide enough acceptance (the *New York Times* finally approved its use in 1986) that you can use it freely. A correspondent who has not indicated whether she is "Miss" or "Mrs." will probably not be offended by "Ms.," but you can also simply write "Dear Frieda Smythe," omitting the title. See Appendix A for additional tips on letter salutations. *See also* mademoiselle; Miss; Mrs.

muezzin always a man.

mugger woman or man. Although the majority of muggers are men, it is not safe to write generically "a mugger/he."

mum's the word nonsexist; has nothing to do with "mum" ("mother").

murderess *murderer.*

my brother's keeper *See* I am not my brother's keeper.

my proud beauty/me proud beauty use only in melodramas where the villain has a particularly long and twirly mustache.

n

In reality, all communication that debilitates females also debilitates males, for if any system diminishes a part of the species, it diminishes all of it.

Bobbye D. Sorrels

nabob in the narrow historical definition (a deputy, governor, or district ruler in India) this word refers to a man, and there is no parallel term for a woman; in the broad sense of a very wealthy and/or prominent person, it can be used of both women and men.

nag (noun) this word should be avoided; it is used almost exclusively to refer to women (with no parallel word for men). To describe someone—either a man or a woman—who complains or incessantly finds fault, use *grouch, grump, grumbler, fussbudget, crosspatch, faultfinder, complainer, nitpicker, sorehead, grouser, squawker, crank, griper.*

nag (verb) although not sexist per se, this word has become sexist since it is used primarily of women, while in the same situation men are said to bully, chew out, complain, or just plain talk. Use instead *complain, gripe, criticize, scold, badger, pick on, find fault, pester, harass, grumble, grouse, irritate, harp at, harp on, bicker, drive up the wall, fuss, raise a fuss, have a bone to pick with.* Do not use "bitch," "henpeck," or "whine," all of which see.

namby-pamby (noun/adj.) this sexist term is almost exclusively reserved for men. It comes from a nickname given to the poet Ambrose (thus the rhyme with "Amby") Philips (1674–1749), whose poems were much parodied. For the noun use instead *softie, pushover, weakling, doormat, lightweight, featherweight.* For the adjective use *insipid, inane, shallow, flimsy, watery, weak, indecisive, anemic, wishy-washy, colorless, milk and water, farcical, frivolous, simpering.* Avoid such traditional alternatives as "baby," "mama's boy," "sissy," or "weak sister," all of which see.

nanny historically this sexist term (because there are no biological, only cultural, reasons for its being limited to women) described a woman servant who had charge of young children. Today it refers to a woman professionally trained in the United States or in Great Britain in child-care skills; the title carries a certain prestige, and the pay and benefits are better than many comparable positions held entirely or mostly by women.

natural/nature look twice when using these words in reference to sex roles. It is extremely difficult to know (scientifically, psychologically, philosophically, etc.) whether something is indeed "natural" and, secondarily, whether being natural makes it a good in and of itself. "We could achieve a refreshing advance in clarity by trading in our uses of 'natural' so that our value choices and explanatory claims would at least be made explicit" (Pierce 1971, p. 242). Instead of "natural," consider *automatic, instinctive, essential, idiosyncratic, usual, often-seen, common, habitual, accustomed, customary, established, time-honored, regulation, traditional, general, prevailing, frequent, popular, predictable, expected.* Instead of "nature," consider *character, personality, individuality, essence, identity, quality, kind, type.*

"natural" father/"natural" mother *biological mother/father, birth father/mother.*

NCO *See* noncommissioned officer.

Neanderthal man *archaic human, the Neanderthal, Neanderthals, Homo erectus, early human.*

née this French construction, indicating the name a woman was born with and weighted with sexist implications, has outlived its usefulness in most cases. Simply give both names: Joanna Morganthau Celletti or Joanna Morganthau-Celletti.

needlewoman *needleworker, tailor, mender, alterer, stitcher, alterations expert, custom tailor, garment worker/designer.*

ne'er-do-well although this term could apply to either a man or a woman, society tends to reserve it for men. Most of the alternatives—nonsexist in themselves—suggest in our culture that we are speaking of men. For example, one virtually never hears or reads of a woman described as a good-for-nothing, black sheep, bum, reprobate, layabout, rascal, scapegrace, blackguard, scalawag, or rapscallion. Choose alternatives for "ne'er-do-well" that most people view as more sex-neutral: *lazybones, washout, loser, born loser, do-nothing, shirker, failure, hard-luck case, prodigal, spendthrift.*

Negress *black.* If gender is necessary: *black woman.* Note that although current style lowercases "black," some people may prefer it capitalized.

nerd this relatively new word (1965) can refer to anyone, but it tends to be used almost invariably for men and boys. Two possible alternatives that are used for both sexes and are also fairly new are *wimp, twinkie.*

nervous Nellie *worrywart, handwringer, worrier, fussbudget, nervous person.*

newsboy *newspaper carrier/vendor, news/street/street news vendor.*

newsman/newspaperman *reporter, newspaper reporter, journalist, news representative/writer, correspondent, representative/member of the press, newsmonger.* Or, be specific: *war/special/foreign correspondent, columnist, commentator, wire/roving/investigative reporter, feature writer, stringer, editor, sportswriter, reviewer, gossip columnist, photojournalist.* **See also** anchorman.

night watchman *night guard/watch, guard, watch, guardian, security guard, caretaker, custodian, sentinel, sentry, lookout, patrol, patroller.*

nobleman *noble, member of the nobility; noblewoman and nobleman* if the context allows for gender-fair usage. Or, be specific: *countess, duke, princess, earl, marquis, baroness,* etc.

no man is an island unless quoting Donne, use *no one is an island.*

no man is a prophet in his own country unless quoting the Bible, use *we are slow to see the prophet in our midst; prophets are not without honor, save in their own country and among their own kin and in their own house; prophets are seldom recognized in their own land; the prophet goes unhonored at home; people rarely recognize the prophet in their midst; prophets are seldom recognized by their friends and neighbors; no one is a prophet in their own country* (see Appendix A for a discussion of the singular "they").

no-man's-land *limbo, dead zone, Death Valley, dead space, uninhabitable/lawless/noncombatant/unclaimed land, hostile country, nowheresville, buffer zone, vacuum, in the crossfire, arid/ noncombatant zone, the desert.* This is a difficult phrase to replace at times, not so much because there are no alternatives, but because we are blinded by its familiarity and seduced by the ease with which it springs to mind.

nomenclature nonsexist; the "men" comes from "nomen," the Latin word for "name."

noncommissioned officer woman or man.

normal man this catch-all convention is used, particularly in medical and some scientific writings, to designate a generic person. Use instead *normal individual/person.*

Norseman *ancient/early Scandinavian, Scandinavian, peoples of old Scandinavia, Norseman/Norsewoman, Northwoman/Northman.* It's generally not possible to replace words like "Norseman," "Irishman," and "Dutchman" with one pithy inclusive term; either circumlocute or use the longer phrases: "Norsewoman and Norseman/Norsemen and Norsewomen."

nosey Parker whether Parker was male or female has not survived in the literature; use the term for a man or a woman, but if the faint clinging odor of the masculine bothers you, use instead *busybody, snoop, tattletale.* **See also** nosy.

nosy this word is too often used to describe women when men in the same situation are simply said to be curious. Use of both sexes: *interested, curious, overcurious, supercurious, interfering, intrusive,* *officious, snoopy, prying, spying, eavesdropping, tending/minding other people's business.*

not a fit night for man or beast *not a fit night to be out in/for two-legged creatures nor four-legged ones either/for humans or beasties, not a night to leave your fire by.*

not by bread alone does man live *not by bread alone do we/do you/does one live.*

nubile avoid; there is no parallel for a man. Another problem with this word is that it defines a woman primarily in terms of her readiness for a relationship with a man.

nun/nunnery the use of "nun" (or "sister") is correct although they are sex-specific terms. This "sexist" system (i.e., restricted to one sex for other than biological reasons) has in fact been a positive one for women, unlike other less formal systems, because (1) women themselves often chose to live this way; (2) inasmuch as the hierarchical church allowed any group autonomy, these women governed themselves; (3) religious orders offered women the first alternative to "belonging" to earthly father or husband; (4) nuns were some of the first women to work professionally outside the home (as teachers and nurses). Many nuns today consider themselves Christian feminists and were among the pioneers in the women's movement. The word "nunnery" is outdated; today nuns live in convents (or sometimes at the motherhouse), although increasing numbers live in apartments, shared houses, and other nonconvent homes. In writing and speaking about nuns, be careful of stereotypes and try to reflect their contemporary work and status.

nuncio for now and probably some time in the future, all nuncios are men.

nurse man or woman.

nursemaid *child care worker, child monitor/minder.*

nursery governess *teacher, private teacher, child monitor/minder.*

nurserymaid *See* nursemaid.

nurseryman *nursery owner/manager/operator, tree grower, landscaper.*

nurture (verb) both men and woman can nurture.

nymphomaniac this sex-specific term is defined as a woman who has excessive sexual desire. The parallel term is "satyr": a man with abnormal or excessive sexual craving. This female/male word pair is perfectly well balanced in theory; in practice, we hear the word "nymphomaniac"—or "nympho"—much more often (and used much less precisely) than we do "satyr." Unless you are using both terms gender-fairly, choose words that apply equally to both sexes: *sexually active/promiscuous/insatiable person, "sex maniac/fiend," someone who sleeps around, bedhopper, indiscriminate lover.*

O

A very great part of the mischiefs that vex this world arises from words.

Edmund Burke

oarsman *rower, boater, paddler, canoer, canoeist.*
oblate woman or man.
odd-job(s)-man *odd-jobber, do-all, factotum, fixer-upper, repairer.*
odd man out *odd one out, loner, left out, third wheel, extra.*
Oedipus complex OK; parallel for father-daughter complex is "Electra complex."
office boy/office girl *office worker/assistant/helper, assistant, secretary, right hand, aide, bureau assistant, co-worker.* Or, be specific: *clerk, bookkeeper, typist, receptionist, switchboard operator.* It is also just barely possible to use—although it's not recommended very highly—*woman Friday/man Friday* if they are used gender-fairly (too often the only use of that convention turns out to be for women, and even then users have a hard time saying "woman Friday" instead of "girl Friday").
officer man or woman.
ogress *ogre.*
oilman use specific titles: *oil company executive/sales representative, oil field worker, petroleum engineer, driller, wildcatter, wholesaler, retailer, refinery operator,* etc.
old as Methuselah *old as the hills/as history/as time, an old chestnut.* See Appendix A for the rationale on avoiding sex-linked metaphors, expressions, and figures.
old-boys' network there may be times when this phrase is the one you want. However, it is becoming rare that a network is composed without exception of one sex, so it is generally more correct—and more acceptable—to use *network, professional/career network, connections, business connections, contacts.* **See also** old-girls' network.

old-girls' network a tongue-in-cheek takeoff, but ultimately very useful to women, on the powerful and long-established old-boys' networks. In certain circumstances the phrase still says something important to women who use one, but the trend will be to free the idea from sex roles. Use instead *network, professional/career network, connections, business connections, contacts.*

old maid *woman.* Unless a person's marital status is at issue, avoid the expressions "unmarried woman" and "single woman" because they perpetuate the marriage-as-norm stereotype. Also examine closely your reasons for needing to mention a person's age, even in such an apparently innocuous phrase as "older woman" or "older man."

old maid (card game) because the commercial decks of cards for this child's game clearly mark the key card, which shows an old woman, as the "Old Maid," it is difficult to be anything but ageist and sexist when using a dedicated deck. However, the game can also be played with a regular deck by removing one face card, and the remaining unpaired figure is called the Old Miser. Note that the dreaded leftover card has not always been female; at times the game has been called Le Vieux Garçon (French for "the old boy") or Black Peter. Since the only known nonsexist name for the game is ageist (Old Miser), those who are passing it on to the next generation are encouraged to re-name the game. One could, for example, remove three aces (leaving the ace of hearts or the ace of diamonds to avoid creating a negative association for black) and call the game simply *Ace.* Or add a joker to the deck and call the game *Joker, Wild Card,* or *The Cheese Stands Alone.*

old-maidish replace this vague term with adjectives that precisely illustrate the quality or qualities you intend: *particular, fussy, finicky, fastidious, pernickety, set in one's ways, solitary, precise, old-fashioned, repressed, nervous, fearful,* etc.

old maids (popcorn) *unpopped corn, no-pops.*

Old Man River/Ol' Man River leave as is.

old masters the old masters were all men, and they *were* masters in the Western European system of master-apprentice relationships. Use of this term is therefore historically correct. Replacing this hierarchical construct today among some artists is the shaman concept of the artist as healer and priest whose art is placed in the service of society. If you are not referring to those painters and works specifically known as the old masters, use: *distinguished painters/paintings, the classics, thirteenth-/fourteenth-/fifteenth-/ sixteenth-/seventeenth-century artists/works.* The word pair "master/mistress" is a good illustration of what commonly happens to sex-specific words that begin as equals: the masculine word expands and takes on new and broader meanings while the feminine word shrinks, often to be restricted to a woman's sexual nature, as it does in this case. The ultimate absurdity of this word pair is seen in the facetious words of Lord Beaverbrook: "Buy Old

Masters. They fetch a much better price than old mistresses." See
Appendix A for a discussion of unequal male/female word pairs.

old wives' tale *superstitious folklore, superstition, myth, misconception,*
tale.

old woman this sexist phrase does triple duty: it not only insults the
man being so described and makes an epithet of "woman," but it
is also ageist. Use instead for both sexes *fussbudget, fuddy-duddy,*
weakling, worrywart, handwringer, worrier.

ombudsman *ombuds, ombud, ombudscommittee, watchdog, investigator,*
referee, representative, surveillant, intermediary, go-between, censor,
monitor, guardian of the public good, regulatory agent,
troubleshooter. The Swedish word itself is inclusive—the "man"
means "one"—but its English use is not. The *Oxford English*
Dictionary lists "ombudsman," "ombudswoman," and
"ombudscommittee," which would indicate that "ombudsman" is
gender-specific, especially when "ombudswoman" is defined as "a
female ombudsman." A particularly good solution is found on
university campuses across the country where the term "ombuds"
(or "ombud") is used (for example, the University of Minnesota
has a Student Ombuds Service).

one-man/two-man/three-man, etc. (adj.) *one-person,* or other
appropriate substitute. For example, *two-seater boat, three-person*
tent, four-passenger plane. For "one-man show": *one-person/solo/*
individual/single-artist show/exhibition/exhibit/performance. For
"one-man band," there is probably no widely recognized
gender-free phrase, so use *one-woman band* or *one-man band.*

one man, one vote *one person/citizen/voter, one vote.*

one man's meat is another man's poison *one's meat is another's poison,*
one person's meat is another person's/another's poison.

one of the boys *one of the gang, a regular person.*

one small step for man, one giant leap for mankind unless quoting
astronaut Neil Armstrong, use *one small step for a human being,*
one giant leap for the world/human race.

oneupmanship *going one better, keeping a jump ahead, getting the*
jump on, trying to get the best of, competitiveness, competition,
rivalry, outdoing someone, quest for superiority, keeping up with the
Joneses, vying for top honors.

only man is vile unless quoting Reginald Heber, use *only we/we*
mortals/humans are vile, only humankind is vile.

open 'er up! *open it up!*

opposite sex not sexist in itself, this phrase is sometimes used coyly in
a sexist context. Give it a second look. Dorothy L. Sayers (see
Appendix B) wonders why it has to be "opposite" sex; why not
"neighboring" sex?

orchardman *orchardist, tree grower, nursery owner/manager/operator,*
citriculturist, arborist, arboriculturist.

orderly *nursing/nurse assistant, N.A.* Traditionally aides and orderlies did the same work, but all aides were women and all orderlies were men. Many hospitals and nursing homes now use inclusive terms.

organization man "One of the interesting changes that has taken place in today's business climate is that many organization 'men' are now women" (Don Ethan Miller, *The Book of Jargon.* New York: Macmillan, 1981, p. 148). Until a more compact, inclusive term appears, use *organization woman/women and organization man/men.* "Organization man/men" should not be used generically, that is, assuming that all members of the set are male.

ottoman nonsexist; the "man" has nothing to do with gender. "Ottoman" comes from the French for "Turk."

Our Father (prayer) *See* Lord's prayer, the.

outcall service *prostitution business.* See Appendix A for a discussion of our language on prostitution.

outdoorsman *hunter, nature-lover, fresh-air lover/type, fan of the great outdoors; outdoorswoman and outdoorsman* if used gender-fairly. Or, be specific: *camper, fisher, hiker, birdwatcher, canoer, mountain climber,* etc.

out-Herod Herod *beat all comers, beat all hollow, outdo, outweigh, surpass, excel, exceed, transcend, outrank, get ahead of, be superior to, outstrip, beat one's own record, put into the shade, put someone's nose out of joint, have the upper hand, go to any length, ride roughshod.* See Appendix A for the rationale on avoiding sex-linked metaphors, expressions, and figures.

ovenman *oven tender/operator, malt roaster.*

overlord *supervisor, overseer, boss. See also* master.

overman (noun) *leader, arbitrator, referee. See also* foreman.

overman (verb) *overstaff, oversupply. See also* man (verb).

overmaster *overpower, overcome, overset, outwit, outflank, outmaneuver, defeat, conquer, vanquish, discomfit, confound.*

overmastering *overpowering, overwhelming, all-powerful, irresistible, invincible, unconquerable, indomitable, unquenchable, incontestable.*

overseer woman or man.

oversensitive this is sexist insofar as it is usually reserved for women. For both sexes use *sensitive, considerate, thoughtful; thin-skinned, touchy, easily hurt, petulant, temperamental.*

oysterman *oyster farmer/grower/cultivator.*

p

In many patriarchies, language, as well as cultural tradition, reserve the human condition for the male . . . general application favors the male far more often than the female as referent, or even sole referent.

Kate Millett

packman *peddler.*

page boy *page.*

pageboy (hairstyle) *bob, page-style hairdo, roll-under hairstyle.*

pal man or woman. "Pal" comes from the Romani for "brother" or "friend," and although it is more often used of boys and men, it is also correctly used of girls and women.

paladin historically paladins were men. In the sense of an outstanding champion of a certain cause, a paladin could be either a man or a woman.

pallbearer woman or man.

Pandora's box *opening a can of worms, the curiosity that killed the cat, unforeseen consequences, the unknown, mischief, the ills that flesh is heir to, machinations of the devil, all hell breaking loose.* See Appendix A for the rationale on avoiding sex-linked metaphors, expressions, and figures.

panjandrum woman or man.

pansy avoid this disparaging term; if you mean "gay man," say so.

pantryman *pantry worker/clerk.*

paperboy *newspaper/paper carrier, newspaper vendor, paperboy/ papergirl* (if gender-specificity is necessary for some reason and if the carriers are under the age of thirteen or fourteen).

paramedic man or woman.

paramour woman or man.

parent too often the parent is assumed to be a woman; be sure the context is inclusive.

parlormaid *servant. **See also*** cleaning girl/cleaning lady/cleaning woman; maid.

parson depending on the denomination, this may be a man or a
woman.

parts man *stock clerk, parts clerk/worker.*

pasha historically there were no female pashas; use this term as a
sex-specific word in the context of Turkish or North African
political life. However, there is no contraindication to the colorful
and metaphorical use of "pasha" to describe a powerful or
high-ranking official, male or female.

paste-up man *paste-up/copy editor, camera operator.*

past master *acknowledged expert, expert, adept; ex-champion;
experienced/accomplished artist/writer/bricklayer,* etc. This may
also refer to the holder of a Freemason office or to a specific title
in a guild or society, in which case it should be used as it is.

pastor depending on the particular denomination, a pastor may be a
woman or a man.

pater/paterfamilias OK to use when also using "mater/materfamilias,"
although the tendency is to avoid Latin forms. Use instead father/
patriarch, if you are sure that the terms are correct in your
context. This is an area in which unthinking and unwarranted
assumptions about male-as-norm tend to surface.

paternalism *parentalism, authoritarian parentalism, authoritarianism,
political intrusion.* "Paternalism" has a long history and
entrenched acceptance in academic, philosophic, and political
circles, and is thus difficult (but not impossible) to replace with a
commonly recognized one-word term. The concept is particularly
offensive to many women; although paternalism has come and
gone for many societies and segments of society, this kind of
misguided "protection" has been an invariable fact of life for
women as a group throughout history. Retain the term when you
want to emphasize male hierarchical domination.

paternity leave *parental leave.*

patient as Job *long-suffering, stoical, forbearing, uncomplaining,
longanimous, abiding, patient, extraordinarily patient, patient as
the grave, through fire and water, keeping the faith.* Job's opposite
number is probably patient Griselda, q.v., but she does not, to put
it mildly, provide a particularly acceptable or admirable model for
today's woman, and it is better to avoid her. For the rationale on
avoiding sex-linked metaphors, expressions, and figures, see
Appendix A.

patient Griselda *someone who is long-suffering/submissive/humble/
patient/extraordinarily patient/patient as the grave/passive/abiding/
stoical/forbearing, someone who endures through thick and thin/
through fire and water.* See Appendix A for the rationale on
avoiding sex-linked metaphors, expressions, and figures. *See also*
patient as Job.

patriarch/patriarchy use these terms when you are also using "matriarch/matriarchy," but be sure that the terms are used fairly in the context. This is an area in which unthinking and unwarranted assumptions about male-as-norm tend to surface.

patrician (adj.) although this word doesn't sound so heavily patriarchal today and thus can be used without giving overt offense, it shares the same Latin root ("pater") as other "father" words. Alternatives include *elegant, well-bred, formal, stately, graceful, courtly, debonair, delicate, decorous, majestic, exquisite, polite, seemly, refined, genteel, cultivated, urbane, sophisticated, worldly, stylish, cosmopolitan, classy.* The best alternative for the noun is *aristocrat,* although we tend not to use "patrician" in that sense, perhaps because of our democratic underpinnings.

patrilineal use this word when referring to descent through the father's line; use "matrilineal" when referring to descent through the mother's line. These are useful and necessary sex-specific words when used correctly.

patrimony *inheritance, heritage, legacy, inherited property, estate, family estate, portion, share, lot.* Notice the nonparallel word pair "patrimony/matrimony."

patriot/patriotic man or woman. Although these words come from the Latin meaning "land of my father," they are functionally nonsexist today.

patrolman *patrol officer, patroller, state trooper, trooper.*

patron *benefactor, sponsor, backer, supporter, promoter, philanthropist, booster, partisan; customer, shopper, buyer, purchaser, subscriber, client.* "Patron" comes from the Latin for "father," and although its gender-specific root does not much affect its use for both women and men today, it is still considered sexist because it is more often used of men than women and it is also the male half of a very unbalanced word pair: "patron/matron." In addition it has some fairly sexist first cousins: "patronage," "patronize," "patronymic," etc., and it is better to avoid the whole "pater" family.

patronage *sponsorship, support, auspices, advocacy, defense, championship, assistance, encouragement, promotion, protection, influence; business, trade, custom, commerce.* Although "patronage" is not often perceived as a sex-specific word today, it comes from the Latin for "father" and reflects centuries of male domination; these associations suggest it is better to avoid the word. *See also* patron.

patroness it would be better to use "patron" than to use "patroness," but "patron" is not a prime choice either. *See* patron.

patronize *support, favor, promote, defend, sponsor, show favor to; condescend to.* "Patronize" is not a functionally sexist word today, but its roots and associations are sexist and it is probably better avoided. *See also* patron.

patron saint *namesake saint, special saint* (e.g., "Saint Appollonia, special saint of dentists").

patronymic *surname, birth name.* Avoid "patronymic," which comes from the Latin for "father" and which emphasizes the historic importance of the male name, except when you are using it (1) in a context that also includes "matronymic"; (2) in its narrowest sense; (3) to discuss sexist practices.

patsy although the origins of this word are not entirely clear, they seem gender-free, and the word is not perceived as particularly gender-specific. However, for a more neutral-appearing term, use *scapegoat, goat, loser, born loser, sucker, dupe, nebbish, victim, mark, target, laughingstock, sad sack, doormat, sap, hard-luck story, pigeon, pushover, fool. See also* fall guy/fall man; whipping boy.

Paul Pry *busybody, stickybeak, nosey Parker.* For the rationale on avoiding sex-linked metaphors, expressions, and figures, see Appendix A.

pawnbroker woman or man.

paymaster *pay/payroll agent, payroll supervisor, purser, treasurer, bursar, receiver, steward, accountant, cashier, teller.*

peacock/peafowl/peahen use the generic "peafowl" instead of the male "peacock" when referring to both males and females.

Peck's bad boy *enfant terrible,* q.v., *in the avant garde, innovative/ unorthodox/unconventional/nonconforming director/artist/musician,* etc., *heretic* (in nonreligious sense), *questioner; embarrassment; mischievous child.*

Pecksniffian from the name of one of Charles Dickens's male characters. Use instead *pharisaical, hypocritical, insincere, crocodilian, mealy-mouthed, double-dealing, two-faced, smooth-tongued, sanctimonious, self-righteous, unctuous, canting, pietistical.* See Appendix A for the rationale on avoiding sex-linked metaphors, expressions, and figures.

pedant man or woman.

pederast *child molester/abuser, habitual child molester.* Although the Greek root word can mean either "child" or "boy," "pederast" is defined today as a man who uses boys as sex objects, and thus is sex-linked; there is no parallel for women and girls. The foregoing substitutes for "pederast" are not only inclusive, they clarify rather than obscure the nature of the pederast's activities. *See also* pedophile.

pedophile *child molester/abuser, habitual child molester.* "Pedophile" is not a sexist word per se, but it is often associated with men since they are the principal abusers. Use the alternatives instead of "pedophile" because: (1) they appear more inclusive; (2) they do not dress up an ugly practice with a fancy name that is indecipherable to many people. *See also* pederast.

peeping Tom *window peeper, voyeur, eavesdropper.* Although "peeping Thomasina" is seen occasionally, it is unnecessarily coy and probably not a very precise opposite for "peeping Tom." Note that the male "peeping Tom" is not the harmless voyeur he has traditionally been thought to be. Statistics indicate that the individual is usually involved or will be involved in more harmful deviant behavior. You may therefore need to use terms that more accurately reflect reality than the supposedly pitiable and innocuous "peeper/voyeur."

peeress *peer.*

Peking man *early human, Peking fossil, Homo erectus.*

penman *scribe, calligrapher, author, writer.*

penmanship *handwriting, writing, hand, script.*

pensioner woman or man.

person not a sexist term; "son" is part of the Latin "persona" meaning "human being." Although "person" has at times been used to mean only men (in spite of its neutral derivation), it is accepted today as nonsexist. Although using "-person" as a suffix has been very helpful in initiating inclusive language, such words should be kept to a minimum, and whenever possible inclusive terms without the betraying/identifying band-aid of "-person" should be used, for example, "chair" instead of "chairperson," "city council member" instead of "city councilperson." See Appendix A for a discussion of -woman, -man, -person.

persona grata/persona non grata man or woman.

peter/peter out (verb) although the origins of "peter" do not appear to be sexist, it has an obvious male look and you may want to use an alternative: *give out, become exhausted, run out, trail off, dry up, use up, dissipate, drain off.*

Peter Pan collar the association of this phrase with a very specific type of collar is so entrenched and immediately evocative that it is difficult to replace it with a phrase that does the same work. Sometimes you can use *round collar.* See Appendix A for the rationale on avoiding sex-linked metaphors, expressions, and figures.

Peter's pence *church tax, donation, alms, honorarium, gratuity, offering.* Use "Peter's pence" when it refers specifically to the (in most dioceses) annual papal collection in the Roman Catholic Church.

Peter to pay Paul, borrow from *See* borrow from Peter to pay Paul.

petite avoid this word; it is used only to describe a female body. The masculine form of the word, "petit," has a rather important and meaningful life in the legal world. This is an example of yet another female/male word pair that bit the dust.

petticoat (woman) this is rarely seen anymore. Thank goodness.

petty officer woman or man.

pharaoh   pharaohs were all men (the word means "king"); women married to the pharaoh or who served as regents are called queens.

Ph.D.   nonsexist. *See also* bachelor's degree; master's degree.

pickup (woman)   never use this; it not only says that the woman is passive (she is "picked up") but it also implies (by giving her, but not her partner, a special derogatory label) that she is the guilty party. We pay lip service to the two-to-tango notion, but our language says that a man's actions are literally unremarkable while the woman's actions deserve a judgment. Eliminating words like "pickup" from the language will not also eliminate the double standard, but it is a necessary part of the process.

pied piper   man or woman. In the well-known fairy tale, the pied piper was a man, but the term itself is gender-free.

pikeman   soldier; tollbooth operator; miner.

piker   woman or man.

Pilgrim Fathers   *Pilgrims.*

pillar of the community   man or woman.

pimp   by definition a man.

pink collar job/pink collar worker   pink collar jobs make up that small portion (20 out of 427) of jobs into which 80 percent of all salaried women fit: secretaries, household workers, nurses, waiters, librarians, health technicians, elementary school teachers, bank tellers, etc. As of 1985, for example, 98.4 percent of all secretaries, 91.5 percent of all bookkeepers, 84 percent of all teachers, 83.1 percent of all cashiers, and 80.1 percent of all office clerks were women (U. S. Bureau of Labor Statistics). Today sex-specific words like "pink collar jobs" are valid sociological terms; the hope is that a changing reality will eventually render them obsolete.

pink ladies (drugs)   *barbiturates.*

pin money   an outdated term for an outdated concept whereby men gave their wives spending money (literally to buy pins); be careful of your intentions and your presentation if you feel you need to use this.

pinup girl   *model, photographic/calendar model.*

pioneer   woman or man. Note that in addition to being sexist, our notions about the pioneers are also often racist; we too often incorrectly assume that all pioneers were not only male, but white.

pirate   man or woman. Noted pirates include Anne Bonney, Mary Read, and Grania O'Malley.

pitchman   *sidewalk vendor/seller, barker.*

pitman (automobile)   *connecting rod.* The "man" in "pitman" refers to the adult male, so the word's origins are sexist.

pitman (industry)   *pit/underground miner, miner.*

pivotman (basketball)   *post/pivot player, center.*

placeman   *bureaucrat, government official, functionary.*

plainclothesman   *plainclothes officer/detective, detective.*

plainsman   *plains dweller/inhabitant; plainswoman and plainsman* if used gender-fairly.

platform man   *platform attendant/loader.*

playboy   *swinger, bedhopper, mover, hustler, free spirit, libertine, high-roller, dissolute person, someone who sleeps around, make-out artist. See also* ladies' man; man about town; rake; womanize/ womanizer/womanizing.

playfellow   *playmate.*

playgirl   this is not an exact parallel for "playboy," but if you mean it in that sense, see "playboy" for alternatives. In any case, avoid the term.

playmate (woman)   avoid referring to a woman this way.

playing lord of the manor   *swagger, give oneself airs, act big, ride a high horse, act the high-and-mighty, be insolent/haughty/overbearing/ pretentious/self-important/pushy/snobbish/pompous/high-handed. See also* lord it over someone.

pledge (fraternities, academies, etc.)   woman or man.

plowboy/plowman   *farm worker, farmer, cultivator, sower.*

plumber   man or woman (although less than one percent of U.S. plumbers are women at this time).

poetess   *poet.*

poilu   this World War I French soldier was always a man, with one notable exception: Marie Marvingt, the Frenchwoman known as the Fiancée of Danger, disguised herself as a poilu and fought in the front lines for three weeks until she was discovered.

policeman   *officer, police/peace officer, officer of the law; policewoman and policeman* if used gender-fairly. Or, be specific: *police sergeant/detective, beat officer, traffic officer,* etc.

policeman of the world   *watchdog of the world, police officer of the world.* Those who most often use "policeman of the world" (political scientists, for example) may object to changing it because of its specific and instantly recognizable sense. However, with a little effort, one could get used to one of the alternatives or construct a new one.

politics makes strange bedfellows   unless quoting Charles Dudley Warner, use *politics makes strange bedmates.*

Pollyanna   *eternal/persistent/unflagging/perennial/cock-eyed/foolish/ incurable optimist, daydreamer, romantic, visionary, castlebuilder, utopian, idealist, victim of terminal cheerfulness, one who lives in a fool's paradise, wearer of rose-colored glasses.* For the rationale on avoiding sex-linked expressions, metaphors, and figures, see Appendix A.

polyandry/polygamy   correct sex-specific terms.

pom-pom girl   *pom-pom twirler/artist.*

pontiff   so far, always a man.

pooh-bah although the original character from *The Mikado* (1885) was a man, this term can be used to describe a self-important person of either sex who occupies a high position, holds several positions at once, or wields great influence.

poor as Job/poor as Job's turkey *poor as a church mouse, destitute, penniless, indigent, poverty-stricken, on one's uppers, down and out, out at the elbows, down at the heels.* See Appendix A for the rationale on avoiding sex-linked metaphors, expressions, and figures.

population control *reproductive responsibility/freedom/rights/ information.* The term "population control" reveals a paternalistic, patronizing attitude (masculine terms are intended) toward people in general, toward Third World peoples, and most particularly toward women. The alternatives shift the emphasis to the control people have over their own choices.

portress *porter.*

poseur although the French is masculine, it is used (in France and in English-speaking countries) for either a man or a woman. If it feels too masculine to you, try these alternatives: *pretentious person, mannerist, lump of affectation, charlatan, quack, humbug, pedant, pedagogue, pseudo-intellectual.*

postboy *postilion.*

postman *See* mailman.

postmaster leave as is when it is a title in current use; otherwise use *postal chief, post office supervisor.*

postmaster general leave as is when it is a title in current use; otherwise use *federal postal chief/supervisor.*

postmistress *postal chief, post office supervisor.* Where the official title for men in the same position is "postmaster," use that (it is less sexist than "postmistress") but you might want to add [sic] after it.

potboy leave as is in historical contexts. Otherwise use *barroom attendant, tavern helper, bar assistant.*

potentate in certain contexts today, this could be a woman or a man; historically, it was always a man.

poultryman *poultry farmer/breeder, chicken farmer.*

poundman *angler, fisher.*

poundmaster leave as is when it is an official title or add [sic] after it; otherwise, use *poundkeeper, pound officer/chief/supervisor.*

powder room *restroom, washroom, lavatory, bathroom, lounge.* This word is paradoxically sexist: the "powder" in the phrase comes from the powder men used on their wigs in colonial times, yet today the powder room is reserved for women. Avoid the term; it is coy and exclusive. *See also* john.

prattle a sexist word insofar as only women and children are said to prattle. The problem with "prattle" and its alternatives is one that goes beyond words: most synonyms for prattle ("chatter," "babble," "jabber," etc.) tend to be used more of women than of men. Examine your material to see if by choosing "prattle" or one of its synonyms, you are not making a subtle statement about women. Some alternatives that seem more inclusive are *rattle, ramble, blabber, blather, spout, spout off, run off at the mouth, talk nonsense, shoot the breeze.*

preacher depending on the denomination, may be a woman or a man.

preadamite *prehuman.* In any case, the term "preadamite" is not a scientific anthropological term.

pregnant there is nothing sexist in this word; the only caution is being aware of the context and attitudes that surround it. Is pregnancy generally treated as an illness, handicap, misfortune, or inferior state of being? Is the pregnant woman assumed to be more moody and less capable than other people? Are expectant mothers penalized in the workplace? When using the word "pregnant" to indicate fullness or suspense, use gender-nonspecific words: *meaningful, profound, momentous, ominous, expectant, suspenseful, waiting, teeming.*

prehistoric man *prehistoric/early peoples/humans, prehumans, fossil humans.*

prehominid nonsexist. *See* hominid.

prelate so far, always a man.

premenstrual syndrome/PMS acceptable sex-specific term that describes a recognized medical condition.

premier man or woman.

premier danseur "ballet dancer" is an inclusive term that covers anyone who dances the ballet. However, ballet companies assign strict meanings to dancers' titles. A "premier danseur" is the principal male dancer in a company; his opposite number is the "prima ballerina." Retain "premier danseur" for its narrow meaning within ballet companies, but describe a man who dances ballet nonprofessionally as a *lead dancer, principal dancer, first dancer. See also* ballerina; danseur/danseuse; prima ballerina.

pressman *press operator/tender/feeder, presser.*

priest in some churches (Episcopalian, The Reorganized Church of Jesus Christ of Latter Day Saints, for example) a priest may be a man or a woman. Priests in other churches (Anglican, Roman Catholic, for example) are men. Addressing female priests is problematic; although one is properly hesitant to call them by the traditional "Father," one isn't too sure what to replace it with. The most widespread practice so far seems to be the use of first names for both female and male clergy. In the Episcopalian Church, although women clergy have not resolved the problem, some are very comfortable being called "Mother," while others choose the first-name convention. (Some female priests say they are not disturbed when they are called "Father"; they accept it pro tem in the spirit in which it is said.) Note that neither male nor female priests are properly addressed orally as "Reverend." It is never in poor taste to ask a priest what she or he likes to be called. This is a time of transition and few people, including the clergy themselves, have hard and fast guidelines as yet.

priestess *priest.* You may need to retain "priestess" in historical contexts, however. At certain times in the past the word reflected a reality that was not demeaning to women, for example, in the goddess religions. And in some instances the term is not second-best but one that offers a model of power and inspiration for women.

prima ballerina gender-specific terms are still used in professional ballet companies to distinguish between the female first dancer ("prima ballerina") and the male first dancer ("premier danseur"). Retain the narrow usage when referring to members of professional ballet companies, but use inclusive language for others: *ballet dancer, first dancer, star dancer, principal dancer.* **See** *also* ballerina; danseur; premier danseur.

prima donna *lead, leading role, opera/lead/principal singer.* Since there is no parallel for men, this is a sexist term, but it will no doubt remain in use until change comes from within the opera community. When the term is used to describe an overly self-absorbed and temperamental person, it is used (in spite of its plainly feminine cast) for both sexes, and it's a toss-up as to who is put down more thoroughly, men or women.

primitive man *early/primitive peoples.*

primogenitor *ancestor, forebear.* Because the "genitor" comes from the word for begetting, "primogenitor" refers to male ancestors only.

primogeniture in its narrowest sense (the inheritance rights of the firstborn son), "primogeniture" is the correct term to use, although the concept is very sexist. In the larger sense of being the firstborn of all the children of the same parents, use *firstborn, firstborn child, eldership, seniority, the rights of the firstborn.*

prince use only for royalty. The supposed equivalent for "prince" ("princess") has very different connotations. Expressions such as "he's a prince," "a real prince," "a prince of a fellow," "a prince among men," etc. have no equivalents for women. Inclusive alternatives are *a real paragon, an ace, the acme of perfection, a trump, a marvel, a one-off, one in a million, the ideal.*

princess use only for royalty. **See** *also* prince.

prioress this is the correct term; the male equivalent is "prior." Like the word "abbess," q.v., "prioress" denotes a woman with power and stature that were usually equal to that of a prior's.

prisoner woman or man.

prison guard man or woman. Note that women can be guards in male prisons.

private/private first class (armed forces) woman or man.

prizeman *prizewinner, prizeholder.*

prizemaster *prize officer.* Use as is in historical contexts.

pro-abortion **See** pro-choice.

pro-choice this is the term preferred by those who believe that women (not government, not doctors, not clergy) should make the choice for or against an abortion; the term "pro-abortion" is offensive to this group, which includes both men and women.

proconsul Roman proconsuls were all men, as are almost all modern administrators of colonies, dependencies, and occupied areas.

procreate procreation is shared equally by men and woman. When speaking of it, sometimes use "beget" and sometimes use "give birth to."

procurer woman or man. See Appendix A for a discussion of our language on prostitution.

procuress *procurer.*

prodigal son *returned prodigal, the prodigal one, the prodigal, one who returns to the fold; profligate, wastrel, squanderer, scattergood, waster, spendthrift, high liver.*

professional man *professional. See also* businessman.

professor emeritus "emeritus" is the male form; women are called "professor emerita" at this time.

pro-life the term that describes those who oppose abortion; pro-life stances range from those who oppose abortion for any reason whatsoever (and who also oppose birth control) to those who favor birth control and accept abortion as a possibility in a few narrowly delimited instances. You may want to be sure which type of pro-life group you are referring to. In addition, some pro-lifers are one-issue people (abortion only) while others define "pro-life" by a wide spectrum of issues (death penalty, poverty and justice, nuclear arms race, etc.). Both men and women are involved in the pro-life movement.

promiscuous applies to both men and women.

propertyman *property coordinator/handler.*

prophet woman or man.

prophetess *prophet.*

prop man *prop handler.*

proprietress *proprietor.*

prostitute/prostitution applies to both women and men. These are the terms of choice (rather than the multitude of words that tend to mask the impact and significance of prostitution). See Appendix A for a discussion of the language on prostitution.

protagonist man or woman.

protectress *protector.*

protegé/protegée *protegé* for either a man or a woman. Although these words come from the French and "protegé" is the male form, it is better to have one word for both sexes. For example, "protegée" is defined in most dictionaries as "a female protegé," thus removing women one step from "the real thing." *See also* divorcé/divorcée; fiancé/fiancée; habitué.

provocateur *See* agent provocateur.

provocative when describing ideas or intellectual properties, the word is entirely nonsexist. In a social or sexual situation, however, the word has connotations that make it difficult to use fairly and factually. If you must use it, do so equally of men and women. Too often it is women who are "provocative"—eternal Eves luring endless numbers of passive Adams.

prudent man (legal) *prudent person/individual.*

Pullman car nonsexist; named after George Pullman.

pullman porter this is a nonsexist term (from Pullman car named after George Pullman) but you can avoid the masculine look by substituting *train attendant, porter, red cap.*

pull oneself up by the bootstraps both women and men do this.

pumpman *pumper.*

q

Syllables govern the world.

John Selden

◆ ◆ ◆

Quakeress *Quaker.*

quarryman *quarrier, quarry worker.*

quartermaster this term is used officially only in the Army and in the Navy. In the Army it refers to a field of specialization, but no individual member of the Army is called a quartermaster. The Navy has quartermasters, but they may be called *navigators.* Other possibilities include *supply officer; petty officer in charge of the quarterdeck; petty officer, quarterdeck.*

queen (gay man) *gay, gay man.*

queen (verb) women apparently "queen it over" their friends while men "lord it over" theirs. For both sexes use the inclusive alternatives: *wear the crown, hold over the head of, get the upper hand, have it all one's own way, have the ball at one's feet, have the game in one's own hand/corner.*

queen consort in referring to the wife of a reigning king, it is generally acceptable to drop the word "consort" entirely except in some very narrow circumstances (legal, historical, official titles).

queer (referring to a woman's or man's sexual orientation) *lesbian, gay.*

quizmaster *quiz show host*

r

One of the difficulties in the language is that all our words from loose using have lost their edge.

Ernest Hemingway

rabbi there are women rabbis in the Conservative, Reform, and Reconstructionist branches of Judaism, and they are addressed in the same manner as men rabbis: "rabbi." There are no women rabbis in the Orthodox branch.

racketeer man or woman.

raconteur woman or man. This French word is masculine in gender (the female "raconteuse" stayed in France) although it is used in English for both sexes. More inclusive-sounding alternatives are *storyteller, anecdotist, teller of tales, taleteller, talespinner, spinner of yarns, romancer, narrator.*

radioman *radio operator/repairer.*

raftsman *rafter.*

ragman *ragpicker, rag collector, junk dealer/collector.*

raise Cain *kick up/make a fuss, carry on, lose one's temper, fly off the handle, flare up, run amok, raise a rumpus/ a storm/a hue and cry/the devil/hell, castigate, lecture, rail, fulminate, find fault; be boisterous/loud/rowdy/disorderly, disturb the peace.* For the rationale on avoiding sex-linked metaphors, expressions, and figures, see Appendix A.

rajah always a man; his wife is a "rani."

rake this term seems reserved for men, and there is no parallel for women. Use inclusive terms instead: *libertine, swinger, bedhopper, free spirit, high-roller, dissolute person. See also* ladies' man; man about town; playboy; womanize/womanizer/womanizing.

rallymaster *rally director/organizer.*

ranchman *rancher. See also* cattleman; cowboy.

rapscallion *See* ne'er-do-well.

"real" father/"real" mother *biological mother/father, birth father/mother.*

rear admiral man or woman.

reasonable and prudent man (law) *reasonable and prudent person/individual.*

recruit woman or man.

rector depending on the denomination, this may be either a woman or a man.

red hot mama avoid.

red-light district *prostitution district.* See Appendix A for a discussion of our language on prostitution.

red man *American Indian, Native American, first American, Indian.* The term "Native American" is in disfavor with many Indian groups because the federal government now includes Samoans and Hawaiians in that category. When possible, refer to a specific tribe.

redneck applicable to both women and men, but probably to be avoided as inflammatory and judgmental.

referee man or woman.

reinsman *driver, coach/sulky driver, horse racer.*

remainderman *remainderer, remainder agent, reversioner.* The term "remainderperson" has appeared in print and is a possibility but should be reserved as a last choice due to its awkwardness.

remember, man, that thou art dust and unto dust thou shalt return *remember that thou art dust, and unto dust thou shalt return.*

Renaissance man *a multi-talented/well-rounded, self-actualizing individual, a person of many talents/parts; Renaissance woman and Renaissance man* if used gender-fairly.

renegade woman or man.

repairman *repairer, technician.* Or, be specific: *car mechanic, plumber, electrician, carpenter, roofer,* etc.

resident (advanced medical student) man or woman.

restaurateur woman or man.

retreat master *retreat director.*

reverend (adj.) depending on the denomination, this title may be used for a woman or a man, and the person might be a priest, deacon, minister, pastor, etc. In most cases, men and women are addressed similarly. Use "The Reverend Carson Smathers" when writing, but in general do not use "reverend" as a noun, as in "How are you today, Reverend?" Use instead the person's first name, "Father," "Mother" (*see* priest), or whatever title the person prefers. Clergy today welcome a question like "What shall I call you?" or "How do you like to be called?"

rewrite man *rewriter. See also* newsman/newspaperman.

Rhodesian man *See* Neanderthal man.

rich as Croesus *well-to-do, made of money, worth a bundle/a pretty penny, rolling in money, on Easy Street, has a goldmine, has money to burn, flush, someone whose ship has come in.* For the rationale on avoiding sex-linked metaphors, expressions, and figures, see Appendix A.

rich man's sport *rich person's sport, a sport for the rich, a sport for rich blood.*

rifleman *sharpshooter, carabineer, crack shot, sniper, sharpshooter.* **See also** gunman.

right-hand man *right hand, deputy, assistant, right-hand assistant, aide, helper, attendant, co-worker, sidekick, subordinate.*

ringman *bettor, gambler, gamester.*

ringmaster *ringleader, host, circus leader, leader, announcer.* **See also** master of ceremonies.

Rise of Man, the *the Rise of Civilization, the Rise of Culture, the Rise of Humanity.*

roaring boy *noisy bully.*

rob Peter to pay Paul *See* borrow from Peter to pay Paul.

rodman *See* gunman.

rogue nonsexist in itself, this word is still used almost exclusively for men. Use instead *outcast, fallen angel, villain, mischief-maker, scamp, cheat.* **See also** bad guy; ne'er-do-well.

Romeo *lover, great/doomed lover.* For the rationale on avoiding sex-linked metaphors, expressions, and figures, see Appendix A.

rookie man or woman.

rough and ready this term has long been reserved for men, but there is no reason not to use it for women when appropriate.

roughneck although culturally reserved for men, particularly because one of its meanings is "an oilfield worker" (which has been an all-male field), this term may also be used for women when appropriate. Or, use *ugly customer, hoodlum, hood, bully, hooligan, uncouth person.*

roundsman *relief cook.*

roustabout a roustabout is invariably a man, and there is no similar word or occupation for women.

routeman *driver, newspaper carriers' supervisor, delivery person, route supervisor.*

rowdy can be said of women or men.

ruffian woman or man.

rule of thumb this rule—by definition a rule inspired by practical rather than precise scientific knowledge—has been used for nearly three centuries and there are several theories about its derivation. In a letter to the editor of *MS.,* Claire Bride Cozzi wrote that the derivation was painfully sexist: English common law allowed a man to chastise his wife with a switch "no thicker than his thumb" (July 1986, p. 6). Helen Eschenbacher responded that the phrase came from many other references to the thumb besides wife-beating, for example, an artist using a thumb to gauge perspective (October 1986, p. 10). The broadest explanation is that the last joint of the thumb is about an inch and was used as a measure, but since the measurement was imprecise the expression "rule of thumb" resulted.

rule the roost this phrase is functionally sexist on two counts: (1) the roost is invariably "manned" by a rooster, but paradoxically (2) the expression is commonly used to refer to a woman who dominates her family. However, the original expression—and the way it is still used in Great Britain today—is "rule the roast," "roast" possibly being a governing body of some sort. The term itself is thus a nonsexist one that has become sexist. Use instead *call the shots/the tune/the plays, wear the crown, sit on the throne, wield the scepter, have it all one's way, lay down the law, be in the driver's seat, hold all the cards, be in the saddle.*

S

Words have a longer life than deeds.

Pindar

Sabines an ancient people of the Appenines, the Sabines are sometimes mistakenly thought to be women only—probably because of the famous/infamous rape (abduction) of the Sabine women.

saboteur woman or man. This French word is masculine in gender although it is used for both sexes in French and in English.

sacristan depending on the denomination, a sacristan may be a woman or a man.

sad sack man or woman.

safety man *safety inspector/engineer.*

sage woman or man.

sahib always a man; the woman is a "memsahib."

salad girl/salad man *salad maker.* Note the nonparallel "girl/man" word pair.

salesgirl/saleslady *See* salesman.

salesman *salesclerk, clerk, sales associate/rep/agent/representative/ broker, agent, seller, door-to-door seller, vendor, estimator, driver, soliciter, salesperson.* These terms are not all interchangeable. For example, "salesclerk" and "salesperson" are appropriate for someone who works in a retail store, whereas "sales representative" is descriptive of someone employed by a large manufacturing company whose work is a combination of business manager, product specialist, and sales trainer. Instead of "salesmen" use plurals of the above alternatives as well as *salesforce, sales staff, salespeople.*

salesmanship *sales ability/techniques, high sales potential; vendorship; hucksterism.*

saleswoman *See* salesman.

salvage man *salvage worker/inspector/repairer, salvager, parts salvager.*

sampleman *sampler, raw sampler, sample collector/worker/ reworker.*

Samson *strong as an ox/a lion, made of iron, tower of strength, someone with the strength of ten, giant refreshed.* See Appendix A for the rationale on avoiding sex-linked metaphors, expressions, and figures.

samurai always a man.

sandboy *sand/beach flea.* Or, leave as is.

Sandman, the *the sleep/sand fairy, the sleep genie, the Sander, Sandy Eyes.*

sandwich man *sandwich board advertiser.*

sandwich girl/sandwich man *sandwich maker.* Note the nonparallel "girl/man" word pair.

sanitation man *sanitation worker/engineer.*

San Quentin quail (referring to underage female sexual partner) do not use this term. Describe the situation as it reflects reality without incorrectly placing the onus for it on the girl or young woman; referring to her this way perpetuates the Eve-as-tempter/helpless-Adam stereotype and implies a certain victimization and unwilling cooperation on the part of the man, obscuring the fact that he is engaging in criminal activity (and laying the foundation for a statutory rape charge). *See also* jailbait.

Santa Claus "Father Christmas," "Père Noel," "Saint Nicholas," and "Santa Claus" are better left as they are, even with the acknowledgment that these (once again) male heroes reinforce the cultural male-as-norm system. Mrs. Claus goes largely unrecognized; she does not even have a first name. There is nothing inherently wrong with a male Santa Claus; the problem is that nearly every cultural rite of this magnitude is male-dominated. The solution is to promote female heroes along with rituals that feature women.

sarge woman or man.

Satan refer to as "it" rather than "he."

satyr replace this sex-specific word with inclusive terms: *libertine, corrupter, fun-lover, bedhopper, swinger, lover, seducer.* *See also* nymphomaniac.

savant man or woman. The French word is masculine in gender but is used in French and English for both sexes.

savage woman or man. Note: this is usually very racist; check your usage.

say uncle *surrender, give up, throw in the sponge, knuckle under, raise the white flag, draw in one's horns, cry barley, strike sail, throw oneself on the mercy of, pack it in, throw up one's hands, capitulate, eat one's words.*

scalawag *See* ne'er-do-well.

scamp man or woman.

scapegoat woman or man.

scarlet woman avoid. There is no parallel term—nor any expressed condemnation—for the men who are the "partners in crime" of scarlet women.

scatterbrained one rarely hears this used of men. Use instead inclusive terms: *impractical, irresponsible, slaphappy, woolgathering, dreamy, out to lunch, on another planet, with one's head in the clouds, not all there, missing some marbles, with a mind like a sieve.*

scholar woman or man.

schoolboy (drugs) *codeine.*

schoolboy/schoolfellow/schoolgirl *schoolchild, schoolmate, classmate, peer, youngster, elementary school child.*

schoolman/Schoolman *scholastic, teacher, school administrator, pedagogue, academician, academist, professor, scholar, savant.* "Schoolman" is historically correct when referring to a Scholastic.

schoolmarm/schoolmaster/schoolmistress *teacher, instructor.*

Scotchman *See* Scotsman, which is preferred.

Scotsman *Scot, inhabitant of Scotland, Scotswoman and Scotsman* if used gender-fairly. Plural: *Scots, the Scottish, Scotswomen and Scotsmen.*

scoundrel man or woman.

scout boy or girl. Instead of "girl scout" and "boy scout," the term "youth scout" is appearing more often.

scoutmaster *scoutleader.*

scowman *scow hand/worker.*

scrapman *scrap worker/separator.*

Scrooge *tightwad, money-grubber, penny pincher, pinchpenny, miser, skinflint, cheapskate, piker, cheeseparer.* See Appendix A for the rationale on avoiding sex-linked metaphors, expressions, and figures.

scrubwoman *janitor, cleaner, household helper, custodian, domestic worker, char, charworker, maintenance worker.*

scullery maid use as is in historical context, or *scullery worker.*

sculptress *sculptor.*

seafaring man *seafarer. See also* seaman.

seamaid *See* mermaid/merman.

seaman *sailor, mariner, marine, navigator, pilot, argonaut, seafarer, tar, salt, gob, captain, skipper, mate, first mate, crew member, deck hand, boater, yachter.* "Seaman" is the official term for the Navy rank, but note that a "seaman" might be either a man or a woman.

seaman apprentice *apprentice sailor/crew member, marine apprentice.* "Seaman apprentice" is the official term for the Navy rank, but it can denote either a woman or a man.

seamanlike/seamanly *shipshape, sailor-like.* Or, be specific: *tidy, orderly, skilled,* etc.

seaman recruit this is the official term for the Navy rank, but it could refer to either a man or a woman.

seamanship *navigation/ship-handling skills, marine strategy, sailing techniques, navigational expertise.*

seamstress *tailor, mender, alterer, stitcher, alterations expert, custom tailor, fashion sewer, garment worker/designer, needleworker.*

second lieutenant woman or man.

second-story man *cat burglar, burglar, housebreaker.*

secretary man or woman (although this is a pink-collar occupation, 98.4 percent of all secretaries being women).

seductive both women and men can be said to be seductive; the term should not be limited to women.

seductress *seducer.*

see a man about a dog/horse *see somebody about about a dog/horse.* Or, replace the phrase with whatever you really mean. Originally this was a Victorian circumlocution designed to avoid mentioning anything inconvenient or embarrassing: visiting the restroom, going to a bar or tavern for a drink, seeing a prostitute.

seedsman *sower, seed dealer, seed store owner, seed company representative.*

selectman *representative, board officer; selectwoman and selectman* if used gender-fairly.

self-made man *self-made person/individual, entrepreneur; self-made woman and self-made man* if used gender-fairly.

self-mastery *self-control.*

seminal *germinal, germinative, creative, original, inventive, primary, primordial, prototypal, prototypical, exemplary, innovative, fresh, novel, unprecedented, precedent-setting, first of its kind, initial, earliest, primal, unorthodox, nonconforming, unconventional, rudimentary, inceptive, fundamental, productive, catalytic, far-reaching, potential, possible, probable, likely, unrealized.* Alternatives are given for "seminal" because it is the adjectival form of "semen," than which nothing could be more male. Using the word underscores the notion that only men have important, "seminal" ideas.

seminary although both sexes have attended seminaries in the past, their experiences have not been parallel: seminaries for women have included those for high school-aged girls while seminaries for men have been for the training of clergy. The former type of seminary is becoming a rarity, and the latter now includes women, depending on the denomination.

semination *sowing, planting, cultivating, cultivation.* **See also** seminal.

sempstress *See* seamstress.

senator man or woman.

send a dear John letter *See* dear John letter, send a.

senior airman this is the official term for the rank in the U.S. Air Force, but a "senior airman" could be either a woman or a man.

senior master sergeant woman or man.

senior naval officer man or woman.

sentinel/sentry woman or man.

separate the men from the boys *separate the sheep from the goats/wheat from the chaff/strong from the weak/good from the bad/able from the incompetent/mature from the immature.*

serf man or woman.

sergeant/sergeant at arms/sergeant first class/sergeant major woman or man.

serve two masters *serve God and mammon, have divided loyalties, be torn in two.*

serviceman (military) *service member, member of the service; servicewoman and serviceman* if used gender-fairly.

serviceman (repair) *servicer, service contractor, repairer, technician, maintenance/repair worker.*

service wives *military/soldiers'/service members' spouses.* These are inclusive terms that are also used for men married to servicewomen.

session man (music recording sessions) *session player/musician, free-lance musician; session man and session woman* if used gender-fairly.

set-up man *set-up mechanic/operator, setter, preparer, press/kick press/ machine setter, setter mechanic/worker; denture mounter.*

sewing woman *tailor, mender, alterer, alterations expert, stitcher, garment worker/designer, fashion sewer, custom tailor, needleworker.*

sex see Appendix A for a discussion of the differences between sex and gender, a concept crucial to understanding and using inclusive language.

sex object use equally for men and women or not at all.

sex roles a nonsexist term, but most sexist writing and speaking is based on false ideas of sex roles. See Appendix A for a discussion of them.

sexton woman or man.

sexual assault/sexual harassment although these are nonsexist terms in themselves, a number of sexist attitudes, behaviors, and reactions surround them. The major offenses are to imply that the victims "asked for it," that they should have been flattered, and that it wasn't such a big deal anyway. These insidious assumptions make their way into the writings and speech of even those who think they are clear-sighted on the issue. Addressing these topics requires reasonable people to examine their material extra carefully.

sexual revolution "In the 1960s, any sex outside marriage was called the *Sexual Revolution,* a nonfeminist phrase that simply meant women's increased availability on men's terms. By the end of the seventies, feminism had brought more understanding that real liberation meant the power to make a choice; that sexuality, for women or men, should be neither forbidden nor forced" (Steinem 1983, p. 153).

shaman woman or man.

shamus although technically this could refer to either sex, it tends to be heard as masculine. Unfortunately, so do its nonsexist alternatives: *cop, copper, flatfoot, gumshoe, private eye, shadow,* *sleuth, tail.* Only when women fill more of these roles will we be able to perceive the terms as inclusive.

shantyman   *shanty dweller.*

shaver (little boy)   *See* little shaver.

sheikh/sheik   always a man. When you mean a man who is very attractive to women, use inclusive words: *heartthrob, knock-out, someone who is easy on the eyes.*

shepherdess   *shepherd.*

she wears the pants   avoid. *See* rule the roost.

shipman   *sailor. See also* seaman; shipmaster.

shipmaster   *ship captain/commander.*

shoeshine boy   *shoeshiner.*

shogun   always a man; no parallel for women.

shoot the bull   this phrase doesn't refer to the male animal, but is thought to come from "boule" meaning "fraud/deceit." However, to avoid its masculine feel, you could use *shoot the breeze. See also* gossip.

shop girl   *shop clerk/assistant/employee/manager/owner, salesclerk, clerk.*

shop steward   man or woman.

shoreman   *shorehand, dockworker, dockhand, stevedore, shoreworker, longshore worker, wharfworker, wharfhand.*

shovelbill/shovelman   *shoveler, shovel hand.*

showgirl   *dancer, performer, performing artist. See also* showman.

showman   *performer, entertainer, limelighter, razzle-dazzle/stage artist, theatrical person, exhibitionist, someone with a flair for the dramatic, ham, show manager/producer, impresario, showperson.* Note the differences between "showman" and "showgirl." Not only is there a nonparallel pair ("man/girl"), but the definitions show a profound inequality in station, prestige, and type of work.

showmanship   *showcraft, razzle-dazzle, performing/staging skills, production genius.* None of these terms carries the precise flavor of "showmanship." You may need to use the old show-don't-tell technique to get your point across.

shrew   *grouch, grumbler, crosspatch, faultfinder, fire-eater, complainer, pain in the neck, nitpicker, troublemaker, bad-tempered/peevish/ cranky/petulant person.* "Shrew" is reserved almost exclusively for women; avoid it.

shrinking violet   woman or man.

shylock   *loan shark, usurer, extortionist, shyster, moneylender, parasite.* The term "shylock" is not only sexist; it is offensive in its anti-Semitism. Avoid it.

sibyl   *prophet, fortuneteller* when you are using the term in a broad sense. (See Appendix A for the rationale on avoiding sex-linked metaphors, expressions, and figures.) Retain it in historical contexts where it emphasizes the significance and power of certain women or in present-day contexts where some women have found richness and validation in the concept.

sideman *member of the band/orchestra, band/orchestra player.* Or, be specific: *bassist, drummer, clarinetist, violinist,* etc.

sight-effects man *sight-effects specialist/technician.*

signalman *signaller.*

silk stocking district *posh neighborhood, wealthy/aristocratic area, deluxe section/fashionable part of town, the Gold Coast.*

simon-pure *pure, genuine, untainted, sterling, honest, truthful, pure-hearted, flawless, upright, highminded, reliable, real, veritable, authentic, exact, precise, credible, worthy.* See Appendix A for the rationale on avoiding sex-linked metaphors, expressions, and figures.

sins of the fathers are visited on the children, the *the sins of the parents are visited on the children* (if you can stand to use this expression in the first place).

sir "sir" and "dame" are parallel sex-specific titles for those raised to knighthood. And "sir" and "madam" are parallel and useful sex-specific terms for everyday social exchanges.

siren avoid. The picture here is of Woman luring Man to destruction—a stereotype that belittles both sexes. Use instead *tempter,* which at least implies the possibility of the temptee resisting the temptation— something that is not possible with a siren.

sissy *coward, weakling, pushover, wimp, doormat, easy mark, weak stick.* Avoid the term "sissy." Note that it comes from "sister" and is a negative term denoting excessive timidity, whereas "buddy" comes from "brother" and indicates a warm, close relationship. The word most often considered a pair with "sissy" is "tomboy," but since it has the masculine connotation, society is much more tolerant of so-called tomboy behavior than it is of so-called sissy behavior.

sister do not use "sister" as a form of address for a woman unless it is a title of respect for a religious (e.g., Sister Anne).

sisterhood *society, association, organization, social organization, common-interest group, kinship, shared kinship, companionship, friendship, comradeship, unity, community.* There are times when the sex-specific word "sisterhood" should be retained; it says something important to women. "Brotherhood" does not have the same effect because it has been used for so long as a false generic.

sisterly sometimes this is the precise word you want, but many times it should probably be replaced with a word that says more exactly what you mean: *affectionate, loving, open, warm, understanding, accepting, close,* etc.

skinflint man or woman.

skirt (referring to a woman) avoid; this turns a woman into an object, by inference a sex object. There is also no parallel for men.

sky-girl *flight attendant. See also* steward/stewardess.

skyjack *See* hijack/hijacker.

slagman *slag worker.*

slattern if you mean a prostitute, use *prostitute*. Otherwise use inclusive terms: *slovenly person, slob.*

slave girl "the glorification of forced sex under slavery, institutional rape, has been a part of our cultural heritage, feeding the egos of men while subverting the egos of women—and doing irreparable damage to healthy sexuality in the process" (Brownmiller 1975, p. 184). Avoid perpetuating the false notion that most women secretly enjoy being enslaved. Be sensitive to speech and writing that uses slave metaphors and references.

slugger woman or man.

slut *prostitute. See also* slattern.

smart aleck although this expression comes from the man's name Alexander and seems to be used more often of men than women, it is acceptable for both sexes. For alternatives that have no masculine associations, use *know-it-all, blowhard, egomaniac, braggart, big/swelled head, arrogant/conceited/mouthy person/ individual.*

sneaky Pete *cheap wine.* See Appendix A for the rationale on avoiding sex-linked metaphors, expressions, and figures.

snowman *snow figure/sculpture/creature, snowwoman* or *snowman* if it really is.

sob sister *sob story writer/journalist, yellow journalist, advice columnist, bleeding heart.*

socman *See* sokeman.

socmanry *socage.*

soda jerk man or woman, girl or boy.

sokeman *tenant, landholder.* Use "sokeman" in historical contexts to refer to an individual male landholder by socage.

soldier man or woman.

soldier of fortune generally a man.

soldier-statesman *soldier-politician/-diplomat/-lawmaker.*

solicitor woman or man.

solon *See* statesman for alternatives. Also, see Appendix A for the rationale on avoiding sex-linked metaphors, expressions, and figures.

sommelier *wine steward/waiter.* "Sommelier" has been associated with men only, but there is a long tradition of using male-gender French words for both sexes in English, so there is nothing to say a sommelier couldn't be a woman.

sonarman *sonar technician.*

songbird *singer.*

songster/songstress *singer.*

sonny avoid this patronizing and sexist (there is no parallel expression for girls/women) term.

son of a bitch avoid. This insult actually reflects on someone's mother. When you need an interjection or exclamation, use *son of a gun! doggone! doggone it! rats! shoot! damn! good grief!* There is generally no dearth of good swear words; replacing this expression is a matter of choice. When you want to refer to a person this way, use *devil, stinker, creep, louse, bum, lowlife, jerk, cheat, shyster, crook.* When describing a difficult job or situation, use *a tough one.*

Son of Man (referring to Christ) In the original phrase, which meant simply "member of the human race," the intent was to emphasize the humanity as well as the divinity of Christ. Christ describes himself often with the phrase, underscoring its profound significance, and those rendering "Son of Man" inclusively will want to find a way to express "member of the human race" in a way that is theologically correct, scripturally sound, and acceptable to congregations as well as to hierarchies. For many reasons this is a difficult phrase to change, but there do exist several acceptable alternatives: *the One who became human/flesh, Son/Child of the People, the Incarnate One, Son of Humanity/Humankind, the One made human/flesh, one of you.*

sons ("generic") *children, heirs, offspring, progeny, daughters and sons/ sons and daughters.*

sonship *parent-child relationship.* There does not seem to be an inclusive alternative for "sonship" that captures the fullness (or would-be fullness if it were inclusive) of this word. Until some creative mind comes up with a pithy inclusive word, circumlocution is the best bet.

sons of God *daughters and sons/sons and daughters of God, children of God.* "Children of God," although more attractive because of its brevity, is not always the best choice because of the difference in meaning between "children" and "adult children."

sons of man *children/daughters and sons of humanity/humankind, daughters and sons/children of the earth, our children/sons and daughters.*

sorceress *sorcerer.*

soubrette leave as is; this is a fairly well-defined role on stage and in the opera. There is, however, no parallel for a man.

soul brother/soul sister use gender-fairly.

sound-effects man *sound-effects specialist/technician.*

sound man *sound controller.*

sow wild oats both men and women do this.

spaceman *astronaut, cosmonaut, member of the space program/space exploration team, space explorer/traveler/aviator/ranger, celestial navigator, astronavigator, spacewoman and spaceman; extra-terrestrial, person from outer space.*

spearman *spear thrower.*

special-effects man *special-effects technician.*

spend money like a drunken sailor *throw money around, squander one's money, spend foolishly/extravagantly/outrageously/lavishly/ imprudently/immoderately.* This phrase is to be avoided because of its masculine overtones and because it unnecessarily vilifies today's sailors who do not fit the old stereotype.

sperm donor a legitimate sex-specific term.

spinster if you need to refer to a person's marital status and sex, use *unmarried woman, single woman.* However, these terms, as well as *single person, single,* are better avoided. They perpetuate the marriage-as-norm stereotype, and too often the information is unnecessary or irrelevant. Note the positive connotations of the word "bachelor," q.v., and the negative connotations of the word "spinster."

spoilsman *spoils advocate, supporter of the spoils system.*

spokesman *speaker, representative, advocate, proponent, voice, agent, press agent, proxy, stand-in, mouthpiece, intermediary, mediator, medium, go-between, negotiator, arbitrator, speechmaker, keynoter; spokesman and spokeswoman* if used gender-fairly. Avoid "spokesperson." It is awkward and contrived, and it is generally used only for women.

sponsor man or woman.

spoonerism switching the initial sounds of two or more words ("half-warmed fish" for "half-formed wish" and "one swell foop" for "one fell swoop") results in a spoonerism, named after Oxford educator William A. Spooner. Although the term is thus sex-linked, there exists no substitute and "spoonerism" should be retained. A sort of sexual linguistic balance exists thanks to Mrs. Malaprop and the term that describes her own brand of confusion: malapropism, q.v.

sportfisherman *sportfishing boat.*

sport of kings *royal/noble sport.*

sportsman *sports lover, sports/outdoor enthusiast, athlete, gamester, gambler, honorable competitor, good sport, honest/fair player; sportswoman and sportsman* if used gender-fairly. Or, be specific: *angler, hunter, tennis player, canoer, ballplayer, golfer,* etc.

sportsmanlike/sportsmanly *sporting.*

sportsmanship *fair play, sporting behavior, being a good sport, playing fair.*

sportsman's license *sporting/sports license.*

spot man *spotter.*

spouse woman or man. "Spouse" has had a straightforward history; it has always referred to the marriage partner of either sex. Use it rather than "husband" or "wife" when the sex of the person is irrelevant to your material.

spy man or woman.

squadron commander/squadron leader woman or man.

squaw/squaw man these terms may be sexist, racist, and incorrect; be sensitive to their connotations and use them only in historical, scholarly—not casual—writing and speech. *See also* red man.

squire (noun) always a man; there is no parallel for a woman.

squire (verb) *accompany, escort* (used of either a man or a woman).

stableboy/stableman *stable hand/attendant.*

staff officer/staff sergeant/staff sergeant major woman or man.

stage man *stagehand, stage manager.*

stand pat nonsexist; the "pat" is not a person.

starlet *neophyte/novice/rookie actor, rookie/young performer, tyro screen star, newcomer to the stage/screen, star.* Instead of "starlet," use whatever term you would use to refer to a male actor at the same level of professional competence.

statesman *political/world/government leader, diplomat, legislator, politician, political/government strategist, public servant; stateswoman and statesman* if used gender-fairly.

statesmanlike/statesmanly *diplomatic, politically savvy.*

statesmanship *statecraft, diplomacy, government/world leadership, leadership.*

stationmaster *station manager.*

steeplejack this term comes from the man's name, and there seems to be no inclusive term to replace it. Use it for both men and women.

steersman *pilot, steersmate.*

stenographer woman or man.

stepmother, wicked save for old fairy tales; do not write any new ones using this phrase. It is sexist because there is no highly developed wicked stepfather persona.

sterile/sterility there is nothing sexist about these words, which are used gender-fairly of both men and women. *See also* barren; infertile/infertility.

sternson nonsexist; from a Scandinavian word that has nothing to do with a male offspring.

stevedore nonsexist; comes from the Spanish word meaning "to pack."

steward/stewardess *flight attendant, crew member.* Plural: *flight crew.*

steward (keeper) man or woman.

stickman (gambling) *casino employee, stick/craps boss.*

stickman (sports) *stick player.* There is no substitute for this term in some games.

stiff upper lip, keep a *See* keep a stiff upper lip.

stillman (liquor) *distiller.*

stillman (oil) *refinery operator.*

stock boy/stock girl *stock/stockroom clerk/assistant, stock gatherer.*

stockman *rancher, cattle owner/raiser/breeder, sheep owner/raiser/breeder.*

storageman *storage agent.*

storeman *storekeeper.*

straight (referring to a heterosexual person) this term is acceptable to gay men, lesbians, and heterosexuals.

straight man *comedian, stooge, entertainer, the straight, comic's partner, feeder of straight lines.*

straw man *diversionary tactic, hoax, nonexistent problem, carefully set up just to be knocked down, front; red herring; nonentity, hot air, ineffectual person, weakling; sitting duck.*

streetwalker *prostitute.* See Appendix A for a discussion of our language on prostitution.

strident *harsh, jarring, raucous, dissonant, discordant, unharmonious, clashing, sharp.* "Strident" is more commonly heard today than it used to be, and its prime use is in describing women, particularly feminists. Because it has been used indiscriminantly and discriminatingly, it has become devalued and stereotypical and should be avoided.

stripper/striptease artist/stripteaser woman or man.

strongarm man *the muscle, strongarm guard, bodyguard.*

strongman *dictator, tyrant, military dictator.*

strumpet *prostitute.* See Appendix A for a discussion of our language on prostitution.

stud (man) *sexual athlete, promiscuous person.* **See also** ladies' man; man about town; playboy; rake; womanize/womanizer/womanizing. The street use of "stud" to refer casually to any man or young man is probably here for awhile.

stuffed shirt this term is acceptable for both sexes, but you may prefer more neutral-sounding alternatives: *big head, someone who is pleased with oneself, prig, person who is stuck-up/conceited/smug/self-important/parochial/provincial/supercilious/snobbish/puffed-up/complacent/self-satisfied.*

stunt woman/stunt man *stunt performer, professional acrobat, daredevil, breakneck.* "Stunt woman" and "stunt man" are acceptable if used gender-fairly.

subassemblyman *subassembler.*

subkingdom retain this biology term as it is.

submissive use cautiously with reference to women. Consider whether your usage makes certain false assumptions. Justification for submissiveness as a "natural" attitude for women has often been based on the biblical injunction for wives to be submissive to their husbands. That this use of "submissive" may have arisen from factors in the mid-Eastern culture of the first centuries A.D. or from subsequent translations is sometimes not taken into account.

suffragette *suffragist.* Although women in Great Britain chose to call themselves "suffragettes," American women did not want the "-ette" ending that indicated a sub-species ("majorette," "usherette," "farmerette," etc.) and were called "suffragettes" only by those periodicals and speakers who were hostile to the women's goals. The difference between "suffragist" and "suffragette" can be seen in the dictionary definitions where a "suffragist" is "one who advocates extension of suffrage esp. to women" and a "suffragette" is "a woman who advocates suffrage for her sex" (*Webster's Ninth New Collegiate Dictionary.* Springfield, MA: Merriam-Webster, 1985). **See also** suffragist.

suffragist this is an inclusive term that may describe anyone who works for the voting rights of others, especially women's. Most often, however, "suffragist" is assumed to refer to a woman. For example, Mark Twain wrote of suffragists: "For forty years they have swept an imposingly large number of unfair laws from the statute books of America. In this brief time these serfs have set themselves free—essentially. Men could not have done as much for themselves in that time without bloodshed, at least they never have, and that is an argument that they didn't know how" (quoted in Fawcett 1912).

sugar daddy avoid. Note that there is no word in the language to describe a woman who supports a younger man.

suitor in affairs of the heart, this term has traditionally been reserved for men. Today, it is not so much the case that women may also be suitors as that the term is no longer necessary because forming a relationship tends to be a mutual activity. No longer is one person the supplicant, the pursuer, while the other is the "sued."

superhero/superheroine these denizens of popular comic book/strip genres might seem to be equals, but as long as "heroine" is defined as "a female hero," she is a subset and thus the lesser of the two. The ideal would be to call all such characters "superheroes." There is at least one tradition supporting female heroes: Although the word "hero" is the masculine form of its Greek root word, one of Greek mythology's best known couples was Hero and Leander, and Hero was *not* the man.

superman/superwoman *superhero.* However, these are fairly equivalent and useful gender-specific terms, and they can be used as they are.

surrogate mother a legitimate sex-specific word.

suttee in this Indian rite, widows were ceremoniously burned alive on their husbands' funeral pyres. Be certain you fully understand the rite if you choose to refer to it. For an excellent discussion of this custom from a feminist viewpoint, see Mary Daly, *Gyn/Ecology* (Boston: Beacon Press, 1978), pp. 113–33.

swagman *vagrant.*

swain *admirer.* "Swain" comes from "swein" meaning "boy" or "servant." *See also* boyfriend; girlfriend; suitor.

swami this word comes from the Hindi and means "owner, lord," and is perceived as being exclusively male. Unless you are using it in its narrowest sense, substitute *teacher, religious teacher, ascetic, pundit, seer, mentor, leader, guide, spiritual guide.*

swashbuckler this term seems ineradicably associated with men, although there have been women who have behaved like swashbucklers, among them pirates Anne Bonney, Mary Read, and Grania O'Malley and the French daredevil Marie Marvingt. Use instead *daredevil, adventurer, sensation-seeker, thrill-seeker, show-off, exhibitionist, fire-eater.*

swear like a trooper *turn the air blue, cuss a blue streak, curse up hill and down dale/up one side and down the other, badmouth.* Troopers include both women and men now, but the phrase retains a strong male tone, which is why alternatives are suggested.

sweater girl if it is necessary to describe a woman in terms of her voluptuousness, use adjectives ("curvaceous," "well-built," "voluptuous") instead of a noun so that a piece of clothing (emphasizing one *part* of a woman) does not become the *whole* woman ("sweater girl" implies a great deal more than what the woman looks like: it also hints at her lifestyle, her intelligence, etc., all on the basis of how she looks in a sweater). Avoid making an issue of a woman's physical appearance more often than you do for a man.

sweetheart woman or man.

sweet sixteen (and never been kissed) as this always refers to a young woman, it is sexist. Avoid it. No sixteen-year-old wants to hear it anyway.

sweet william leave as is.

switchman *switcher, technical equipment operator/technician, switching equipment technician/operator.*

swordsman *sword fighter, fencer; swordswoman and swordsman* if used gender-fairly.

swordsmanship *fencing/sword fighting skills/expertise.*

t

Our native language is like a second skin, so much a part of us we resist the idea that it is constantly changing, constantly being renewed.

Casey Miller and Kate Swift

tailor woman or man.

take it like a man *meet/confront with courage/bravery/valor/boldness, put on a bold face, bear up against, hold up one's head, screw one's courage to the sticking point, look in the face, nerve oneself, make bold, hold out against, take heart, defy, have plenty of backbone, meet danger/trouble head on, come up to scratch, face the music.*

talesman *substitute juror.*

talisman nonsexist; this word developed from Greek to Arabic to the modern Romance languages from a word meaning "consecration."

talk to like a Dutch uncle *talk to bluntly, rebuke, upbraid, admonish, admonish sternly, chide, reprove, reprimand, reproach, scold, chew out, lecture, lay down the law, remonstrate, rake over the coals.*

tallboy nonsexist; "boy" comes from the French word for wood, "bois."

tallyman *tally keeper.*

tapman *taproom attendant.*

tart *prostitute.* See Appendix A for a discussion of our language on prostitution.

taskmaster/taskmistress *supervisor, boss, job boss, disciplinarian, inspector, instructor, overseer, monitor, martinet, surveyor, superintendent, director, manager, employer.*

taximan *taxi driver.*

teach one's grandmother to suck eggs *teach a bird to fly/fish to swim, reinvent the wheel, take coals to Newcastle.*

tease (referring to a woman) avoid.

technical sergeant man or woman.

tegmen nonsexist; from the Latin word for "covering."

teleman *communications officer; petty officer in charge of communications or petty officer, communications; sparks.*

tell it to the marines this is nonsexist since marines are now both women and men. Or use: *pull the other one.*

temptress *tempter.*

tenderfoot woman or man.

termagant *loud, overbearing person, faultfinder, grouch, grumbler, crosspatch, fire-eater.* Avoid this word as it is reserved for women and there is no parallel word for men. *See also* shrew.

testatrix *testator.* "Testatrix" is still used for certain legal matters, however.

thinking man *thinker, thinking/reflective/intelligent/learned person, thinking/intelligent being, intellectual, philosopher, sage, scholar, brain, highbrow.*

thresherman *thresher.*

thug man or woman.

ticket girl *ticket taker, pricing clerk.*

tied to [someone's] apron strings *dependent/overly dependent on, clinging, immature, timid, youthful, hang on the sleeve of, dance attendance on, can't make a move without, no mind of one's own.*

tillerman *tiller, tiller operator.*

timberman *timber cutter/worker, logger, tree cutter, woodcutter, log roller; timberwoman and timberman* if used gender-fairly.

time waits for no man *time waits for no one.*

timothy grass leave as is.

tinker woman or man.

tinman *tinsmith.*

tirewoman *personal attendant.*

T-man *Treasury agent.*

toady man or woman.

to a man *without exception, unanimous, like-minded, of one mind/ accord, with one voice, every last one of them, everyone, at one with each other, willing, agreed on all hands, in every mouth, carried by acclamation/unanimously, to a one, to a man and to a woman.*

toastmaster/toastmistress these terms are difficult to replace as they have a very specific meaning and are deeply entrenched in the language because of the many toastmasters clubs around the country; when possible, replace with *speaker, lecturer, talker, guest lecturer, orator, declaimer, speechmaker, rhetorician, elocutionist, preacher, interlocuter.*

to each his own *to each their own* (see Appendix A for a discussion of singular "they"), *there's no accounting for tastes, it takes all kinds, chacun à son goût, to each her own/his own.*

toff an exclusive term referring to men only; there is no parallel for women.

tollman *toll collector, toll booth operator.*

tomato (referring to a woman) avoid. See Appendix A on using names of foods to refer to people.

tomboy *active/boisterous/adventurous/physically courageous/competitive child, live wire, strong/vigorous/direct/spirited/self-confident child, rude/blunt/messy/rough/tough child, logical/mechanically minded child,* etc. "Tomboy" used to refer just to a boy, then to both girls and boys, and now only to a girl. *See also* sissy.

Tom, Dick, and Harry, every *See* every Tom, Dick, and Harry.

tomfool (noun) *fool, blockhead, scatterbrain, rattlebrain, flake, dumbbell, meathead, bonehead, knucklehead.*

tomfool (adj.) *foolish, imprudent, irresponsible, unwise, hasty, shortsighted, foolhardy, reckless, pointless, nonsensical, cockeyed, ridiculous, silly, crazy, daft, simpleminded, scatterbrained, stupid, mindless, thick-witted.*

tomfoolery/tommyrot *foolishness, nonsense, rubbish, shenanigans, monkeyshines, monkey business, mischief, hanky-panky, trick, buffoonery, silliness, malarkey, baloney, poppycock, balderdash, moonshine, gobbledygook, garbage, stuff and nonsense, hogwash, bunkum, craziness, goofiness.*

Tommy leave as is for British soldier.

tommy gun nonsexist; submachine gun named after John T. Thompson.

Tom Thumb *hop-o'-my-thumb.* For the rationale on avoiding sex-linked metaphors, expressions, and figures, see Appendix A.

tom-tom nonsexist; comes from the Hindi word "tamtam."

too big for one's britches can be said of a woman or a man.

tootsie (referring to a woman) avoid.

top sergeant woman or man.

torch singer this has always been a female singer with a husky, passionate voice who has generally lost her man. The term may include in the future male singers in gay bars. An inclusive alternative (although it is not an exact synonym) is *blues singer.*

totem pole, high man on the/low man on the *See* high man on the totem pole; low man on the totem pole.

tough guy *toughy, tough.*

tout man or woman.

towerman *tower tender/operator/erector/attendant.*

townsman *town-dweller, local, native, resident, citizen, townie, city slicker, urbane person; townswoman and townsman* if used gender-fairly.

trackman *track layer/inspector, trackwalker; runner, track athlete/event entrant, athlete who competes in track events.*

tradesman *shopkeeper, store owner/manager/worker/employee, small business owner, merchant, retailer, dealer, tradesperson; tradeswoman and tradesman,* if used gender-fairly; *skilled worker.* Plural: *tradespeople.*

tradevman *training devices personnel.*

tragedienne *tragedian.*

trainman *train worker/operator/crew member, railroad employee, rail worker.*

traitress *traitor.*

tramp (hobo) woman or man.

tramp (referring to a woman) *prostitute.* See Appendix A for a discussion of our language on prostitution.

trashman *trash collector.*

traveling salesman *traveling sales agent/rep/salesperson, commercial traveler.*

trawlerman *trawler, trawler owner/operator.*

trencherman *hearty/heavy/serious eater; sponger, hanger-on.*

tribesman *tribe/tribal member, member of a tribe; tribeswoman and tribesman* if used gender-fairly. Use the word "tribe" only when referring to American Indian tribes; when applied to people living in the Third World, it is generally considered ethnocentric and racist.

trickmaster *trickster, magician, conjurer, illusionist, sleight-of-hand artist; hoodwinker, faker, cheat, imposter, swindler, fraud, bunko artist, charlatan, quack, sharpie.*

triggerman *professional/armed killer, killer, gangster, gun, hired gun, gunner, gunfighter, gunslinger, assassin, slayer, gun-wielder/-toter, sharpshooter, sniper, attacker, outlaw, bank robber, bandit, terrorist, racketeer, mobster, hoodlum, cutthroat, liquidator; triggerwoman and triggerman* if used gender-fairly.

trollop *prostitute.* See Appendix A for a discussion of our language on prostitution.

trooper man or woman.

troop sergeant an outdated term, but if used today it could refer to a woman or a man; if using it in a historical context, it was undoubtedly a man.

troubadour woman or man. For more on the little-known women troubadours, see Meg Bogin, *The Women Troubadours* (New York: Norton, 1976).

truck driver man or woman (two percent are women).

truckman *trucker, truck driver; ladder truck firefighter.*

truckmaster historically always a man.

trull *prostitute.* See Appendix A for a discussion of our language on prostitution.

trustee woman or man.

turfman *racetrack regular, horseracing/track fan, devotee of horseracing.*

tutoress *tutor.*

twerp man or woman, girl or boy.

two-man (adj.) *See* one-man/two-man/three-man, etc. (adj.).

tycoon woman or man.

typist man or woman.

Let us be very clear on this matter: if we condemn people to inequality in our society we also condemn them to inequality in our economy.

Lyndon B. Johnson

ugly customer (dangerous person) man or woman.
ugly duckling woman or man.
umpire man or woman.
unbrotherly replace this vague term with words that convey your meaning precisely: *unkind, cold, uncaring, unfeeling, uncharitable, hostile, distant,* etc.
Uncle Sam leave as is. While some countries are personified by men (England's John Bull, for example), others are personified by women (France's Marianne).
uncle, say *See* say uncle.
Uncle Tom it is probably better to forego this term entirely; you may know exactly what you mean by it but your audience may not. As well as being sexist (there is no equivalent for a woman), it can be highly racist as well in many contexts. Gender-nonspecific substitutes include: *sycophant, collaborator, subservient/obsequious person, traitor to one's race, backscratcher, bootlicker.*
underclassman *undergraduate.* Or, be specific: *first-year student, sophomore, junior, senior.* **See also** freshman.
underlord *second in command, subordinate.*
undomestic a nonsexist word in itself, but sometimes used in sexist ways. Give it another look.
unfeminine avoid this vague, self-contradictory cultural stereotype. A woman's clothes, behavior, words, feelings, and thoughts are, by definition, "feminine" because a woman is wearing them, saying them, feeling them, etc. Words such as "womanly/unwomanly," "manly/unmanly," "feminine/unfeminine," "masculine/ unmasculine," "ladylike/unladylike," and "gentlemanly/ ungentlemanly" are based on cultural, not biological, givens. If a woman's behavior is labeled unfeminine, it is society, not biology,

that makes an entirely subjective judgment about what a woman may or may not do. Language should not underwrite this sort of illogic. The only truly unfeminine things that can be imputed to a woman are things she is incapable of doing—those things biologically reserved to men. If you find yourself wanting to use "unfeminine," try to pin down the characteristics you need to describe: *cold, hard, selfish, abrupt, analytical, direct, squarish,* etc. Note that these adjectives can apply equally well to a man. For an explanation of the difference between gender and sex, see Appendix A.

ungentlemanly *See* unmasculine for an explanation of the subjective cultural meanings attached to this word. Zero in on the characteristics you are trying to describe with the word "ungentlemanly," for example: *impolite, crude, rude, insensitive, thoughtless, discourteous, poorly behaved, ill-mannered, uncivil, disagreeable, inconsiderate,* etc. Note that these adjectives can apply equally well to a woman. For an explanation of the difference between gender and sex, see Appendix A.

Union Jack (British flag) leave as is.

union man *union member, labor/trade unionist, unionist, member of a union; union woman and union man* if used gender-fairly.

Unknown Soldier, the this World War I soldier was a man.

unladylike *See* unfeminine for an explanation of the subjective cultural meanings attached to this word. Clarify for yourself and your audience the precise characteristics you are trying to describe with the word "unladylike": *insensitive, indelicate, awkward, uncharming, unkind, rude, undignified, ill-mannered, ungracious, impolite, abrupt,* etc. Note that these adjectives apply equally well to a man. For an explanation of the difference between gender and sex, see Appendix A.

unman *unnerve, frighten, disarm, disable, deprive of courage/strength/ vigor, appall, horrify, petrify, terrorize, incapacitate, deprive of power, undermine, paralyze, unhinge, draw the teeth of, render hors de combat, devitalize, attenuate, weaken, shatter, exhaust, disqualify, invalidate, muzzle, enervate, tie the hands of, spike the guns of, take the wind out of one's sails, clip the wings of, put a spoke in one's wheel, undo.* In the narrower sense of emasculate or castrate, use "unman" sparingly as it often implies, unflatteringly, that the man is a passive victim. Note that there is no parallel term referring to women for such words as "unman," "emasculate," and "castrate."

unmanliness/unmanly *See* unmasculine for an explanation of the subjective cultural meanings attached to these words. Identify the characteristics you are trying to describe: *dishonesty/dishonest, cowardice/cowardly, deviousness/crooked, weakness/weak, fearfulness/fearful, timidity/timid,* etc. Note that these words can be applied equally well to a woman. For an explanation of the difference between gender and sex, see Appendix A.

unmanned *unstaffed, having no staff aboard, unpeopled, uninhabited, lacking crew, crewless, remote control, on automatic pilot; frightened, undone.* **See also** unman.

unmasculine avoid this vague, self-contradictory cultural stereotype. A man's clothes, behavior, words, feelings, and thoughts are, by definition, masculine because a man is wearing them, saying them, feeling them, etc. Words such as "womanly/unwomanly," "manly/unmanly," "feminine/unfeminine," "masculine/unmasculine," "ladylike/unladylike," and "gentlemanly/ungentlemanly" are based on cultural, not biological, givens. If a man's behavior is labeled unmasculine, it is society, not biology, that makes an entirely subjective judgment about what a man may or may not do. Language should not underwrite this sort of illogic. The only truly unmasculine things that can be imputed to a man are things he is incapable of doing—those things biologically reserved to women. If you find yourself wanting to use "unmasculine," try to pin down the characteristics you need to describe: *timid, craven, weak, indirect, fearful, soft, faint-hearted, gentle, overemotional, comfort-loving,* etc. Note that all these adjectives can apply equally well to a woman. For an explanation of the difference between gender and sex, see Appendix A.

unsportsmanlike *unsporting, unfair, unfair play/playing, unsporting behavior, behavior of a poor loser.*

unstatesmanlike *undiplomatic, impolitic, imprudent, lacking grace and diplomacy, showing poor political strategy/ineffective government leadership.*

unwed mother *mother, woman, head of household, single parent.* **See also** housewife; working mother/wife/woman.

unwomanly **See** unfeminine for an explanation of the subjective cultural meanings attached to this word. Clarify for yourself and your audience the precise characteristics you are trying to describe with "unwomanly": *cold, hostile, sharp, unloving, ungentle, uncharming, ungiving, unsupportive, ill-mannered, unmannerly, ungracious, undignified, indecorous, unattractive, unappealing,* etc. Note that these adjectives apply equally well to a man. For an explanation of the difference between gender and sex, see Appendix A.

unworkmanlike replace this vague word with a word or words that convey exactly what you want to say: *unprofessional, unskillful, unskilled, inexpert, inexperienced, untrained, inefficient, unsystematic, unbusinesslike, incompetent, sloppy, careless, unsuitable, unhandy, imprecise, unproficient,* etc.

upperclassman *junior, senior, upperclass student, third-year/fourth-year student.*

usherette *usher.*

utility girl/utility man *utility worker/hand/cleaner, typewriter repairer.* Note the nonparallel "girl/man."

V

The beginning of wisdom is the definition of terms.

Socrates

Valentino *heartthrob, great/dashing lover, paramour.* For the rationale on avoiding sex-linked metaphors, expressions, and figures, see Appendix A.

valet *personal attendant.*

valet de chambre *room attendant.*

vamp (referring to a woman) *seducer.* Short for "vampire," this term emphasizes the seductiveness of women and the helplessness of men, which does a disservice to both of them. There is no term like "vamp" for a man.

varlet historically varlets were always young men. Alternatives include: *attendant, menial, page.*

vassal woman or man. Although taken to mean a man, this word is actually defined as "a servant, slave, dependent, or subordinate," and historically it included all members of the household of the feudal tenant, male and female.

vegetable man *vegetable peddler/vendor.*

venireman *venire member.*

venturesome can refer to a woman or a man.

verger man or woman.

verseman *versifier, poet, maker of verses.*

vestryman *vestry member, member of the vestry.*

veteran man or woman.

vicar depending on the denomination, a vicar may be a woman or a man.

vice admiral man or woman.

vice-chairman *vice-chair, second in command, deputy, deputy director, vice-president.* Use "vice-chairperson" rarely, if ever.

viceroy this has traditionally been a males-only rank. The "roy" comes from the French "roi" for "king."

victory for mankind *victory for the world, victory for humankind/all peoples/everyone, our common victory.*

victress *victor.*

vigilante woman or man.

villainess *villain.*

virago most people asked to define this word would remember only its first dictionary definition ("a loud, overbearing woman: termagant"). Its second definition is "a woman of great stature, strength, and courage" (*Webster's Ninth New Collegiate Dictionary.* Springfield, MA: Merriam-Webster, 1985) and as such has been reclaimed by some members of the women's movement.

virgin/virginity use for both men and women. Be sensitive to the double standard that still expects virginity or at least some measure of virginal behavior from women while rewarding men in subtle and unsubtle ways for being experienced.

virgin forest/virgin soil, etc. use these terms as they are, although you might want sometimes to use *unspoiled, untouched, pristine.*

virile this is a properly sex-specific word when it refers to a man's ability to function sexually. In its broader sense, alternatives that can refer to both sexes should be used: *energetic, vigorous, forceful, strong, powerful, dynamic, spirited, daring, fearless, venturesome, courageous, intrepid, tough, audacious, dashing, potent, hardy, hearty, rugged, bold.*

virtue virtue for a woman has most often been defined by her chastity, while for men it has always been far more free-ranging and has included such "manly" attributes as valor, courage, and a sense of morality. When using the word "virtue," assign it in its broadest sense equally to women and to men, and be sensitive to subtle imbalances in your context.

visiting fireman *visiting firefighter.*

visual-effects man *visual-effects specialist/technician.*

vizier has always been a man.

votaress *votary.*

voyageur history records only male voyageurs—employees of the fur companies who transported goods and travelers to and from outpost stations.

voyeur man or woman.

W

Whatever you want to say, there is only one word that will express it; one verb to make it move; one adjective to qualify it. You must seek that word, that verb, and that adjective, and never be satisfied with approximations, never resort to tricks, even clever ones, or to verbal pirouettes to escape the difficulty.

Gustave Flaubert

wage earner woman or man.

waitress *waiter, server, table server.* Also used in some areas: *wait, waitron, waitperson.*

wallflower (referring to a woman) avoid; there is no parallel for a man, and the origins of the phrase reflect outdated customs and attitudes.

Walter Mitty *daydreamer, escapist, secret adventurer.* See Appendix A for the rationale on avoiding sex-linked metaphors, expressions, and figures.

wanton can describe both men and women, but use sparingly, objectively, and gender-fairly. It is more correct to describe behavior as wanton than to describe a person as wanton.

war bride sexist; where are the war grooms? There may, however, be times when it is correct to use this phrase in certain historical contexts.

warden man or woman.

warder woman or man.

wardress *warden.*

warehouseman *warehouse operator, warehouser.*

war hawk man or woman.

warlock *witch; conjurer, sorcerer, magician.* Because "witch" and "warlock" are strong, evenly balanced, and not particularly sex-biased words, they may be retained even though they are sex-linked.

warlord *supreme military leader, military leader/commander.*

warmonger woman or man.

warpaint (referring to a woman's makeup) avoid.

warrant officer man or woman.

washerman/washerwoman *launderer, cleaner, drycleaner.*

washwoman *See* washerman/washerwoman.

watchman *watch, guard, security guard, guardian, sentry, sentinel, lookout, caretaker, keeper, custodian; crossing tender/guard; patroller, patrol.*

watchman's rattle *sentry's/lookout's rattle, alarm, warning, distress/ danger signal.*

waterboatman (bug) leave as is.

water boy *water carrier.*

waterman *boater, ferry/watercraft operator.*

watermanship replace this vague word with a more specific one: *swimming/boating/rowing/sailing/water sports skills, canoeing expertise,* etc. Or, reword to describe the person with these skills: *competent swimmer, professional boater, skilled canoeist, veteran rower, proficient/expert/talented/knowledgeable/skillful swimmer/ boater,* etc.

water witch *water dowser.*

way to a man's heart is through his stomach, the *the quickest way to the heart is through the stomach, the way to the heart is through the stomach, the way to a person's heart is through their stomach* (see Appendix A for a discussion of singular "they").

weaker sex, the avoid.

weak sister *weak link in the chain, weak reed to lean on, weak spot, weakling, one who blows hot and cold, unreliable/untrustworthy/ half-hearted/wishy-washy/fickle person, someone who is weak as a child/weak as water.* Although this term is used to refer (very unflatteringly) to both men and women and is thus in that sense gender-fair, the underlying assumption is extremely prejudicial to women.

wear the pants (woman assuming "masculine" role) avoid; outdated both in form and content.

weathergirl/weatherman *meteorologist, weather reporter/forecaster/ prophet, weathercaster, forecaster, climatologist; weatherwoman and weatherman* if used gender-fairly. Note the nonparallel "girl/man."

weighmaster *public weigher, licensed public weigher.* Sometimes it is necessary to use "weighmaster" because it is an official job title with no inclusive equivalent.

weightlifter man or woman.

welfare mother *welfare client/recipient.*

Welshman *inhabitant of Wales; Welshman and Welshwoman* if used gender-fairly. Plural: *the Welsh, people of Wales, Welshwomen and Welshmen.* It's generally not possible to replace words like "Welshman," "Norseman," "Irishman," and "Dutchman" with one pithy inclusive term; either circumlocute or use the complete phrases: "Welshwoman and Welshman/Welshmen and Welshwomen."

wench   in the earlier, historical sense of the word ("a young woman" or "a female servant"), use it as is. If you mean prostitute, use *prostitute.*

wet nurse   this is a legitimate gender-specific word.

whaleman   *whaler.*

wharfman   *wharfworker, wharfhand, dockhand, dockworker, stevedore, shoreworker, shorehand, longshore worker.*

wharfmaster   *wharfinger.*

what evil lurks in the hearts of men?   *what evil lurks in our/people's/ human hearts? what evil lurks in the hearts of humans?*

whatman   nonsexist; named after James Whatman.

whatsoever a man sows, that shall he also reap   *whatsoever you sow, that too shall you reap; whatever we sow we will also reap.*

wheelman   *cyclist.*

wheelsman   *pilot, steerer, navigator.*

whine   although not sexist per se, this word is functionally sexist since it is used primarily of women and children, while in similar circumstances men are said to complain, criticize, or just plain talk. Use instead *complain, grumble, grouse, gripe, criticize, harp on, fume, find fault, be dissatisfied, pester, harass, irritate, fuss, raise a fuss. **See also** bitch (verb); nag (verb).*

whipping boy   *scapegoat, victim, target, dupe, tool, goat.* In the historical sense, use as is; it always was a boy.

whirling dervish   woman or man.

white girl   (drugs) *cocaine.*

whore/whoredom/whorehouse   *prostitute/prostitution/house of prostitution.* "Whore" used to be a nonjudgmental term describing a lover of either sex. See Appendix A for a discussion of our language on prostitution.

widow/widower   *surviving spouse.* It may occasionally be necessary to specify "widow" or "widower" for clarity. The ideal would be to have one word instead of two to describe a surviving spouse— "widow" preferably since it is the shorter, base word. Notice, incidentally, that "widower" is one of the very few male words in the language that is the marked term—that is, the female word is the unmarked or "normal" word and the male word is based on it.

widow lady   *surviving spouse, widow.*

widow's mite   *one's last cent/dime, giving of one's all, giving out of one's need, giving till it hurts.* For the rationale on avoiding sex-linked metaphors, expressions, and figures, see Appendix A.

widow's peak   this appears irreplaceable by an equally concise and descriptive term.

wife/wifehood/wifelike/wifeliness/wifely   "wife" is a perfectly acceptable word in itself. The simplest and most neutral explanation of its derivation traces it to a general Germanic term meaning "woman," that is, "female human being" (Baron 1986, p. 37). It is sometimes used, however, in very sexist ways. The best test is to see if you would use "husband" in a similar situation. Very often the use of "wife" is gratuitous and does not advance your story or your information. Our ideas of "wifelike," "wifely," "wifeliness," and "wifehood" are entirely dependent on subjective cultural stereotypes. Replace these terms with words that are gender-nonspecific, precise, and descriptive. For example, for "wifely" use *companionable, helpful, supportive, sympathetic, sensitive, affectionate, intimate, loving, approving, admonishing,* etc. Note that these words would do equally well for "husbandly." ***See also*** woman.

wife/husband *spouse,* unless gender-specific language is necessary. One of the most glaring unbalanced gender pairs in the language is "man and wife." Use instead "woman and man/man and woman," "wife and husband/husband and wife."

wife-beater *spouse-abuser/-beater.* Sometimes it is good to retain "wife-beater" to emphasize the nature of this crime, which tends to be almost entirely directed against women.

wife-swapping *spouse-swapping.*

wimp woman or man.

winchman *wincher.*

wing commander man or woman.

wingman *flyer.* "Wingman" is used in the Air Force for either a woman or a man. ***See also*** airman.

wingmanship *flying skills/expertise.* ***See also*** airmanship.

wino woman or man.

win one's spurs this expression has strong masculine overtones, probably because knights were given golden spurs for their exploits. Use instead *earn one's wings, come of age, triumph, succeed, arrive, make a hit, pull it off, carry the day, come off with flying colors, have it all one's own way, have the world at one's feet, turn up trumps, have one's star in the ascendant.*

wireman *wirer.*

wise as Balaam's ass/wise as Solomon *wise as an owl/a serpent/a judge.* For the rationale on avoiding sex-linked metaphors, expressions, and figures see Appendix A.

wise father that knows his own child, it is a *See* it is a wise father that knows his own child.

wise man/wise woman *wise person/one, elder, leader, sage, philosopher, oracle, mentor, luminary, learned person, pundit, scholar, savant, authority, expert, guru, thinker.* At times, "wise man" or "wise woman" will be indicated; these are currently used gender-fairly.

wish is father to the thought, the/the wish being father to the thought *the wish gives birth to/begets/engenders/brings forth/precedes/ produces the thought.*

witch woman or man. Avoid any pejorative use, and be careful of writing or speaking about today's witches if you are not knowledgeable about their lifestyles and beliefs.

wizard a wizard is generally a man. For more inclusive terms use *sorcerer, magician, conjurer, witch.*

wolf (referring to a man) *flirt, seducer, someone who comes on strong.*
woman the Old English word from which "woman" is taken
("wif-man") came from "wif" ("woman") plus "man" ("human
being"). What happened was that women continued to be "female
human beings," which is fairly decent, but the word for "male
human beings" ("wer-man") was gradually lost (it survives only in
"werewolf") and men got to be human beings, period, full stop, no
qualifications for sex. Although suggestions are made from time to
time to replace the word "woman," it appears to be well
entrenched in the language. What is more crucial today than
where the word came from is how it is perceived. And
functionally "woman" is a respected, acceptable term that can be
used anywhere, any time, any place, as long as the context in
which it appears is not sexist or exclusive.
woman (adj.) avoid using "woman" if you would not use "man" in a
parallel situation—for example, "a woman driver" or "a woman
scientist" is a no-no.
woman-hater *misogynist/misanthrope, woman-hater/man-hater.* These
sex-specific terms are acceptable as long as they are used equally
frequently and in gender-fair ways.
womanhood both definitions of this word are acceptable—"the state of
being a woman" and "women or womenkind." Note that
"manhood" (q.v.) has *four* definitions, two of which are falsely
generic, the other two of which correspond to the two definitions
for "womanhood."
womanish avoid this vague and pejorative stereotype and use instead
words that more precisely describe the characteristics you want to
convey: *fussy, particular, overparticular, choosy, fastidious, anxious,
overanxious, worried, nervous, timid, weak, indecisive, unathletic,
vapid,* etc.
womanize/womanizer/womanizing *be promiscuous/sexually active/
sexually aggressive/indiscriminate; sensualist, swinger, free-lover,
freethinker, free spirit, voluptuary, sybarite, seducer, bedhopper,
lover; swinging, bedhopping, seducing, sleeping around.*
womankind *See* mankind. There may be a legitimate use for
"womankind" where there is not for "mankind" since "mankind"
is invariably misused as a generic whereas "womankind" refers to
a group composed entirely of women.
womanlike/womanliness/womanly avoid these vague stereotypes that
convey different meanings to different people according to their
perceptions of what a woman ought or ought not do, say, think,
feel, and look like. These judgments are subjective cultural
judgments that have nothing to do with sex and everything to do
with gender. Find instead words that express the characteristics
you want to describe: *gracious/graciousness, warm/warmth, gentle/
gentleness, receptive/receptivity, supportive/supportiveness, tender/
tenderness, charming/charm, sympathetic/sympathy, nurturing/
nurturance, well-mannered/good breeding, considerate/*

consideration, kind/kindness, intuitive/intuition, strong/gentle strength, etc. Note that all these words may be used equally appropriately of a man. See Appendix A for a discussion of the difference between gender and sex.

woman's place is in the home, a when a man's "place" is also in the home and when the woman truly wants to be there, this is a powerful sentiment. It also rings true if we substitute "heart" for "place" and apply it to both sexes. Unfortunately, this dictum has been used with all the finesse of a sledgehammer and promulgated as a "natural" law as well as a test of patriotism, "femininity," conjugal love, and right-thinking. Being physically at home is an excellent choice for many women and one that society ought to be more supportive of in terms of laws, financial arrangements, moral support, and practical assistance. The problem with this expression is that it has become a mandate for all women, and it ignores a man's involvement with the home. Do not use it unless you are sensitive to its use, history, and significance.

woman suffrage movement this term, which is the one used most often by historians, is a legitimate sex-specific phrase.

woman's work avoid this term except when referring to what goes on during childbirth; there is no other work biologically specific only to women. "[I]t is a retrogressive idea to call any particular sphere of work 'Women's'. We do not know what women's work will be, we only know what it has been" (Caroline Boord, *The Freewoman,* December 14, 1911, p. 70).

woman's work is never done, a neither is a man's, although in some homes and workplaces, this is still much truer for a woman.

women "Women are half the world's adult population. They comprise one-third of the paid labor force and they perform two-thirds of the world's work hours. For this they earn one-tenth of the world's income, but they only own one percent of the world's property" (United Nations Commission on the Status of Women, 1980). Sexist language both shapes and reflects statistics like these.

women and children avoid using these words together. Pairing women with children is inaccurate and belittling to women. It is also a paternalistic attempt to perpetuate the subordination and powerlessness of women.

women and children first *those who need extra assistance first; children, frail elderly, and infirm first.*

womenfolk OK when also using "menfolk." Otherwise use *folk, folks, people. See also* Man/man ("generic").

women's lib *women's liberation movement, women's movement, feminism, feminist movement.* The expression "women's lib" is trivializing and condescending; avoid it.

women's libber *feminist, supporter/member of the women's movement. See also* women's lib.

women's liberation *See* women's movement.

women's movement this term is not synonymous with "feminist movement" or with "women's liberation movement," although all three have much in common. The women's movement is a broad, generic grouping covering all issues that affect women. The emphasis in the women's liberation movement, which grew out of leftist politics in the 1960s, is the obvious one of liberation. The feminist movement, which has been around for several centuries at least, has had different focuses and is generally more politicized and radicalized than the women's movement. These definitions are inadequate; the caveat here is not to use the three terms interchangeably and to inform yourself about the differences before writing or speaking about these groups.

women's rights movement this movement commonly dates from 1848 when women met in Seneca Falls, New York, to draw up the first public protest in the United States against the political, social, and economic repression of women.

women's page(s), the (newspaper) there is no rationale for the inclusion of special pages aimed at one sex. The sports pages, even though many more men than women used to read them, were not labeled "the men's pages." What are now sometimes still called "the women's pages" might be designated instead *lifestyle, living section, health and fitness, modern living,* etc.

Wonder Woman Wonder Woman is not, as one might think, the female equivalent of Superman, Batman, or Tarzan. Cheris Kramarae (1980, pp. 85, 89) points out that Wonder Woman is an aberration rather than a super specimen of her gender. "She lives in a community that is dominated by women; however, there are no men living on her island. Even on the island, the queen is given insight, wisdom, and knowledge by two men from another world. All the women except Wonder Woman are spectators to the action of the story." Kramarae adds that this is not to belittle Wonder Woman's strength, magic, courage, and independence, and she recommends reading Gloria Steinem's essay of appreciation of the Wonder Woman comic of the 1940s in the introduction to *Wonderwoman,* a book of reprinted comics of the strip by Charles Moulton (New York: Holt, Rinehart and Winston, 1972).

woodsman *woodworker; forest dweller; woodswoman and woodsman* if used gender-fairly. It is difficult to replace "woodsman" (in the sense of someone who lives and works in the woods) with an inclusive substitute; circumlocution is probably the best solution.

working girl *See* career girl/career woman; working mother/wife/ woman.

working man *worker, employee, laborer, day laborer, jobholder, hand, artisan, average worker, wage earner, average wage earner, blue-collar worker, operator, agent, doer, performer, perpetrator, operative.* Or, be specific: *mechanic, librarian, bricklayer, electrician,* etc.

working mother/wife/woman *worker.* **See** working man for other
inclusive alternatives. Using phrases like "working mother,"
"working wife," or "working woman" to describe women who
work outside the home implies that women who work inside the
home do not really work. To describe the former use
*wage-earning/job-holding/salaried woman, woman employed
outside the home/in the paid workforce,* or her specific job title. To
describe the latter use *nonsalaried woman, woman working/
employed inside the home/at home.* If both partners work, avoid
gender-specific distinctions and describe the couple as *working
parents, a two-income/two-paycheck family, two-earner/dual-career/
dual-income couple.* "The great majority of wives are devoting
their time to unpaid work, and when the importance of the work
is considered, it appears extraordinary that the services of wives
have no money value placed on them. . . . A wife who works
diligently and devotedly to the family service should be entitled to
such wages of a servant or housekeeper as are usual in that station
of life in which she lives and this in addition to her board" (Lady
L. McLaren, 1908, quoted in Garner 1984, p. 15).

workman *artisan, worker.* **See also** handyman; odd-job(s)-man;
repairman; working man.

workmanlike/workmanly replace these vague words with a word or
words that convey exactly what you want to say: *skillful, expert,
professional, competent, careful, precise, proficient, first-rate,
top-flight,* etc.

workman quarrels with his tools, a bad *See* bad workman quarrels with
his tools, a.

workmanship *work, construction, handiwork, handicraft, artisanry,
artisanship, skilled-craft work, skill, technique, style, expertness,
competence, finish, polish, execution, performance.* "Workmanship"
may need to be retained in the legal sense as there is a great deal
of case law that uses it.

workmen's compensation *workers' compensation.*

worth a king's ransom *beyond price, worth its weight in gold, above
rubies, invaluable, matchless, peerless, inestimable, costly, of great
price, precious, worth a pretty penny.*

wrestler woman or man.

y

In fact, you will never make your mark as a writer unless you develop a respect for words and a curiosity about their shades of meaning that is almost obsessive.

William Zinsser

yachtsman *yacht owner, yachter; yachtswoman and yachtsman* if used gender-fairly.

yachtsmanship *yachting skills/techniques, yacht sailing techniques.*

Yahweh (YHWH) because this personal name for God is not gender-specific, it has grown popular with groups seeking inclusive terms for God. However, practicing Jews neither use nor speak this sacred word, and out of respect for this belief system, it is recommended that others forego its use also. Jews use instead the term "Ha-Shem" ("The Name"). Variant forms of address that Jews use for God include "Adonai," "Lord," and "Elokeinu"—but never "Jehovah," which was a hybrid name introduced by European Christian scholars centuries ago (Bob Epstein, Hennepin County Library, Minnetonka, MN; *Encyclopaedia Judaica*, vol. 7. New York: Macmillan, 1971, pp. 679–80). *See also* Father (God); God.

yardman *yard worker/laborer/supervisor; stockyard handler/laborer; railroad worker; gardener, landscaper.*

yardmaster *yard manager/supervisor, railroad yard operations supervisor.*

yeoman/yeomanly/yeomanry/yeoman of the guard/yeoman's service although some of these terms can be replaced (*retainer, attendant, military corps personnel attached to the British royal household, smallholding farmer, petty officer,* etc.), in most cases there are no good substitutes, and unless you are knowledgeable enough about their precise meanings to tamper with them, use alternatives at your peril.

yeoman's job *impressive/remarkable/extraordinary/outstanding/valiant/ heroic job, superexcellent/first-class/bang-up/A-number-one job, massive/enormous effort.*

yes man *yes person, toady, sycophant, flunky, stooge, brown-noser, apple polisher, bootlicker, backscratcher, flatterer, tool, hanger-on.*

yogi woman or man. Indians call the woman a "yogini."

yokefellow *yokemate, companion, opposite number, partner.*

yokel man or woman.

young lady *young woman.*

young shaver *See* little shaver.

youth girl or boy.

Appendixes

Appendix A
Writing Guidelines

INTRODUCTION

Language both reflects and shapes society. A young woman who has grown up hearing the word *policeman* does not consider that she herself might become one. She doesn't somehow think of being a mailman or a fireman or a newspaperman either. When she was growing up these words reflected society; there were few or no women in these fields. But those words did more than reflect society: they shaped it. Many young women like this one based career decisions on the language, which said: Do not apply here.

"Contrary to the assumption that language merely reflects social patterns such as sex-role stereotypes, research in linguistics and social psychology has shown that these are in fact facilitated and reinforced by language" (Hellinger 1984, p. 136).

When you use inclusive language you are doing two things: (1) you ensure that any shaping done by the language is bias-free; (2) you ensure that the language reflects reality.

Accuracy and Realistic Writing

"People are beginning to realize that non-sexist language is more than a token gesture of good will to feminists. It is a matter of accurate communication" (Nilsen 1979, p. 367).

Inclusive language is logical, accurate, and realistic. Exclusive language is not. Where is the logic in dividing versifiers into poets and poetesses? Where is the accuracy in writing "Dear Sir" to a woman? Or in speaking of "the development of the uterus in rats, guinea pigs and men" or of a law that says "No person may require another person to perform, participate in or undergo an abortion of pregnancy against his will" (quoted in Key 1975, p. 89)? Where is the realism in the full-page automobile advertisement that says in big bold letters, "A good driver is a product of his environment," when more women than men influence car-buying decisions? Or how successful is the ad for a dot-matrix printer that says, "In 3,000 years, man's need to present his ideas hasn't changed. But his tools have," when many of these printers are bought and used by women, who also have ideas they need to present? And when we use stereotypes to talk about people ("just like a woman"), our speech and writing will be inaccurate and unrealistic at least some of the time.

Better Writing

One of the most rewarding—and, for many people, the most unexpected—side effects of breaking away from traditional, sexist patterns of language is a dramatic improvement in writing style. By replacing fuzzy, over-generalized, cliche-ridden words with explicit, active words and by giving concrete examples and anecdotes instead of one-word-fits-all descriptions, you can express yourself more dynamically, convincingly, and memorably.

"If those who have studied the art of writing are in accord on any one point, it is on this: the surest way to arouse and hold the attention of the reader is by being specific, definite, and concrete" (Strunk and White 1972, p. 15). Writers who talk about brotherhood or spinsters or right-hand men miss a chance to spark their writing with fresh descriptions; they leave their readers as uninspired as they are. Thoughtless writing is also less informative. Why use, for example, the unrevealing *adman* when we could choose instead a precise, descriptive, nonsexist word like *advertising executive, copywriter, account executive, ad writer,* or *media buyer.*

The word *manmade,* which seems so indispensable to us, doesn't actually say very much. Does it mean artificial? handmade? synthetic? fabricated? machine-made? custom-made? simulated? plastic? imitation? contrived?

As you examine sexist words from the standpoint of good writing you will notice that they fail the test nearly every time.

Sensitivity

Communication is—or ought to be—a two-way street. For example, a speaker may use the "generic" *man* to mean *human being,* but the audience hears it as *adult male.* This is communication gone awry. In the same way, when you use inclusive language, be sensitive to your audience, so that your message is received the way you mean it. Words that alienate or irritate people do not allow for true communication. Like the young dentist who renamed her local group's fellowship hour the personship hour, those who sprinkle their speech with *spokesperson, salesperson, chairperson,* and *councilperson* in the mistaken belief that they are educating people to inclusive language are not stacking up converts in the corner. These terms *are* inclusive, but they are also contrived, distracting, and unlovely. The point is that there are dozens of inoffensive ways of speaking and writing inclusively, and it seems only sensitive and effective to seek them out.

Some nonsexist terms are still very jarring for some people. Choosing a milder nonsexist word or circumlocuting the problem will help effectuate the transition to prejudice-free language more easily and quickly. For too many years, the users of our language have been insensitive to all the people who felt the pain of being excluded. Inclusive language is intended to end the pain, not shift it to other people.

This is not a brief for timidity or even for compromise. The fact is that it is possible to use inclusive language without offending or startling people and without sounding like someone with a poor command of the language. It's not always easy, but it becomes less troublesome with practice and the acquisition of a few skills.

Sometimes we encounter a sexist word that seems so *right,* so irreplaceable (look, for example, at the difficulty we have with *manned space flight*). These problems are very real—not insuperable, but real. The more subtle problem is words that don't sound right to us. We may even suspect that they are ungrammatical. But in fact, they are only unfamiliar. Computers have added many bizarre terms to the language—words that were once new and unlovely that we have appropriated for ourselves in strange and wonderful ways. One rarely hears anyone fussing about, for example, the use of *access* as a verb. Before 1966 we had access *to* things but we did not—ever!—access them. In inclusive language there is no coining of new words, and there is very little that is shocking if the changes are made properly. We have only to use words we already know in ways that allow all human beings to be equally visible.

DEFINITION OF TERMS

Sexist/Nonsexist

Sexist language is language that promotes and maintains attitudes that stereotype people according to gender. It assumes that the male is the norm—the significant gender. Nonsexist language treats all people equally and either does not refer to a person's sex at all when it is irrelevant or refers to men and women in symmetrical ways when their gender is relevant.

"A society in which women are taught anything but the management of a family, the care of men, and the creation of the future generation is a society which is on the way out" (L. Ron Hubbard). "Behind every successful man is a woman—with nothing to wear" (L. Grant Glickman). "Nothing makes a man and wife feel closer, these days, than a joint tax return" (Gil Stern). These quotations display various characteristics of sexist writing: (1) stereotyping an entire sex by what might be appropriate for *some* of it; (2) assuming male superiority; (3) using nonparallel terms (*man and wife* should be either *husband and wife* or *man and woman*).

The following quotations clearly refer to all people: "It's really hard to be roommates with people if your suitcases are much better than theirs" (J. D. Salinger). "If people don't want to come out to the ball park, nobody's going to stop them" (Yogi Berra). "If men and women of capacity refuse to take part in politics and government, they condemn themselves, as well as the people, to the punishment of living under bad government" (Senator Sam J. Ervin). "I studied the lives of great men and famous women, and I found that the men and women who got to the top were those who did the jobs they had in hand, with everything they had of energy and enthusiasm and hard work" (Harry S Truman).

Inclusive/Exclusive

Inclusive language *includes* everyone; exclusive language *excludes* some people. The following quotation is inclusive: "The greatest revolution of our generation is the discovery that human beings, by changing the inner attitudes of their minds, can change the outer aspects of their lives" (William James). It is clear that James is speaking of both women and men.

Examples of exclusive writing fill most quotation books: "Man is the measure of all things" (Protagoras). "The People, though we think of a great entity when we use the word, means nothing more than so many millions of individual men" (James Bryce). "Man is nature's sole mistake" (W. S. Gilbert).

Gender-Free/Gender-Fair/Gender-Specific

Gender-free terms do not indicate sex and can be used for either women or men, boys or girls. Examples are *teacher, bureaucrat, employee, hiker, operations manager, child, clerk, sales rep, hospital patient, student, grandparent, chief executive officer.*

Writing or speech that is gender-fair involves the symmetrical use of sex-specific words and it promotes fairness to both sexes in the larger context. If you are describing the behavior of children on the playground, you will want to refer to girls and boys an approximately equal number of times, and you will be careful to observe what the children actually do and not just assume that only the boys climb to the top of the jungle gym and that only the girls play quiet games.

Researchers studying the same baby described its cries as "anger" when they were told it was a boy and as "fear" when they were told it was a girl (cited in Kramarae 1981). This sort of subtle bias has skewed much research in the past and continues to be seen in the language today.

Gender-specific words (for example, *alderwoman, businessman, altar girl*) are neither good nor bad in themselves. However, they must be used gender-fairly; that is, terms for women and terms for men should be used an approximately equal number of times in contexts that do not discriminate against either of them. One problem with gender-specific words is that they identify and even emphasize a person's sex when it is not necessary (and is sometimes even objectionable) to do so. Another problem is that they are so seldom used gender-fairly. In most cases, gender-free terms are preferable by far.

Generic/False Generic

A generic term is an all-purpose, gender-free word that includes everybody. Some examples of generic nouns are *workers, immigrants, people, voters, civilians, church members, elementary school students.* Generic pronouns include: *we, you, they.*

A false generic is a word that is claimed to include all people, but that in reality does not. Some examples: *man, mankind, chairman, forefathers, brotherhood, alumni.* Although some speakers and writers say that when they use *mankind* they mean *everybody*, their listeners and readers do not perceive the word that way and it is thus a false generic (see "Special Problems," p. 175, for a discussion of the "generic" *man* and *men*). The pronoun *he* is another false generic. Defenders of this convention maintain that the use of *he* to mean *he and she* is simply correct grammatical usage (see "The 'Generic' He," p. 173). However, these voices have weakened considerably as a growing body of research and usage shows that these terms are not true generics.

SEX AND GENDER

One of the understandings most basic to the correct use of inclusive language is the difference between sex and gender.

Sex is the biological status of the person; people with male genitals are male and people with female genitals are female. Words like *male* and *female* are used to indicate the objective fact of a person's sex. *Sex is biological.*

Gender is the cultural notion of what it is to be a woman or a man. Words like *masculine* and *feminine* describe these notions. In our society we describe people as womanly or manly, as a tomboy or a sissy, as unfeminine or unmasculine. These words have nothing to do with the person's sex; they are culturally acquired, subjective concepts about character traits and expected behaviors that vary from one place to another, from one individual to another. *Gender is cultural.*

Lucile Duberman writes that "the truth is our gender roles are not innate and God-given, nor are they necessarily irrevocable. Society creates gender roles, and society can alter them" (Duberman 1975, p. 58).

It is important to distinguish between sex and gender because much sexist language arises from cultural determinations of what a woman or man "ought" to be. Once a society decides, for example, that to be a man means to hide one's emotions, bring home a decent paycheck, and be able to discuss football standings, while to be a woman means to love pretty clothes, little children, and new recipes, much of the population becomes a contradiction in terms—unmanly men and unwomanly women. Crying, nagging, gossiping, and shrieking are assumed to be limited to women; rough-housing, ogling the other sex, telling dirty jokes, and being unable to find one's socks and keys are laid at the men's collective door. Lists of stereotypes appear silly because very few people fit them.

As you write and speak, check to see if the way you describe men and women is related to their sex (that is, to the biological fact of their being women or men) or if it is related to gender. The surest way to keep your writing nonsexist is to see that the people you speak of come across as individuals, not as members of a set.

There are two types of legitimate gender-specific words. One depends on sex. For example, *wet nurse, sperm donor,* and *surrogate mother* are defined by the person's biology. Other terms, such as *displaced homemaker, battered woman,* or *nanny,* are dependent on cultural conditions rather than on sex, but we use them because they reflect some present reality.

GENERAL RULES

Gender-Free Language

The ultimate goal of inclusive language is to speak of people as persons irrespective of their sex. Just as we do not see "the black lawyer for the defense" or "the Roman Catholic artist" we should not have to read "the female nuclear arms activist" or "the male model."

In a land of equal opportunity, of what importance is a person's race, sex, age, or creed? The moment we mention one of these characteristics—without a good reason for doing so—we enter an area mined by potential linguistic disasters. Although there may be instances in which a person's sex is germane (for example, "A recent study showed that female patients do not object to being cared for by male nurses"), most the time it is not.

Avoid using *lady, woman,* or *female* before a job title. (The same is true for men, except that it hardly seems necessary to say so since one rarely sees "A gentleman artist," "a man physician," or "a male minister.") Eliminate feminine forms of job titles because they simply call attention to the sex rather than to the role of the person (see "Special Problems," p. 175).

When you need to let your audience know someone's sex, reveal it through the use of proper names or pronouns rather than job titles or "feminine"/"masculine" nouns. For example, "Anna Truro/the mailcarrier/she" is far better than "the female mailcarrier."

Parallel Treatment

When sex-specific words must be used, maintain sexual symmetry in their treatment. To ensure true gender-fairness, ask yourself often: Would I write the same thing in the same way about a person of the opposite sex? Would I mind if this were said of me?

One potential for asymmetry exists in male-female word pairs. There are three ways in which they can be nonparallel. (1) Certain words are used as parallel pairs, but are in fact asymmetrical, for example, *cameragirl/cameraman, man Friday/girl Friday, mermaid/merman, makeup girl/makeup man.* The worst offender in this category is *man/wife*; the correct pairs are *man/woman* and *wife/husband.* (2) Other words are so unequivalent that few people confuse them as pairs, but it is revealing to study them, knowing that they were once equals: *governor/governess, patron/matron, courtier/courtesan, master/mistress, buddy/sissy, patrimony/matrimony, call boy/call girl, showman/showgirl, Romeo/Juliet,* etc. We all know what a *Romeo* is, but if we didn't we could look it up in the dictionary; this is not true of a *Juliet.* A *call boy* is a page, while a *call girl* is a prostitute. *Buddy* is a term of affection, while *sissy* is a derogatory one. A study of word pairs bears out the theory that words that are primarily associated with women ultimately become discounted and devalued. (3) Acceptable words and constructions sometimes become unacceptable because of the way they are used. For example, in the same paragraph a man might be referred to by his last name, Lahti, while a woman is referred to as Mrs. Henson; refer to men and women in parallel ways. If he is Sam, she should be Ella, and vice versa. Such expressions as *two girls and a man, a male and three women,* and *aldermen and women* should read: *two women and a man* (or *two girls and a boy!*), *a man and three women,* and *aldermen and alderwomen.*

Hidden Bias/Context

Writing may be completely free of sexist words and yet carry a sexist message if the context is biased. A sentence like this passes the first test but fails the second: "Seventy people were killed in the derailment yesterday including fourteen women."

Women may be correctly called mailcarriers, business executives, and actors, but if they are also described as nags and gossips (words rarely applied to men), the material is sexist.

Are those in positions of power and prestige generally men? Are men quoted and deferred to more often than women? Are women usually passive, dependent, and limited to pink-collar jobs? Are women's physical appearance, personality traits, and character referred to when they are not mentioned for men? Does the material exploit people? Does it deal in stereotypes (what "all" men and women "ought" to be like)?

When you speak and write of women and girls, at least some of them should be engaged in activities that are highly valued in the culture, activities that are exciting, physically challenging, and that demonstrate leadership, creativity, and initiative. Men and boys should be seen sometimes in secondary activities, or showing some concern about their appearance, or expressing emotions. They can be observers, supporters, nurturers. Speak of whole people—complex, multifaceted, nonstereotypical human beings.

If you can easily (in most cases) substitute a man for a woman or vice versa and not discover some linguistic or psychological absurdity in your material, you are probably avoiding hidden sexism.

Sexist Quotations

Sometimes you need to use a quotation, but it is sexist; for example: "The best use of laws is to teach men to trample bad laws under their feet" (Wendell Phillips). There are several ways of handling this.

You can omit the quotation marks and paraphrase the remark (still attributing it to the author): Wendell Phillips suggested that the best use of laws is to teach people to trample bad ones underfoot.

You may replace the sexist words or phrases with ellipsis dots and/or bracketed substitutes: "The best use for laws is to teach [people] to trample bad laws under their feet" (Wendell Phillips).

Use [sic] to show that the sexist words come from the original quotation and to call attention to the fact that they are incorrect: "The best use of laws it to teach men [sic] to trample bad ones under their feet" (Wendell Phillips).

Or quote only part of it: Wendell Phillips said the best use for laws was to teach people "to trample bad laws under their feet."

And, of course, you always have the choice of omitting the quotation entirely.

Generic Nouns

Certain generic nouns are often assumed to refer only to men, for example, *politicians, physicians, lawyers, voters, legislators, clergy, farmers, colonists, immigrants, slaves, pioneers, settlers, members of the armed forces, judges, taxpayers.* There are references to "immigrants, their wives, and children," or "those clergy permitted to have wives," etc.

In a historical context it is particularly damaging for young people to read about settlers and explorers and pioneers as though they were all white men. Our language should describe the accomplishments of the human race in terms of *all* those who contributed to them.

Animals/Things

If the sex of an animal is known (and is important to your material), specify it. When the sex is unknown or unimportant, refer to all animals as *it*. Things are also *it*. Avoid using *she* and *her* to refer to nature, nations, churches, battleships, boats, cars, engines, gas tanks, etc. The enemy is not *he,* but *it* or *they.*

Generally leave nonhuman items with "sexist" names as they are, for example, *timothy grass, daddy longlegs, alewife, mandrake, sweet william, myrtle.*

Women as Separate People

Identify women by their own names, not by their connections to husband, son, or father. If a connection is relevant, make it mutual. Instead of writing "Frieda, his wife of seventeen years," write "Frieda and Eric, married for seventeen years." One of the most sexist maneuvers in the language is the way we oblige women to label themselves in relationship to a man. Marie Marvingt, a Frenchwoman who lived around the turn of the century, was an inventor, adventurer, stunt woman, superathlete, aviator, and all-around scholar. She chose to be affianced to neither man (as a wife) nor God (as a religious), but it was not long before an uneasy male press found her a fit partner. She is still known today by the charming but revealing label "the Fiancée of Danger."

It is difficult for some people to accept women doing unconventional things with their names. For many years, the pattern has been unvarying, and etiquette books were able to tell us precisely how to address a single woman, a married woman, a divorced woman, or a widowed woman. We all felt very secure with such rules. But now some women are married but keeping their birth names; others are hyphenating their last name with their husband's. And some women have constructed names for themselves that are different from, but perhaps based on, either their birth name or their married name or both.

Ever since the apocalyptic naming of Eve by Adam, human beings have recognized that there is power in naming. Some Native

Americans have two names, one of which is never made public because of the power it would give another person over them.

The problem of women's names is not easily solved. In some families today the husband has his birth name, the wife her birth name, and a child might have a last name different from either of them because she is living with her stepfather and mother. Some women have two sets of letterhead stationery: one for their professional life, one for their family life. So, yes, it is confusing. And, no, there are no guidelines that can be summarized for the etiquette books.

A woman who had been nicknamed "Betty" early in life had always liked her full name, "Elizabeth," and resolved that by the time she was forty she would be known as "Elizabeth." When one of her friends heard about the change, she said sharply, "I'll call her Betty if I like!"

We too can call them Betty if we like, but it's not very sensitive and it breaks the only rule we have in this area: call the woman what she wants to be called.

Miscellaneous

Avoid changing official titles (for example, a U. S. Department of Labor division used to be known as the Manpower Administration) although you may want to add [sic]. And be sensitive about rewriting history. Fathers of the Church *were* men. However, we now refer to the Founding Fathers as the Founders. Many compounds with *-man (liegeman, yeoman,* etc.) are historically accurate and are used as they are.

Although this book is about sexist language, it should be emphasized that language must also be free from bias based on race, age, creed, ethnic group, disability, or socioeconomic background. Eliminate irrelevant and inaccurate communications about what it means to be male or female, black or white, young or old, rich or poor, disabled or temporarily able-bodied, or to hold a particular belief system.

The following words can be used in conjunction with more specific words to arrive at nonsexist phrases:

agent	coach	engineer
anyone	colleague	-er words
artisan	commissioner	everybody
artist	companion	everyone
assistant	consumer	executive
associate	contractor	expert
attendant	correspondent	fabricant
builder	counselor	facilitator
chief executive	crew	folks
citizen	customer	guide
civilian	dealer	hand
clerk	deputy	handler
clinician	employee	individual

inhabitant	one	representative
inspector	operator	retailer
intermediary	owner	retainer
laborer	patriot	scientist
loader	performer	servant
machinist	person	someone
maker	planner	specialist
manufacturer	politician	student
mechanic	practitioner	subscriber
member	producer	technician
messenger	professional	tender
motorist	program director	tutor
nobody	promoter	vendor
nominal head	proprietor	worker
no one	purveyor	writer
notable	repairer	
officer	reporter	

THE "GENERIC" HE

The use of the third person singular pronoun *he* as a generic (that is, using it to mean *he and she*) is to be strictly avoided. It is ambiguous, the grammatical justification for its use is problematic, and it is not perceived as including both women and men (see "Special Problems," p. 175, for a related discussion on "generic" *man*). Donald G. McKay points out that each of us hears the "generic" *he* over a million times in our lifetime and that the consequences of this kind of repetition are "beyond the ken of present-day psychology" (McKay 1980, p. 47). He says the "generic" *he* has all the characteristics of a highly effective propaganda technique: repetition, covertness/ indirectness, early age of acquisition, and association with high-prestige sources; "Although the full impact of the prescriptive *he* remains to be explored, effects on attitudes related to achievement, motivation, perseverance, and level of aspiration seem likely."

Defenders of the convention most often claim that it is a point of grammar and certainly not intended to offend anyone. That it does in reality offend large numbers of people does not appear to sway some grammarians, nor does the fact that their recourse to the laws of language is on shaky ground. While *he* involves a disagreement in gender, singular *they* involves a disagreement in number. For example, in "to each his own" the gender is wrong half the time; in "to each their own" there is a disagreement in number. Eighteenth-century (male) grammarians decided that number was more important than gender, although the singular *they* had been in favor until that time (Bodine 1975, pp. 131–33).

The pronoun *he* (when used in any way except to refer to a specific male person) can be avoided, replaced, or defused in several ways.

- One of the easiest ways is to rewrite your sentence in the plural: "Everyone is a genius at least once a year; a real genius has his original ideas closer together" (G. C. Lichtenberg). Everyone is a genius at least once a year; real geniuses have their original ideas closer together.
- Rewrite the sentence using *we/us/our*: "From each according to his abilities, to each according to his needs" (Karl Marx). From each of us according to our abilities, to each of us according to our needs.
- Rewrite the sentence in the second person: "No man knows his true character until he has run out of gas, purchased something on the installment plan and raised an adolescent" (Mercelene Cox). You don't know what your true character is until you have run out of gas, purchased something on the installment plan and raised an adolescent.
- Recast in the passive voice: "Pessimist: One who, when he has the choice of two evils, chooses both" (Oscar Wilde). Pessimist: One who, when given the choice of two evils, chooses both.
- Omit the pronoun entirely: "Repartee: What a person thinks of after he becomes a departee" (Dan Bennett). Repartee: What a person thinks of after becoming a departee. "The American arrives in Paris with a few French phrases he has culled from a conversational guide or picked up from a friend who owns a beret" (Fred Allen). The American arrives in Paris with a few French phrases culled from a conversational guide or picked up from a friend who owns a beret.
- Replace the masculine pronoun with an article: "Can't a critic give his opinion of an omelette without being asked to lay an egg?" (Clayton Rawson). Can't a critic give an opinion of an omelette without being asked to lay an egg?
- Replace the pronoun with such words as *someone, anyone, one, the one, no one*, etc.: "He who can take advice is sometimes superior to him who can give it" (Karl von Knebel). Someone who can take advice is sometimes superior to one who can give it. "Everyone can master a grief but he that has it" (Shakespeare). Everyone can master a grief but the one who has it. Or, as La Rochefoucauld put it: "We all have the strength to endure the misfortunes of others."
- Use *he and she* or *his and her,* but only if there are not a great many of them. *S/he* is not recommended for anything but memos, notes, or the most casual communications. "Education is helping the child realize his potentialities" (Erich Fromm). Education is helping the child realize his or her potentialities. Note that there are instances in which it is better to use *he or she* than it is to use gender-nonspecific words, as, for example, when you want to raise consciousness about both sexes being involved in a certain activity: the new parent . . . he or she; the plumber . . . she or he.

- Replace the pronoun with a noun (or a synonym for a noun used earlier): "He is forced to be literate about the illiterate, witty about the witless and coherent about the incoherent" (John Crosby). The critic is forced to be literate about the illiterate, witty about the witless and coherent about the incoherent. "To find a friend one must close one eye—to keep him, two" (Norman Douglas). To find a friend one must close one eye—to keep a friend, two.
- When the *he* refers to an animal whose sex is unknown or irrelevant, replace *he* with *it*: "When you see a snake, never mind where he came from" (W. G. Benham). When you see a snake, never mind where it came from. "When you have got an elephant by the hind legs and he is trying to run away, it is best to let him run" (Abraham Lincoln). When you have got an elephant by the hind legs and it is trying to run away, it is best to let it run.
- The singular *they* ("to each their own") has strong supporters. Ann Bodine says, "Despite almost two centuries of vigorous attempts to analyze and regulate it out of existence, singular *they* is alive and well" (Bodine 1975, p. 131). In less formal language, its acceptance rate is fairly high. There are so many other ways of replacing the "generic" *he* that you should not have to rely on singular *they* too often. However, when nothing else works and you need to use it, keep in mind that at that point you can either make an error of gender (use *he* when you really mean *he and she*) or you can make an error of number (using plural instead of singular). "Only a mediocre person is always at his best" (Somerset Maugham). Only a mediocre person is always at their best.
- You may also use masculine and feminine pronouns in alternating sentences, paragraphs, examples, or chapters, although this technique should be used sparingly as it can be annoying to read. Or you can use specific genderless nouns (*the average person, workers,* etc.) or substitute job titles or other descriptions for the pronoun.

SPECIAL PROBLEMS

"Generic" Man/Men

Much of the debate on inclusive language centers on the use of *man*. Those who want to retain the use of the "generic" *man* say that *man* is defined not only as "an adult male human being" but also as "a human being," "a person," "an individual," or "the whole human race." They also claim that the use of *man* does not exclude women and is nothing more than a grammatical convention: man embraces woman.

The problem with this approach is that not everybody reads dictionaries or, having read them, uses words the way they are defined there. Researchers who studied the hypothesis that *man* is generally understood to include women found "rather convincing evidence that when you use man generically, people do tend to think male, and tend not to think female" (letter from Joseph Schneider and Sally Hacker, quoted in Miller and Swift 1976, p. 19). According to Miller and Swift, that study and others "clearly indicate that *man* in the sense of male so overshadows *man* in the sense of human being as to make the latter use inaccurate and misleading for purposes both of conceptualizing and communicating" (p. 23).

Citing dictionary definitions as proof of a word's meaning in society is an iffy business at best. One definition of the word *virago* is: "a woman of great stature, strength, and courage" (*Webster's Ninth New Collegiate Dictionary.* Springfield, MA: Merriam-Webster, 1985). But the average person is almost certainly more likely to think of a virago in terms of the word's other definition, "a loud overbearing woman: termagant." If you use the word *virago* in its positive sense and your audience "mis-hears" you, it's unproductive to insist that what you really meant was the other definition.

Far more important than a word's etymology, history, or dictionary definition is its usage: How do people *hear* the word? Jeanette Silveira says "there is ample research evidence that the masculine 'generic' does not really function as a generic. In various studies words like *he* and *man* in generic contexts were presented to people who were asked to indicate their understanding by drawing, bringing in, or pointing out a picture, by describing or writing a story about the person(s) referred to, or by answering yes or no when asked whether a sex-specific word or picture applied to the meaning" (Silveira 1980, p. 167). In all these studies (fourteen of them are summarized in *Women's Studies International Quarterly,* vol. 3, no. 2, 1980), women and girls were perceived as being included significantly less often than men and boys. Both women and men reported that they usually pictured men when they read or heard the masculine "generic."

Saying that man embraces woman is illogical on two counts: (1) In terms of language alone, it would seem more sensible to have woman embrace man since the word *man* is found in the word *woman,* but not vice versa. (2) The justification for man becoming the set and woman the subset is linguistically, sociologically, and psychologically arbitrary. The term *human being* clearly embraces both man and woman. With such a simple, commonsensical alternative available, it seems unnecessary to defend a convention that is almost surely on its last manly legs.

In addition, note that Greek, Latin, and Old English have all had three very different words to talk about people: *human, woman, man* (Greek: *anthropos, gyne, aner;* Latin: *homo, femina, vir;* Old English:

man, female, wer). It is only relatively recently that the distinctions have become blurred, and we expect one word (*man*) to do double duty.

An associated situation would seem to involve words that end in *-boy*. But there is little opposition to changing such words as *altar boy, bellboy, busboy,* and *messenger boy* to accommodate the girls who now share these roles. Apparently the man-embraces-woman concept does not extend to "boy embraces girl."

The author of a syndicated column on language usage wrote, "Contrary to what some feminists tell us, the suffix 'man' means a human being, not necessarily a man" (Bright 1986, p. 5G). The problem here is the "not necessarily a man." In other words, when you see the suffix *-man* it *could* refer to an adult male human being. It might not, of course. But it might. Each time people encounter this convention, they must decide which meaning is intended. Clarity of thought and expression demands that this ambiguous use of the word be eliminated.

Sanford Berman says that "words can powerfully harm people, as amply demonstrated by bigots' and tyrants' deliberate attempts to linguistically de-humanize and demean groups they intend to exploit, oppress, or exterminate. Calling Asians 'gooks' made it easier to kill them. Calling blacks 'niggers' made it simpler to enslave and brutalize them. Calling Native Americans 'primitives' and 'savages' made it okay to conquer and despoil them. And to talk of 'fisher*men*,' 'council*men*,' and 'longshore*men*' is to clearly exclude and discourage women from those pursuits, to diminish and degrade them" (letter to the editor, *Minnesota Monthly,* in press).

Finally, Dennis Baron says in *Grammar and Gender* that attempts today to justify the use of the masculine generic "are but thin masks for the underlying assumption of male superiority in life as well as language; despite the attempts of the wary language commentators to include women under masculine terms, the effect is to render women both invisible and silent" (Baron 1986, p. 100).

Sex-Role Words

Certain sex-linked words depend for their meanings on cultural stereotypes: *feminine/masculine, manly/womanly, boyish/girlish, gentlemanlike/ladylike, husbandly/wifely, fatherly/motherly, brotherly/ sisterly, unfeminine/unmasculine, unmanly/unwomanly,* etc. These words' meanings may vary from culture to culture and even within a culture. No two people will understand exactly the same thing when they hear one of these terms, and because the words depend for their meanings on interpretations of average behavior or characteristics, they may be grossly inaccurate when describing individuals. There are only a very few biological functions that are limited to one sex or the other (only women can give birth or nurse a baby; only a man can donate sperm or impregnate a woman). Somewhere, sometime, men and women have said, thought, or done everything the other sex has said, thought, or done except for certain sex- linked biological activities. Therefore to describe a woman as unwomanly is a contradiction in terms; if a woman is doing it, saying it, wearing it, thinking it, it must be—by definition—womanly. (See "Sex and Gender," p. 167.)

Avoiding cultural stereotypes allows writers and speakers to use more precise language, to define human behavior, speech, and thought in ways that communicate their ideas more powerfully. F. Scott Fitzgerald did not use the word *feminine* to describe the unforgettable Daisy in *The Great Gatsby.* Instead, he wrote, "She laughed again, as if she said something very witty, and held my hand for a moment, looking up into my face, promising that there was no one in the world she so much wanted to see. That was a way she had." Daisy's charm did not belong to Woman; it was uniquely hers. Replacing vague . sex-linked descriptors with thoughtful words that describe an individual instead of a member of a set can lead to language that touches people's minds and hearts.

"Feminine" Endings

Suffixes such as *-ess, -ette,* and *-trix* do three things: (1) They perpetuate the notion that the male is the norm and the female is a subset, a deviation, a secondary classification. Consider the difference in definition between a poet ("one who writes poetry") and a poetess ("a female poet"). In other words, men are "the real thing" and women are sort of like them. (2) They specify a person's sex when gender is irrelevant. (3) They carry the sense of littleness or cuteness. Suffixes are added to root words to qualify them. A poet should be a poet—without qualification. Marlis Hellinger says these suffixes have "a weakening, trivializing or even sexualizing effect on an occupational activity which for a man may connote power and prestige" (Hellinger 1984, p. 138). Which would you rather be, a governor or a governess?

If the individual's sex is critical to your material, use the adjectives *male* and *female* ("At a time when male actors played female roles . . .") or use pronouns ("The poet interrupted her reading . . .").

The following words with "feminine" endings should be replaced as shown.

actress/actor
adulteress/adventurer
ambassadress/ambassador
ancestress/ancestor
anchoress/anchorite
authoress/author
aviatrix, aviatress/aviator
benefactress/benefactor
canoness/canon

coadjutress/coadjutor
coheiress/coheir
comedienne/comedian
deaconess/deacon
directress/director
enchantress/enchanter
equestrienne/equestrian
executrix/executor
farmerette/farmer

goddess/god
governess/governor
heiress/heir
heroine/hero
hostess/host
huntress/hunter
inheritress/inheritor
inspectress/inspector
instructress/instructor
Jewess/Jew
laundress/launderer
majorette/major
manageress/manager
mayoress/mayor
mediatress, mediatrix/mediator
murderess/murderer
Negress/black
ogress/ogre
patroness/patron
peeress/peer
poetess/poet
portress/porter
priestess/priest

procuress/procurer
prophetess/prophet
proprietress/proprietor
protectress/protector
sculptress/sculptor
seductress/seducer
shepherdess/shepherd
songstress/singer
sorceress/sorcerer
starlet/star
stewardess/steward
suffragette/suffragist
temptress/tempter
testatrix/testator
tragedienne/tragedian
traitress/traitor
tutoress/tutor
usherette/usher
victress/victor
villainess/villain
votaress/votary
waitress/waiter
wardress/warder

Sex-Linked Metaphors, Expressions, and Figures

Our rich and colorful language contains thousands of striking, evocative, and useful metaphors, expressions, and figures. Some of the most familiar ones are sex-linked, that is, they identify a real or fictional person by a feminine or masculine name.

As is true of the rest of the language, these phrases are dominated by male images. There is nothing wrong with any of them in themselves. However, their cumulative effect tends to be overpowering. This dictionary lists alternatives for many of these expressions, not so that they can be removed from the language, but so that you can attempt to balance your writing and speaking with both female and male images or use alternatives when gender-fairness is not possible. In addition, there are times when it is awkward and illogical to use a male metaphor for a woman. There is nothing ungrammatical or wrong about saying, "She's a real Johnny-come-lately," but it grates. And it doesn't have to be that way.

Some sex-linked metaphors, expressions, and figures are irreplaceable and many more are so colorful and useful that they are nearly indispensable. However, if you are sensitive to the problem, you can be more selective in your use of such phrases, retaining only the most dynamic, the most appropriate, and creating original ones of your own or using listed alternatives for the less important ones.

Compare the length of the following lists of male and female expressions (this is a partial but proportionate listing). Male: *according to Hoyle; Achilles' heel; benjamin; before you can say Jack Robinson;*

Bluebeard; Bob's your uncle; borrow from Peter to pay Paul; cabbages and kings; Casanova; charley horse; David and Goliath; Dear John letter; Don Juan; Don Quixote; doubting Thomas; drunk as a lord; Dutch uncle; every Tom, Dick, and Harry; Father Christmas; give someone Harry; good Joe; Hobson's choice; Jack Tar; Jekyll and Hyde; John Hancock; Johnny-come-lately; Johnny-on-the-spot; judas goat; judas kiss; King Midas; Lothario; Machiavellian; Montezuma's revenge; Mickey Finn; Mickey Mouse; Milquetoast; old as Methuselah; out-Herod Herod; Paul Pry; Peck's bad boy; peeping Tom; poor/patient as Job; Peter Pan collar; Peter's pence; raise Cain; rich as Croesus; Romeo; Samson; the Sandman/Mister Sandman; Santa Claus; say uncle; Scrooge; shylock; simon-pure; smart aleck; sneaky Pete; tommyrot; wise as Solomon; Valentino; Walter Mitty.

Female: *Amazon, black Maria, Caesar's wife, Delilah, Eve, goody two shoes, lazy Susan, Lolita, magdalen, Mrs. Malaprop, nervous Nellie, Pandora's box, patient Griselda, Pollyanna.*

Fellow, King, Lord, Master

Fellow, king, lord, and *master* have three things in common: (1) Whether from definition, derivation, or people's perceptions of them, they are very male-oriented words. (2) They are root words: many other words, phrases, and expressions are formed from them, thus extending their reach. (3) Not everyone agrees whether all forms of them are sexist. Someone who might admit that a fellow sitting next to them at the lunch counter can only be a man might see nothing sex-specific in the expression *fellow student.* Or those who agree that the master of a certain house is a man might believe that speaking of the mastery of a subject in school is acceptable language. In this dictionary, the premise is that these four words are acceptable only in their narrowest, male-defined terms; all other uses of the words are given alternatives. Consider, for example, the cumulative effect on the language when such a masculine word as *master* is encountered in so many everyday ways: *master bedroom, master builder, master class, masterful, master hand, master key, master list, mastermind, masterpiece, master plan, master stroke, master switch, master tape, master teacher, masterwork, mastery, overmaster, past master, postmaster, poundmaster, prizemaster, self-mastery, trickmaster, truckmaster, weighmaster, wharfmaster, yardmaster.*

See the dictionary entries under these words for more information about them.

Prostitute/Prostitution

The words that we use to describe people involved in prostitution are some of the most interesting and revealing in the language.

Prostitution, which generally involves two consenting adults, is a takes-two-to-tango operation and could not survive without the active and continued participation of both parties. Yet our language does not reflect this reality: it does not treat prostitute and partner equally. If there is an imbalance, if anyone is a victim, it is the prostitute: she or he is often disadvantaged, compelled by circumstances, a pimp, or drugs to maintain the system. The prostitute's "client" is not similarly compelled. Yet by naming prostitutes pejoratively, society apportions to them all the blame, all the "badness." Julia Penelope Stanley found 220 terms in our language that describe a sexually promiscuous woman, but only twenty-two for a sexually promiscuous man. She notes that there is no linguistic reason why the first set is large and the second set small (Stanley 1977).

Following are a few of the printable words we use to describe prostitutes: *bawd, call girl, camp follower, chippie, demimondaine, drab, fallen woman, fancy girl, fancy woman, floozy, grisette, harlot, hooker, housegirl, kept woman, lady of pleasure, lady of the evening/night, loose woman, madam, slattern, slut, streetwalker, strumpet, tart, tramp, trollop, trull, whore.* There are, of course, male prostitutes but the (male-dominated) language has been slow to name them, which is why all the above words apply only to women.

When it comes to the men who do with prostitutes that which supposedly makes the prostitutes bad women, we presently have only three generally used words for them: *john, trick, date. John* is a nice word. Lots of people name their children John. *Trick* is not too shabby either; it is used a lot (although not in that sense) in polite society. And *date* is even more innocuous.

Until we begin to use words for prostitute and partner that are inclusive or at least symmetrical, there will be no real fairness. However, a good start is to eliminate all words for prostitutes except one: *prostitute.* This is a matter-of-fact word that is as informative and descriptive as it needs to be. It can also be used inclusively for male and female prostitutes.

For want of a better term, the prostitute's partner might be called a *prostitute's "client"* (retain quotation marks to show the dubiousness of the word). What is important here is to make the direct association with the prostitute. Calling people a *john* or a *trick* nicely avoids tainting them with any suggestion of what they are involved in.

Eliminate also such cover-ups as *outcall service, escort service, red light district, call girl service, brothel, bordello, call house.* They are *houses of prostitution* or *prostitution services.* Only by using neutral, symmetrical terms for everyone involved can we begin to remove the wholly inappropriate sexist bias from our language on prostitution.

-Woman, -Man, -Person

In this dictionary every attempt has been made to find alternatives that do *not* include the suffixes *-woman, -man,* and *-person.* These are always possible as a last resort, of course, but they have been rejected as generally useful constructions because (1) *-woman* and *-man* still specify gender, which is often irrelevant and sometimes damaging; (2) *-person* is often weak, awkward, and annoying. It not only sounds contrived, it *is* contrived; (3) too often these suffixes come first to mind, so one looks no further and thus misses some dynamic and descriptive words.

This is not to discount them entirely. Words with *-man* and *-woman* suffixes may be the best choice when you wish to emphasize the presence or participation of both sexes in some activity or position. For example, "Local businesswomen and businessmen donated their weekends to do plumbing, electrical, and carpentry work in the new downtown shelter for the homeless."

When using words with these suffixes, be sensitive to sexual symmetry. *Salesmen and women* should be *salesmen and saleswomen; chairman and chairperson* should be *chairman and chairwoman* (but of course better yet is *chair* for both).

Names of Animals/Foods

Nearly all the animal names we use for people are limited to one sex or the other (most often women), thus making them sexist. "Men's extensive labeling of women as parts of body, fruit, or animals and as mindless, or like children—labels with no real parallel for men—reflects men's derision of women and helps maintain gender hierarchy and control" (Thorne, Kramarae, and Henley 1983, p. 9).

As a general rule, using animal names to refer to people is neither sensitive nor very socially attractive. Words to avoid include: *bat, bird, bitch, bow-wow, brood mare, buck, bull, bunny, cat, chick, chicken, chickie-baby, cow, dog, dumb ox, filly, fox, gay dog, goose, gorilla, grimalkin, heifer, hellcat, kitten, lapdog, mare, old bat, old goat, ox, pig, pussy, pussycat, sex kitten, she-cat, silly goose, sow, stag, stud, swine, tigress, top dog, vixen, wolf.* A few terms seem descriptive without being derogatory, for example, *lamb* tends to be used in an affectionate way of either a woman or a man.

Metaphors that compare people to animals in some particular are seldom sexist and thus are acceptable, for example, *merry as a cricket, wise as an owl, happy as a lark, feeling one's oats,* etc. To distinguish between pejorative descriptions and acceptable descriptions, ask first whether the expression is limited to one sex, and then determine whether a person is being *labeled* an animal or whether the person is being *likened to* some animal characteristic. Calling a man a wolf is different from saying someone—either a man or a woman—is a lone wolf. Calling someone an eager beaver implies not so much that the person *is* a beaver but that the person is eager *as* a beaver is eager.

Names of foods are also used for people, and while many of them purport to be positive, ultimately they are belittling, trivializing, and make objects of people. Reflecting on all the connotations of people as food may help you avoid such terms as: *beefcake, cheesecake, cookie, creampuff, cupcake, dish, honey, marshmallow, peach, sugar, sweetie pie, tomato, top banana.* Again, the difference between positive and negative uses of food terms depends on whether the term is limited to one sex (a man would never be referred to as a *cookie*, nor would the word *beefcake* be used of a woman) and whether the food word is a direct label ("she's a dish!") or whether it is simply comparing the person in some metaphorical way to a food. For example, *apple of my eye* can be said of either sex and it doesn't mean the person *is* an apple in the same way a woman is called a *peach*—but rather that he or she is *like* the best apple from the tree.

Strong writing depends on metaphors—even metaphors based on animals and food—but there is a difference between labeling people and creating vivid word associations.

Name-Calling

Epithets used for name-calling (*bastard, bitch, broad, fag/faggot, fairy, harpy, harridan, hellcat, pansy, queer, son of a bitch*) are generally sex-linked in some way, and they are therefore to be avoided on that ground as well as on others. Only a few of them have been listed in the dictionary because it is assumed that using derogatory, obscene, or vulgar words is probably not a part of most people's public speaking and writing. They are mentioned here in order to underline the fact that they are usually sexist.

Nonsexist Words with Man/Men

Not all words containing *man, men,* or *boy* are sexist. Nonsexist words that could be mistaken for sexist words are listed in the dictionary with notes explaining their usage. Examples of such words are: *amen, boycott, carboy, dragoman, emancipate, highboy, manager, manciple, mandarin, mandate, mandrake, manege, manes, maneuver, mangrove, Manhattan, mania, Manichaeism, manicure, manifest, manifold, maniple, manipulate, manor, mantle, manual, manufacture, manumission, manuscript, menagerie, mendacious, mendacity, mendicant, menopause, menses, menstrual, ottoman, premenstrual, tegmen, whatman.*

Letter Salutations

A state commission on the economic status of women reports receiving a surprising number of letters addressed "Dear Sir" or "Gentlemen." Following are a few of the many inclusive alternatives to traditional sexist letter openings.

Dear Agent

    Boxholder
    Citizen
    Committee Member
    Councillor
    Credit Manager
    Customer
    Director
    Editor
    Employee
    Executive
    Friend
    Homeowner
    Madam or Sir
    Madams and Sirs

Dear Manager

    Mr./Mrs.
    Occupant
    Owner
    Parent or Guardian
    Personnel Officer
    Publisher
    Reader
    Resident
    Sir or Madam
    Sirs and Madams
    Staff Person
    Subscriber
    Teacher

Dear Friends of the Library

    Members of the...
    Parishioners
    Supporters
    Volunteers

Dear Ellen Howard-Jeffers

    Acme Drycleaning
    Robert Jackson
    C. Franciosa
    Tiny Tots Toys

Dear Superintendent Bennett

    Vice-President Morris
    Editor Bernstein
    Senior Research Specialist Jordan
    Administrative Assistant Maki
    Nurse Domenica

Greetings

Hello!
To the President
To the Public Relations Department
To Whom It May Concern
To the Chief Sales Agent
To the Freestyle Credit Department
TO: The Commission on Language Abuse
TO: Parents and guardians of J. J. Hill students
TO: J. G. Frimsted

Or omit the salutation entirely and begin with:
    RE: Account # 4865-1809-3333-0101
    Please send me a copy of the most recent committee report.
    I am ordering six copies of your publication.
    Enclosed please find complete payment for . . . .

Your Help Wanted

Our language is constantly changing, especially perhaps now as we work to make it reflect the fullness and richness of our human diversity and oneness. The material in this dictionary is not written in stone; it needs to be constantly refined and reevaluated. If you disagree with something here, if you find sexist terms not listed, or if you know of additional nonsexist alternatives for sexist terms, please send your comments to: Rosalie Maggio, in care of The Oryx Press, 2214 North Central at Encanto, Phoenix, AZ 85004. Thank you!

Appendix B
Readings

Change and Resistance to Change

Casey Miller and Kate Swift

❖ ❖ ❖

Every language reflects the prejudices of the society in which it evolved. Since English, through most of its history, evolved in a white, Anglo-Saxon, patriarchal society, no one should be surprised that its vocabulary and grammar frequently reflect attitudes that exclude or demean minorities and women.

But we are surprised. Until recently few people thought much about what English—or any other language for that matter—was saying on a subliminal level. Now that we have begun to look, some startling things have become obvious. What standard English usage says about males, for example, is that they are the species. What it says about females is that they are a subspecies. From these two assertions flow a thousand other enhancing and degrading messages, all encoded in the language we in the English-speaking countries begin to learn almost as soon as we are born.

A sizable number of people would like to do something about these inherited linguistic biases. But getting rid of them involves more than exposing them and suggesting alternatives. It requires change, and linguistic change is no easier to accept than any other kind. It may even be harder.

At a deep level, changes in a language are threatening because they signal widespread changes in social mores. At a level closer to the surface they are exasperating. We learn certain rules of grammar and usage in school. When they are challenged it is as though we are also being challenged. Our native language is like a second skin, so much a part of us we resist the idea that it is constantly changing, constantly being renewed. Though we know intellectually that the English we speak today and the English of Shakespeare's time are very different, we tend to think of them as the same—static rather than dynamic. . . .Only recently have we become aware that conventional English usage, including the generic use of masculine-gender words, often obscures the actions, the contributions, and sometimes the very presence of women. Turning our backs on that insight is an option, of course, but it is an option like teaching children the world is flat. In this respect, continuing to use English in ways that have become misleading is no different from misusing data, whether the misuse is inadvertent or planned.

The need today, as always, is to be in command of language, not used by it, and so the challenge is to find clear, convincing, graceful ways to say accurately what we want to say.

Skirting Sexism

Pearl G. Aldrich

◆ ◆ ◆

"But 'the manager . . . he' is correct grammar," the woman insisted. Several classmates had suggested that she should have used "the manager . . . he or she" in her presentation. "You're a manager, aren't you?" challenged one man. "'The manager . . . he' isn't accurate."

Both were right. English-speaking people have been taught for 150 years that "the manager . . . he" is correct grammar, but in the business and professional world today, "the manager . . . he" is no longer accurate, any more than "the teacher . . . she."

Language reflects our attitudes. As we change our attitudes, we change our language. But change never comes smoothly either in life or in language. This discussion among managers attending a workshop to improve their writing abilities illustrates the confused state of linguistic affairs two decades after efforts to eliminate sexism in language began as part of the women's movement.

Though nonsexist language has not yet come of age, important changes have entered the mainstream of day-to-day business writing and speaking.

Reprinted by permission from *Nation's Business*, December 1985, pp. 34-35.

Women executives still receive invitations to professional meetings containing assurances that shopping trips will be planned for their wives, but in the main, we see and hear *spouses* (sometimes it is *mate*—but not often; it is too suggestive of Tarzan swinging from tree to tree with Jane on his hip).

Generally, *supervisor* has replaced *foreman. Workman's compensation* has become *workers' compensation, messenger* has replaced *errand boy, server* is slowly overtaking *waiter* and *waitress,* and *my girl* (meaning my secretary or my assistant) is seldom heard.

Business people, for the plural, is replacing reliance solely on *businessmen,* while *businessman* and *businesswoman* are being used when appropriate. As more women enter sales forces, options for *salesman* already in the language are being used more frequently: *sales rep, sales associate, seller.*

Many people dislike *salesperson* and *chairperson. Person* is used as a suffix primarily for women. A *chairman* is still a *chairman,* while a *chairperson* is a woman. In many organizations, *chair* or *head* is used.

Ms., commonly used now in both speech and correspondence, has entered English textbooks. So have women's names as illustrations for such rules as use of degrees after proper names (Alice Jones, M.D.). And a few recently published reference books for business writers include sections on nonsexist language.

Work hours and *work force* are still struggling to replace *man-hours* and *manpower* in costing jobs and writing proposals. Substitutes for *man* in such expressions as *man-made* (artificial), *a man-sized job* (a big job), and *the common man* (the average person) are hard to find.

However, the most pervasive problem, and the hardest to solve, is the pronoun problem.

Using the single number masculine, *he* and *his,* as the inclusive pronouns when some of the people meant are women is a lesson in traditional grammar that we learn early and thoroughly. The double pronoun, *he/she, his/her,* is now used fairly generally to achieve nonsexist language, but many find it awkward.

And what about this type of awkward? Said the regional manager as he distributed a questionnaire at a sales meeting: "I'm asking every man and woman to answer all questions as accurately as he can."

Lindsy Van Gelder made the suggestion in *Ms.* magazine that the simplest way around the problem was to give "he" a rest and use "she" as the general pronoun. "Instead of having to ponder over the intricacies of 'Congressman' versus 'Representative,' we can simplify by calling them all 'Congresswoman.' And don't be upset by the business letter that begins 'Dear Madam,' fellas. It means you, too."

Well, we need not go that far to solve the pronoun problem. There are several ways to get around it without being absurd or awkward, or wrenching the language into impossible constructions.

Eliminate the pronoun. A woman consultant recently received a contract from a corporation in which she was referred to as *he* and *his* throughout, despite being identified in the first paragraph by the obviously female name of her firm. She says, "Of course it's boilerplate and run off automatically even though the corporation's vendors are male, female and groups of both, but it makes me uncomfortable and it certainly doesn't do the corporation's image any good."

Eliminating *his* in the following excerpt will cover all vendors without damaging the contract's intent or legality: "The independent contractor shall furnish *his* professional consulting services and advice as specified by purchase orders."

In another example, from an investment company letter, eliminating *himself* changes a sexist sentence to nonsexist quickly and easily without changing the meaning: "The investor has in fact reaped more than a dollar of deductions for each dollar invested, often moving *himself* to a lower tax bracket."

Make the sentence plural. The sentence from the investment letter also could have been made plural: "Investors have in fact reaped more than a dollar of deductions for each dollar invested, often moving *themselves* to a lower tax bracket."

The sentence, from an employees' manual, "Each employee completes his time sheet at the end of his shift," would have been better in the plural: "All employees complete their time sheets at the end of their shifts."

Address the reader directly. The employees' manual would have been even better if the writer had said: "Complete your time sheet at the end of your shift."

And the regional sales manager quoted above could have avoided trouble by saying, "I'm asking you to answer all questions as accurately as you can."

The second-hardest problem is deciding on terms of address.

General use of *Ms.* has created awareness of other baffling situations. What can you do when you don't know if your addressee is a man, woman, or computer, and the old reliable, Dear Sir, is obsolete? What term of address can you use in your reply when the original correspondence contains initials rather than a first name before a last name, a unisex name such as Loren Hadley, Blair Rogers, or Page Paxton, or no name at all?

For the first two, if you want to be completely accurate, call the organization and ask the telephone operator or receptionist if Loren Hadley or L. J. Thompson is a man or a woman. If that is impossible or impractical, here are five solutions to choose from.

1. Use the complete name as provided: Dear Loren Hadley or L. J. Thompson.
2. Cover both bases: Dear Ms. or Mr. Thompson.
3. Use his or her title and last name: Dear Vice-President Hadley or Dear Purchasing Agent Thompson.
4. Set up your letter in the form of a memo:

To: L. J. Thompson
From: Lindley Mercer

5. Ignore tradition, eliminate the salutation, and start the first paragraph of your letter.

If your correspondence contains no name at all, chances are you are talking to a computer. Even if the computer is user friendly, it is the reference numbers or code that it responds to. Write the company address and the reference. Then start the first paragraph of your letter.

If the hand of tradition is heavy upon you and eliminating the salutation makes you uncomfortable, address the whole company (Dear Massachusetts General Insurance Company), To Whom It May Concern, or Dear Friends.

Deciding terms of address in writing is infinitely easier than deciding how to speak to people when you can see their gender but don't know their rank. Men grow up learning how to operate in a male hierarchical system and usually can determine with reasonable accuracy which man to address formally and which informally.

Women usually address all men in business suits as Mr., but they have no easier time of it than men in deciding how to address a woman in a professional setting.

The automatic, trivializing use of a woman's first name is on its way out, but incidents like this still abound:

Bill's attempts to interest XYZ Company in his products had finally paid off.

He was invited to make a presentation and was offered the use of a conference room in a letter signed John Liveridge, assistant to the president.

When Bill signaled that he was ready, a woman and a man entered the room.

The woman said to Bill, "I'm Virginia Hancock, and this is John Liveridge, my . . . ."

Bill enthusiastically broke in, drowning her last word, "I'm delighted to meet you, Mr. Liveridge, and you too, Ginny."

Ms. Hancock owned the company. Mr. Liveridge was her assistant. And Bill lost a customer.

One rule fits all: Use Ms. until you are told something different. Do not address women by their first names unless you are on well-established, friendly terms or you have clear-cut signals that it is OK.

And don't assume a Ph.D. or M.D. is a man.

A sexually inclusive language is slowly evolving, and we can achieve it by continuing to work on problem areas.

Is God Purple?

Mary Jo Meadow

✦ ✦ ✦

In the beginning, when God made heaven and earth, God made two different kinds of people: purple people and green people. The holy books say that God made people in the image of God: purple and green. Purple people and green people were really quite a bit alike. The biggest difference was that green people gave birth to new people, and purple people had larger and stronger bodies. Outside that, they were about the same.

As time passed, things did not go as well for the green people as they did for the purple. The greens were often incapacitated with bearing children, and the purples used their greater strength to take control of running things. Some said that purple people were jealous because green people could make new people. Others thought it was just because people tend to use whatever power they have to get themselves into positions of advantage. In a rough world where physical strength easily won out, the purples could dominate the greens.

As different languages developed, a peculiar thing happened in many of them. People had come to think of purple people as being really human, and to consider green people something lesser made to serve purple people. So the languages used the word purple-person to stand for all people. They made a different word—one that meant partner or counterpart of purple people—that was used when only green people were referred to. When both green people and purple people were referred to together, they used the word purple-person. These words reflected how they felt about the value of purple persons and green persons. When these languages talked about God, most of them called God purple. After all, God was the most important person there was, so it certainly would not do to think of God as anything but purple. Calling God purple then made purpleness even more valuable than greenness. Language affects people that way.

Religions usually had control of education and most of them refused to let green people study; they thought that learning was for purple people only, and that green people should take care of the routine things of life so purples would be free to study and run the world. Later, people would say that since green people hadn't made significant contributions to culture, that proved they were really not as capable as purple people. Living this way—with purple people running

the world and making all the decisions, and with the word purple-
person standing for a fully human person and for God—green people
and purple people became even more fully convinced that purples were
more valuable. That's how people are: they tend to think that people
who have the most power and whose names are used the most are
more important than other people. It got so bad that green people were
often treated pretty much like animals. They could be beaten and
abused by purple people without anyone seeing anything wrong with it.
Some people didn't even think that green people were really persons.

One day God decided to become a person, too. God came as a
purple person—probably that was the only way God could get people
to listen. Nobody thought that green people could say anything worth
listening to. The purple-person-God was very kind to green people;
some purples thought this God was too kind to greens and was making
a mistake. But the purple-person-God treated greens as though they
were real people, listening to them, and wanting to be with them—to
actually share ideas with them, not just using them to wait on all the
purple people. Since the purple people who kept the records of God's
visit seldom counted green people at meetings, we don't know all the
things that green people did with the purple-person-God.

After God left, a new religion grew up around God's visit. The purple
people and green people both shared important positions in this religion at
first, but pretty soon the purple people wound up in charge. An important
purple person named Paul said some good things—once Paul even said that
in God there isn't any distinction between purple persons and green persons. But Paul also passed on a lot of the old ideas that green people were
really less than purple people—that they should be kept in their lowly place.

In this new religion, God was always referred to as a purple person.
All of God was called purple—not only God as a human purple person,
but also God high away in heaven. Some important purple persons—like
Jerome, Augustine, and Chrysostom—seemed rather afraid of green persons and said that, because they are weaker and more sinful than purple
persons, they drag down purple people. They thought a very few green
people could rise above their greenness and be worthy of friendship with
purple people—but, of course, most could not. Since these purple persons
said they spoke with God's authority, everybody believed them.

Finally purple people got so confused about green people that they
discussed it at a big meeting called a church council. They wanted to
decide whether green people really have souls like purple people. Of
course, only purple people were allowed to go to such an important
meeting. The purple people had a hard time of it, and the vote was
very close, but they did say that green people have souls. Since the
purple people said so, that made it so. Still, they didn't treat green
people any differently. The purple people kept on making all the
decisions—even those about green people—and the green people kept
on serving the purple people so the purples could fully develop themselves. Nobody—not even the greens—thought that maybe a green
person should also be developed. Later, people would say that since

green people had not developed themselves over the centuries, it proved that they didn't really have a knack for it.

Over all this time, people weren't really aware that they thought less of green people than purple people, but you could tell by the way different people were treated. Most purple people had green people attached to them who left their own lives, gave up their names and identity, and followed the purples around taking care of their daily needs to leave the purple people free for important things. Nobody did this for green people. When green people did get jobs of their own, they were paid less than purples—only about half as much—as though their work was not as valuable. Many jobs and types of education were forbidden them, and they hardly ever got into decision-making places—especially important ones like church and government. Over time, some people realized this could not be how God wanted things. They explained that when the word purple person means human being, it makes people consider purpleness superior. And when God is called a purple person, it makes purple persons seem more godly than green persons. People aren't aware they think this way—and would even deny it—but they keep on treating green people as less valuable—so they must think they are.

Many purple persons don't want to hear this. When people have an advantage, they don't want to lose it and they twist things all around to keep them the same. People are like that. Some purple people said that green people are envious. Others said that they don't understand that God wants different, but equal, roles for purple and green people. One purple person said it might be okay to think of God as both green and purple, except that it wouldn't reflect God's purple majesty properly. A purple religious leader named Paul very carefully explained that since God was a purple person when visiting the earth, it meant that green people couldn't reflect the image of God as well as purple people, and so they couldn't be leaders in the religion. This shows how the way we use language affects our thinking about greenness and purpleness.

Some green people are also against change. They believe so strongly in their own inferiority that they wouldn't feel safe with a God who wasn't purple—and they don't want green persons as religious leaders because they think green people need the guidance and leadership of purple people. That's another thing about people: when they take their own inferiority for granted, they are terrified at the thought of becoming more responsible for themselves and their lives. In another place where people were either black or white, and the whites were considered better than blacks, many black people had wanted to stay under the care of whites until they finally realized how much it was destroying them.

Many people who are against change have said silly things. They said the family would fall apart, or immorality would be widespread, or disease would run wild, or even that green people would take over the world if anything changed. Scholars who study how people and families work try to explain how silly these fears are, but when people are scared they usually can't listen to reason. Others say that change would mess up religion, or would disturb people's faith, or make it impossible to worship. Some even said that, since God is a purple person, it is right to keep green people down. Others said that green people have the better part; they can practice humility and service—very important religious ideals.

The green people who are trying to make things better see the issue as one of justice, as it had been for black people. These green people say—as black people had said—that separate but equal never really works. They point out that the religion lets only purple people make big decisions and allows only purple people to do the very holy things. They also note that if green people really had the better part, at least some of the purples would have been fighting for it—and no purple people seem to want to do the things green people are expected to do. It would be sad if people's faith were hurt because we stopped calling God purple or started treating green people equally, but the religion says that people are supposed to be treated justly. The way green people have been treated is really a big sin of the religion—just as it was a big sin not to try to get justice for black people when white people enslaved them and considered them inferior.

And that's where things stand today. We are left with questions to think about. Are green people really meant to serve purple people? Are green people not able to reflect God's image as well as purple people? Are purple people the "real" people with green people only a tag-on idea? Are green people really treated fairly in their religion when purple people make all the decisions and do the holy things, when their religion uses the word purple person to refer to all people, and when it calls God a purple person? Finally, is God really purple?

Exclusive Wording Can Taint Great Ideals

Ann Daly Goodwin

✦ ✦ ✦

Thomas Jefferson drove me to it. He finally provoked me into flinging on the feminist cloak.

During my teaching years, you see, I had to keep apologizing for him. Apologizing, of all things, for the Sage of Monticello, the Man of the People from whose luminous quill flowed the Declaration of Independence.

He drafted other ringing words as well, words like these: "When the press is free, and every man able to read, all is safe." A nation could cornerstone a life on that phrase. A journalist could anchor a career on it.

Every year of my teaching life, that watchword went up on the blackboard the first day of school. Quotes from other authors followed, quotes from a fat file, quotes given eloquent expression by some of the minds I most admire.

But a dreary many of those well-wrought words delivered the same incomplete, skewed perception: At the center of significant action on planet Earth, search for a heroic figure. A man.

Check out Burke's famous challenge: "The only thing necessary for the triumph of evil is for good men to do nothing." Or Wordsworth's gentle inspiration: "The best portion of a good man's life is his little nameless, unremember'd acts of kindness and of love." Or Emerson's engaging observation: "A good poem goes about the world offering itself to reasonable men, who read it with joy and carry it to their reasonable neighbors."

Granted, the good fellows who penned those stirring sentences lived in an earlier, less enlightened age. But what is a teacher to do who honors the main message, but abhors the unintended slight? Activate the eraser and abandon spirit-kindling quotations? A small-minded solution. Change the words ever so slightly and skirt the sexist images? A scandalous notion.

I used a tiny "X" instead, chalk-whispered under the offending man/men/mankind/he. Then I waited, but never longer than the second week of class. A hand would wave. "We figured out why that mark is there," a beaming student would explain. Point made, quotations continued, sexist sting extinguished.

How easy to avoid that sting in the first place. How simple to say "people," to use the plural, to convert "he" into "they." How creative to employ inclusive options. Gandhi did and out came this kindly creed: "I have tried to make every creature feel secure in my presence." [S]ome ministers expand prayers to encompass all people: "Lord God of our *forebears*, God of Abraham, Isaac and Jacob, *of Sarah, Rebecca and Rachel. . . .*" One needs only a smidgen of imagination to know who gets left out in less sensitive versions.

I have been lucky in my personal life; I remember few shut-out moments—quite the contrary. The earliest conversation I can recall with my father came when I, foolish child, was lamenting my American birth. Everyone else in my family, you see, had been launched in Ireland, India or China, and I complained that, compared to that, seeing first light in St. Louis seemed uninspired.

"Never mind," my father soothed. "You are the only one of us who can be president."

Perhaps he added that the nation's chief executive must be native-born, if I did not know it already. But the enduring lessons went deeper. He taught me what opportunity was before I knew enough to ask. He taught me about women's liberation before the movement had a name.

Maybe that is why I was so selfishly slow to see the need for feminist action; no language, no attitude set limits for me. But gradually, as I greeted that yearly parade of young people in my classroom, the succession of glowing quotes largely ignoring girls and women got through to me in a new way: Not every girl's father helps her grasp her independence. Legions of my sisters-in-spirit must declare their own.

I never did decide to run for president. But with all due respect, Mr. Jefferson, move on over. Some day, depend upon it, a woman's going to win it.

The Human-Not-Quite-Human

Dorothy L. Sayers

The first thing that strikes the careless observer is that women are unlike men. They are "the opposite sex"—(though why "opposite" I do not know; what is the "neighbouring sex"?). But the fundamental thing is that women are more like men than anything else in the world. They are human beings. *Vir* is male and *Femina* is female; but *Homo* is male and female.

This is the equality claimed and the fact that is persistently evaded and denied. No matter what arguments are used, the discussion is vitiated from the start, because Man is always dealt with as both *Homo* and *Vir*, but Woman only as *Femina*.

I have seen it solemnly stated in a newspaper that the seats on the near side of a bus are always filled before those on the off side, because, "men find them more comfortable on account of the camber of the road, and women find they get a better view of the shop windows." As though the camber of the road did not affect male and female bodies equally. Men, you observe, are given a *Homo* reason; but women, a *Femina* reason, because they are not fully human. . . .

Probably no man has ever troubled to imagine how strange his life would appear to himself if it were unrelentingly assessed in terms of his maleness; if everything he wore, said, or did had to be justified by reference to female approval, if he were compelled to regard himself, day in day out, not as a member of society, but merely. . . as a virile member of society. If the centre of his dress-consciousness were the cod-piece, his education directed to making him a spirited lover and meek paterfamilias; his interests held to be natural only in so far as they were sexual. If from school and lecture-room, Press and pulpit, he heard the persistent outpouring of a shrill and scolding voice, bidding him remember his biological function. If he were vexed by continual advice how to add a rough male touch to his typing, how to be learned without losing his masculine appeal, how to combine chemical research with seduction, how to play bridge without incurring the suspicion of impotence. If, instead of allowing with a smile that "women prefer cavemen," he felt the unrelenting pressure of a whole social structure forcing him to order all his goings in conformity with that pronouncement. . . .

In any book on sociology he would find, after the main portion dealing with human needs and rights, a supplementary chapter devoted to "The Position of the Male in the Perfect State." His newspaper would assist him with a "Men's Corner," telling him how, by the expenditure of a good deal of money and a couple of hours a day, he could attract the girls and retain his wife's affection; and when he had succeeded in capturing a mate, his name would be taken from him, and society would present him with a special title to proclaim his achievement. People would write books called, "History of the Male," or "Males of the Bible," or "The Psychology of the Male," and he would be regaled daily with headlines, such as "Gentleman-Doctor's Discovery," "Male-Secretary Wins Calcutta Sweep," "Men-Artists at the Academy." If he gave an interview to a reporter, or performed any unusual exploit, he would find it recorded in such terms as these: "Professor Bract, although a distinguished botanist, is not in any way an unmanly man. He has, in fact, a wife and seven children. Tall and burly, the hands with which he handles his delicate specimens are as gnarled and powerful as those of a Canadian lumberjack, and when I swilled beer with him in his laboratory, he bawled his conclusions at me in a strong, gruff voice that implemented the promise of his swaggering moustache." Or: "I asked M. Sapristi, the renowned chef, whether kitchen-cult was not a rather unusual occupation for a man. 'Not a bit of it!' he replied bluffly. 'It is the genius that counts, not the sex. As they say in *la belle Ecosse*, a man's a man for a' that'—and his gusty, manly guffaw blew three small patty pans from the dresser."

He would be edified by solemn discussions about "Should Men Serve in Drapery Establishments?" and acrimonious ones about "Tea-Drinking Men"; by cross-shots of public affairs "from the masculine angle," and by irritable correspondence about men who expose their anatomy on beaches (so masculine of them), conceal it in dressing gowns (too feminine of them), think about nothing but women, pretend an unnatural indifference to women, exploit their sex to get jobs, lower the tone of the office by their sexless appearance, and generally fail to please a public opinion which demands the incompatible. And at dinner-parties he would hear the wheedling, unctuous, predatory female voice demand: "And why should you trouble your handsome little head about politics?"

If, after a few centuries of this kind of treatment, the male was a little self-conscious, a little on the defensive, and a little bewildered about what was required of him, I should not blame him. If he traded a little upon his sex, I could forgive him. If he presented the world with a major social problem, I should scarcely be surprised. It would be more surprising if he retained any rag of sanity and self-respect.

Why Nonsexist Communication?

Bobbye D. Sorrels

◆ ◆ ◆

Successful contemporary communicators use nonsexist patterns of expression for many reasons, including:

1. Whereas in the past society virtually restricted males to certain roles and females to others, such restrictions no longer exist. Therefore, communication symbols based on past roles simply do not portray current conditions properly. Instead, they distort reality. They constitute an anachronism in the course of human events. Cannot and do not women work as police officers, deliver mail, practice law, and serve in the army? Yet, the words *policeman, mailman, lady attorney*, and *infantryman* deny that they can and do perform these roles.

2. The use of certain words sometimes to mean males and sometimes to mean both males and females creates a great deal of confusion. For example, a national civic organization has gone to court to try to continue to exclude women from its membership, using as its major argument that the "man" words in its constitution and bylaws mean men only. Yet, to refer to all people in their public pronouncements, they use such words and phrases as *man, mankind,* and "brotherhood of man."

3. No set of communication symbols is permanently chiseled in stone. Humans create symbols to serve their needs for active interchange. When the symbols no longer serve those needs, humans change them. Sexist symbols do not serve human needs.

4. An old saying suggests, "Tell me a people's language, and I'll tell you the values of that people." With an English language that portrays males as the norm and females as abnormal or

subnormal, those who analyze and practice the language must believe that females have less value than males.

5. A basic sense of fairness requires the equal treatment of men and women in the communication symbols that so define the lives of the people who use them. Sexist communication limits and devalues all humans with outmoded language.

6. A basic rule for good communication involves analyzing the audience. Therefore, wise communicators understand and apply the knowledge that many people, both females and males, react negatively to sexist communication.

7. Because sexist communication tends to elevate males and debase females, it too often creates a self-fulfilling prophecy of inferiority and failure for women and aggressively insensitive machismo for men. The consequent loss of the potential contributions of both men and women represents a waste that a society can ill afford.

8. The conversion from sexist to nonsexist communication need not involve clumsy, uncomfortable, or ungrammatical expressions. Natural, graceful, and grammatically correct nonsexist patterns come relatively easily to one who has the commitment to see them.

9. Sexist communication patterns expose their users as people who do not stay abreast of contemporary communication practices.

10. Sexist communication patterns may have legal implications. People have won lawsuits when sexist communication has contributed to discriminatory practices.

Solving the Great Pronoun Problem:
14 Ways to Avoid the Sexist Singular

Marie Shear

Consider the sex of the squirrel. Any squirrel. Is it a she or a he? I never gave the matter a thought until one Saturday morning a couple of summers ago. Then I heard a radio news report that a squirrel had precipitated a power blackout somewhere in New York—by running up an electrical wire, gnawing through a cable, or something—frying its furry little carcass in the process. The newscast called the squirrel "he." I was intrigued. Had a reporter been to the morgue, or wherever wayward squirrels go when they fry, to check the corpse's sex?

Of course not. Like lots of other organizations and individuals, the radio station had simply assumed that anything worth mentioning is male, until proved otherwise. That assumption creates The Great Pronoun Problem.

Male pronouns are supposedly the hardest form of sexist language to overcome. Purists insist that *he, his,* and *him* are indispensable when the person in question is unidentified or archetypical. In apocalyptic terms, they warn that nonsexist alternatives are ostentatious and politicized. The purists sound like 15th-century cartographers warning Columbus about the sea monsters.

Despite the humbug, we *can* solve The Great Pronoun Problem. Nonsexist usage, like all first-rate writing and speech, requires skill placed in the service of an educated eye and ear. But we needn't exaggerate the difficulty. Practice is necessary. Genius is not.

Here are six general guidelines and fourteen specific methods that, with a little practice, should enable you to correct the pronoun problem while you continue writing as accurately and gracefully as you did before. Soon after that, you should be able to avoid the problem in the first place.

First, Forget "Company Manners"

Don't save nonsexist language for special occasions that require formal prose. Incorporate it into memos, letters, reports, and conversations. A double standard is hypocritical. Besides, people who treat nonsexist pronouns like "company manners" don't develop enough skill to use them smoothly and swiftly.

Ignore the Ridicule

Biased gentlemen and occasional ladies ridicule the advocates of nonsexist usage, picturing us as zealots who would mutilate English and impose thought control. They fume at a single use of *he or she,* wrongly claiming that nonsexist language is monotonous. Yet they overlook the real monotony in sexist prose like this, from *Esquire* magazine: "When a three-week-old baby hears *his* father's voice, *his* face elongates, *his* shoulders hunch, *his* eyebrows shoot up, *he* becomes still with anticipation—all signs *he* is expecting some excitement [italics mine]." The same critics argue that unbiased prose is imprecise, oblivious to the farcical inaccuracy of a former Senator's statement that abortion is "strictly a matter between the patient and *his* doctor." Such language isn't noble or neutral. It is toxic. Unless you yearn to teach remedial kindergarten, ignore the sniping and get on with your work.

Keep It Simple

Don't make a federal case out of it. Look for the simplest deft solution to the particular problem. There's no need to draft an ingenious revision, combining ten of the fourteen methods below, if a single obvious technique—like using the plural—will do the trick.

Consider the Context

Context helps determine which method is best. For example, if there is a lot of repetition immediately before and after a sexist sentence, you won't want to repeat the noun in it.

When you change from singular to plural, check the words that any pronouns refer to. If it's no longer clear whether *they* or *their* means the new plural or an old one, consider making the old plural singular. It's simpler to do than it sounds . . . .

Avoid/Slashes—and Dashes—

Several proposed remedies for sexist pronouns are forced or fussy. Don't use them.

He/she and *his/her* are visually distracting when they are read silently. Read aloud, they are hiccups. So are *s/he* and *(s)he*.

He (or she) and *his—or her—*and *he, or she,* are patronizing. Parentheses, dashes, and commas treat women as a coy afterthought.

Don't alternate *he* and *she* from paragraph to paragraph, either. As you write and revise, you will inevitably shift paragraphs around for reasons unrelated to sexism. It is distracting to keep readjusting the alternation while you work.

The exclusive use of *she* is occasionally recommended, on the grounds that it includes the word *he* and that turnabout is fair play, anyhow. Despite its ironic charm, the idea is intellectually indefensible. It slights the largest minority in the United States: males.

Coined pronouns seem synthetic. Even I don't use the ones I invented about fifteen years ago. No one else's inventions stand any better chance of winning the popular acceptance already enjoyed by *they, their,* and *them.*

Enjoy the Fringe Benefits

The fresh eye you cast upon pronouns may also spot cluttered or muddy language nearby. Cleaner, crisper writing can result. For instance, you cut half the verbiage when you change "a tenant needs a roof over his head" to "a tenant needs shelter." Similarly, you lessen the tedium in "his employees, his guests, or members of his family" when you substitute "his or her employees, guests, or family members. . . ." Bad writers write badly, with or without sexism. But competent writers who eliminate sexism write as well as before, and some write better.

The Methods

These 14 ways to avoid sexist pronouns are listed in random order.

1. Add the female: *she or* he, *hers or* his, he *or she,* his *or hers.*
2. Use the first person: *I, me, my, mine, we, our, ours.*
3. Use the second person: *you, your, yours.*
4. Move the noun.
5. Repeat the noun.
6. Use a new noun—instead of a pronoun or as a synonym for an old noun.
7. Use the plural—one of the easiest, handiest methods.
8. Delete the pronoun.
9. Use a new pronoun: *it, its, this, that.*
10. Use an article or conjunction: *a, an, the, but, and.*
11. Use *who* with or without a noun—*who, anyone who, someone who, whoever, no one who, one who, any (noun) who, a (noun) who, the (noun) who.* This helps emphasize a single individual.
12. Rewrite—the most work and the least often needed.
13. Use the passive—be cautious; the incompetent use it verbosely; the cunning use it evasively.
14. Use *they, their, them*—the simplest, most sensible method of all. . . .

The Simplest Solution of Them All

Millions of people have been using *they, their,* and *them* as third-person singulars all along. They are eminently sensible. As a reformed pedant, I don't say that casually. Until a few years ago, I agreed with the columnist who called the singular *they* "grammatically repulsive." I scorned people who used it, considering them fundamentally uncouth—like public smokers. But I've seen the light.

Many word-watchers endorse *they.* During the last ten or fifteen years they have alerted us to its surprisingly long and respectable history. Valuable scholarly discussions by Ann Bodine and Rosa Shand Turner teach us that *they* isn't some new, sloppy corruption of "correct" English, but rather a return to venerable usage. George Jochnowitz concludes that it is wrong, even astounding to consider *they* incorrect for formal writing when it predates *he* and is nearly universal in colloquial and spoken English.

Do pronouns matter? President Ronald Reagan thinks so. He calls Christians *we* and calls everyone else *they*. In contrast, Jimmy Carter talks about the typical Presidential candidate *himself or herself.*

Way to go, Jimmy.

State Statutes and Gender

Richard J. Sands and Maryann Corbett

✦ ✦ ✦

In 1984, the Minnesota Legislature ordered the Office of the Revisor of Statutes to remove gender-specific language from the state statutes without changing the meaning of the law. The task of reworking the statutes was done by the attorneys of the revisor's office staff, under the management of Richard Sands, Senior Assistant Revisor, and Maryann Corbett, Assistant for Writing Standards. The work took many months, and the rewritten version of the statutes was adopted as law in February of 1986.

In the law that first called for the revision, the legislature ordered the revisor to keep language as natural as possible, not to do things mechanically, but to preserve normal English word patterns. The revisor's staff has taken extraordinary care to obey those directives and, at the same time, to preserve the legal substance of every sentence in the statutes.

To be sure that our changes would be acceptable to readers, the revisor's staff first produced guidelines that explored all the possible ways of replacing masculine pronouns by changing sentence structure. Then, following those guidelines, we created a model revision of one section of the statutes. We distributed both the original and the revised version to selected groups of readers: first, to state government employees, the people who need to use the statutes but often lack technical legal training, and also an audience of expert technical writers, the members of The Society for Technical Communication. We asked them to tell us what words or groups of words they found objection-

---

Printed by permission of the Minnesota Office of the Revisor of Statutes.

able. Their responses show that the unrevised version of the statutes was far more objectionable than the revised version, often because it contained so many uses of "he," "his," and "him."

Our second survey was distributed to newspaper editors throughout Minnesota and across the country. This survey was a collection of short passages from the statutes, showing both the original and the revised version of each. The passages showed several alternative ways of removing pronouns and tested a few selected pronoun replacements. Responses to this survey showed, among other things, that a small but vocal minority of readers dislikes repeated double pronouns—"he or she," "his or her." We have made a concerted effort not to use them.

Although changes to specific nouns tend to draw the most attention, it was the changes of masculine pronouns that consumed the most staff energy on this project. Some 20,000 nonsubstantive gender-specific pronouns were removed. The word "his" was changed more than 10,000 times and the word "he" was eliminated about 6,000 times. (Only 301 of the 20,000 pronouns were feminine.)

The most frequent method of replacing pronouns was by repeating the noun, but every other conceivable method was used to some extent. Passive voice and plural number were rarely used because those techniques have other disadvantages. No new words were coined.

Concerning the problem of replacing nouns, we first had to decide exactly which words should be considered gender-specific. We consulted a large body of linguistic research to get information about how the words are actually used and, in the end, decided not to change a number of words that contain a masculine element, such as "master" and "journeyman." These were left alone because we found that speakers of English commonly use them to refer to men and women alike, or because we found that there was no commonly used substitute. A few, like "manhole," were left alone because every proposed substitute has drawn so much bad press. "Workmanship" was retained because lawyers felt there was too much case law that specifically defined it.

About 100 gender-specific nouns and adjectives, occurring a total of about 1,400 times, were eliminated. Well over 90 percent of these occurrences involved ten words: chairman (which accounted for 54 percent and which was changed to chair), warehouseman (warehouse operator), policeman (police officer), councilman (council member), nurseryman (nursery operator), patrolman (patrol officer), salesman (salesperson), serviceman (service member), foreman (lead supervisor), and fisherman (changed to various words depending on the context).

To make sure that language remained natural, drafters did nothing in a mechanical fashion. Every instance of a word's occurrence was judged separately to make sure the chosen replacement was right for the context.

The statutes as they were before the revision were not always models of great style. Because the office took care to keep language as normal as possible in this revision, we are confident that the revised statutes are no worse than the originals. In many cases they are improved.

Bibliography

Below are books and articles referred to in the text as well as other special books, although the list is embarrassingly short given the number of well-written and well-researched works that deal with women's issues in general and with nonsexist language in particular. The library catalog classification that will be most helpful to you in finding other works is *Language and Languages—Sex Differences*. More scholarly works are located under *Sociolinguistics*.

Anthony, Susan B., et al. *History of Woman Suffrage.* Vol I. Rochester, NY: Charles Mann, 1889.

Baron, Dennis. *Grammar and Gender.* New Haven, CT: Yale University Press, 1986.

Bebout, Linda. "Asymmetries in Male-Female Word Pairs." *American Speech* 59 (Spring 1984).

Bodine, Ann. "Androcentrism in Prescriptive Grammar: Singular 'They,' Sex-Indefinite 'He,' and 'He or She'." *Language in Society* 4 (1975):129–46.

Bright, Sally. "Our Lively Language." *St. Paul Pioneer Press and Dispatch* (June 8, 1986):5G.

Brownmiller, Susan. *Against Our Will: Men, Women and Rape.* New York: Bantam, 1976.

Bunch, Charlotte, and Pollack, Sandra, eds. *Learning Our Way: Essays in Feminist Education.* Trumansburg, NY: Crossing, 1983.

Capek, Mary Ellen S., ed. *A Women's Thesaurus: An Index of Language Used to Describe and Locate Information by and about Women.* New York: Harper & Row, 1987.

Chesler, Phyllis. *Women and Madness.* New York: Avon, 1973.

Chesler, Phyllis, and Goodman, Emily J. *Women, Money, and Power.* New York: Morrow, 1976.

Daly, Mary. *Gyn/Ecology: The Metaethics of Radical Feminism.* Boston: Beacon, 1978.

———. *Pure Lust: Elemental Feminist Philosophy.* Boston: Beacon, 1984.

———. *The Church and the Second Sex.* Boston: Beacon, 1985.

———. *Beyond God the Father: Toward a Philosophy of Women's Liberation.* Rev. ed. Boston: Beacon, 1985.

De Beauvoir, Simone. *The Second Sex.* New York: Knopf, 1953.

Duberman, Lucile. *Gender and Sex in Society.* New York: Praeger, 1975.

Dworkin, Andrea. *Woman Hating: A Radical Look at Sexuality.* New York: Dutton, 1974.

———. *Our Blood: Prophecies and Discourses on Sexual Politics.* New York: Harper & Row, 1976.

———. *Pornography: Men Possessing Women.* New York: Perigee, 1981.

———. *Right-Wing Women: The Politics of Domesticated Females.* New York: Perigee, 1983.

Emswiler, Sharon Neufer, and Emswiler, Thomas Neufer. *Women and Worship: A Guide to Non-Sexist Hymns, Prayers, and Liturgies.* New York: Harper & Row, 1974.

Farris, James. "The Dynamics of Verbal Exchange: A Newfoundland Example." *Current Anthropology* 4 (1963):307–16.

Fawcett, Millicent Garrett. *Women's Suffrage: A Short History of a Great Movement.* London: T. C. & E. C. Jack, 1912.

"Feminism in America 1848–1986." *The Wilson Quarterly* X (4) (Autumn 1986):88–141.

Firestone, Shulamith. *The Dialectic of Sex: The Case for Feminist Revolution.* New York: Bantam, 1970.

Friedan, Betty. *The Feminine Mystique.* New York: Norton, 1963.

———. *It Changed My Life: Writings on the Women's Movement.* New York: Dell, 1977.

———. *The Second Stage.* New York: Summit, 1981.

Garner, Les. *Stepping Stones to Women's Liberty: Feminist Ideas in the Women's Suffrage Movement 1900–1918.* Cranbury, NJ: Associated University Presses, 1984.

Greer, Germaine. *The Female Eunuch.* New York: McGraw-Hill, 1971.

———. *Sex and Destiny: The Politics of Human Fertility.* New York: Harper & Row, 1984.

Heilbrun, Carolyn G. *Toward a Recognition of Androgyny.* New York: Harper Colophon, 1973.

Hellinger, Marlis. "Effecting Social Change Through Group Action: Feminine Occupational Titles in Transition." In *Language and Power.* Edited by Cheris Kramarae et al. Beverly Hills, CA: Sage, 1984.

Henley, Nancy. *Body Politics: Power, Sex, and Nonverbal Communication.* Englewood Cliffs, NJ: Prentice-Hall, 1977.

Hill, Alette Olin. *Mother Tongue, Father Time: A Decade of Linguistic Revolt.* Bloomington, IN: Indiana University Press, 1986.

Kaufman, Gloria, and Blakely, Mary Kay, eds. *Pulling Our Own Strings: Feminist Humor and Satire.* Bloomington, IN: Indiana University Press, 1980.

Key, Mary Ritchie. *Male/Female Language.* Metuchen, NJ: The Scarecrow Press, 1975.

Kramarae, Cheris. *Women and Men Speaking.* Rowley, MA: Newbury House, 1980.

———, ed. *The Voices and Words of Women and Men.* Oxford: Pergamon, 1981.

Kramarae, Cheris; Schulz, Muriel; and O'Barr, William M., eds. *Language and Power.* Beverly Hills, CA: Sage Publications, 1984.

Kramarae, Cheris, and Treichler, Paula A. *A Feminist Dictionary.* Boston: Pandora Press, 1985.

Kramer, Rita. "The Third Wave." In "Feminism in America 1848–1986." *The Wilson Quarterly* X (4) (Autumn 1986).

Lakoff, Robin. *Language and Woman's Place.* New York: Harper & Row, 1975.

Macmillan Publishing Co., Inc. *Guidelines for Creating Positive Sexual and Racial Images in Educational Materials.* New York, 1975. (Ninety-six-page booklet available from Macmillan at 866 Third Avenue, New York, NY 10022.)

McKay, Donald G. "The Pronoun Problem." In *The Voices and Words of Women and Men.* Edited by Cheris Kramarae. Oxford: Pergamon, 1980.

Merriam, Eve. "Sex and Semantics: Some Notes on BOMFOG." *New York University Education Quarterly* 4 (4) (1974):22–24.

Miller, Casey, and Swift, Kate. *Words and Women: New Language in New Times.* New York: Anchor/Doubleday, 1976.

———. *The Handbook of Nonsexist Writing: For Writers, Editors and Speakers.* New York: Harper & Row, 1980.

———. "Nonsexist Language: Making It More Than a Trend." *The Bookwoman* 50 (1) (1986):1–5.

Millett, Kate. *Sexual Politics.* New York: Avon, 1971.

Moraga, Cherrie, and Anzaldúa, Gloria, eds. *This Bridge Called My Back: Writings by Radical Women of Color.* Watertown, MA: Persephone, 1981.

Murray, Pauli. "The Liberation of Black Women." In *Our American Sisters: Women in American Life and Thought.* Edited by Jean E. Friedman and William G. Shade. Boston: Allyn and Bacon, 1973.

Nilsen, Alleen Pace, et al. *Sexism and Language.* Urbana, IL: National Council of Teachers of English, 1977.

———. "You'll Never Be the Man Your Mother Was." *Et cetera* 36 (4) (Winter 1979).

Nunnally-Cox, Janice. *Foremothers: Women of the Bible.* New York: Seabury, 1981.

Oakley, Ann. *Women's Work: A History of the Housewife.* New York: Pantheon, 1975.

———. *Subject Women.* New York: Pantheon, 1981.

———. *Taking It Like a Woman.* New York: Random House, 1984.

———. *Sex, Gender and Society.* Hants, England: Gower, 1985.

Ochs, Carol. *Behind the Sex of God: Toward a New Consciousness Transcending Matriarchy and Patriarchy.* New York: Beacon/Harper & Row, 1979.

Partnow, Elaine, ed. *The Quotable Woman.* Los Angeles: Pinnacle, 1977.

Pierce, Christine. "Natural Law, Language and Women." In *Woman in Sexist Society: Studies in Power and Powerlessness.* Edited by Vivian Gornick and Barbara K. Moran. New York: New American Library, 1971.

Rich, Adrienne. *The Dream of a Common Language.* New York: Norton, 1978.

Rowbotham, Sheila. *Women, Resistance and Revolution.* New York: Random House, 1973.

———. *Women's Consciousness, Man's World.* London: Penguin, 1974.

———. *Dreams and Dilemmas: Collected Writings.* London: Virago, 1983.

Ruether, Rosemary Radford. *Religion and Sexism.* New York: Simon & Schuster, 1974.

———. *New Woman/New Earth: Sexist Ideologies and Human Liberation.* New York: Harper & Row, 1978.

————. *Sexism and God-Talk: Toward a Feminist Theology.* Boston: Beacon, 1984.

————. *Womanguides: Readings Toward a Feminist Theory.* Boston: Beacon, 1986.

Rysman, Alexander. "How the 'Gossip' Became a Woman." *Journal of Communication* 27 (1977):176–80.

Sanford, John A. *The Invisible Partners: How the Male and Female in Each of Us Affects Our Relationships.* New York: Paulist, 1980.

Sayers, Dorothy L. *Are Women Human?* Grand Rapids, MI: William B. Eerdmans, 1971, 1984. First published in 1947 as two of twenty-one essays entitled *Unpopular Opinions.*

Schaef, Anne Wilson. *Women's Reality: An Emerging Female System in the White Male Society.* Minneapolis: Winston, 1981.

Scott, Anne F., and Scott, Andrew M. *One Half the People: The Fight for Woman Suffrage.* Philadelphia, PA: Lippincott, 1975; Champaign, IL: University of Illinois Press, 1982.

Silveira, Jeanette. "Generic Masculine Words and Thinking." In *The Voices and Words of Women and Men.* Edited by Cheris Kramarae. Oxford: Pergamon, 1980, pp. 165–78.

Sorrels, Bobbye D. *The Nonsexist Communicator: Solving the Problems of Gender and Awkwardness in Modern English.* Englewood Cliffs, NJ: Prentice-Hall, 1983.

Spender, Dale. *Man Made Language.* London: Routledge & Kegan Paul, 1980.

————. *Women of Ideas: And What Men Have Done to Them.* London: Routledge & Kegan Paul, 1982.

————. *There's Always Been a Women's Movement This Century.* London: Routledge & Kegan Paul/Pandora, 1983.

Stanley, Julia Penelope. "Paradigmatic Woman: The Prostitute." In *Papers in Language Variation.* Edited by David L. Shores. Birmingham, AL: University of Alabama Press, 1977.

Steinem, Gloria. *Outrageous Acts and Everyday Rebellions.* New York: New American Library, 1983.

Strunk, William, Jr., and White, E. B. *The Elements of Style.* 2d ed. New York: Macmillan, 1972.

Thorne, Barrie; Kramarae, Cheris; and Henley, Nancy, eds. *Language, Gender and Society.* Rowley, MA: Newbury House, 1983.

U.S. Department of Labor, Manpower [sic] Administration. *Job Title Revisions to Eliminate Sex- and Age-Referent Language from the Dictionary of Occupational Titles, Third Edition.* Washington, DC: Government Printing Office, 1975. (Note that the Manpower Administration has also had a title revision: it is now the Education and Training Administration.)

Wandor, Michelene, ed. *On Gender and Writing.* London: Pandora, 1983.